THE SONORAN DESERT EXPLORER

THE SONORAN DESERT EXPLORER

A Guide to Natural Wonders and Adventures

ARIZONA-SONORA DESERT MUSEUM

Timber Press
Portland, Oregon

Photo and illustration credits appear on page 370.

Timber Press
Workman Publishing
Hachette Book Group, Inc.
1290 Avenue of the Americas
New York, New York 10104
timberpress.com

Timber Press is an imprint of Workman Publishing, a division of Hachette Book Group, Inc. The Timber Press name and logo are registered trademarks of Hachette Book Group, Inc.

Printed in Dongguan, China (TLF), on responsibly sourced paper.
Text and cover design by Leigh Kaisen
Illustrations by Leigh Kaisen and Sara Isasi
The publisher is not responsible for websites (or their content) that are not owned by the publisher.

ISBN 978-1-64326-175-1

A catalog record for this book is available from the Library of Congress.

To the threatened and endangered species of the Sonoran Desert region and the people working to save them and their habitats.

CONTENTS

PART 1

PART 2

PART 3

PREFACE

Welcome to the Sonoran Desert

Known around the world for its saguaros, spectacular sunsets, and vibrant borderland culture, Tucson is the gateway to the Sonoran Desert for many travelers. This book guides you through that portal to the northern reaches of the Sonoran Desert, one of the most biologically and culturally diverse deserts in the world, with explorations of Tucson, Southern Arizona, and beyond. Whether you live in the area or are visiting for a few days, the Sonoran Desert is a sensory cornucopia of extraordinary sights, sounds, stories, tastes, and scents found nowhere else in the world.

The Sonoran Desert sprawls over some 120,000 square miles (320,000 square km) across two countries, five states, and at least seventeen Indigenous nations and ancestral lands. It is home to about 130 species of mammals, more than 500 kinds of birds, and about 20 amphibians and 100 reptiles. It even hosts 30 native freshwater fish in precious rivers, streams, and springs. Approximately 2500 species of native plants occur within the Sonoran Desert proper (the olive green section of the map on page 18), a considerable portion of the more than 4000 that occur in the broader region, including Arizona, Sonora, Baja California, Baja California Sur, and southeast California. At the center of the region is the deep and narrow Gulf of California, a subtropical sea so rich in biological diversity it was called "the world's aquarium" by famed oceanographer Jacques-Yves Cousteau.

▸▸ Summer storm clearing over Brown Mountain in Tucson Mountain Park

▸▸ Saguaros and ocotillos silhouetted by a Sonoran Desert sunset

The Sonoran Desert challenges the pervasive stereotype of deserts as stark, desolate landscapes where life struggles to survive. Rather, plants, animals, and cultures thrive here due to remarkably creative adaptations to the challenges and extremes of the environment. In fact, the diversity of some groups of animals—such as our super-pollinators, the bees—peaks in the Sonoran Desert and similar climates around the Mediterranean Sea.

The authors of this book are scientists and educators at the Arizona-Sonora Desert Museum, an excellent starting place for any exploration of the region. Located in Tucson, the museum is a zoo, botanical garden, natural history museum, aquarium, and art institute that provides visitors with a glimpse of the various biomes, animals, plants, geology, and cultures they may come across in the area. Admittedly, we are all Sonoran Desert superfans, and we hope you'll be inspired by our love and appreciation for this place as you take some of our recommended adventures and learn about the plants and animals you encounter.

▲ The museum has about 2 miles of trails.

What you'll see is a moment in a continuum of change. Ten thousand years ago, the people of this area lived among pines, junipers, scrub oaks, and Joshua trees. The saguaro cactus forests of today took root about 1000 years later. More recently, people are impacting environmental change at a much faster pace, as you will discover on some of the adventures. In that sense, the Sonoran Desert, unique though it is, faces the same major challenge as other ecosystems around the world—rapid loss of biodiversity spurred by human activity. We hope your explorations of the Sonoran Desert will motivate you to support and get involved in efforts to slow the loss of biodiversity in whatever part of the planet you call home.

Clockwise from upper left:
Where the Sonoran Desert meets the sea

Cave exhibit at the Desert Museum

Visitors stop to admire a barn owl.

Fruiting saguaros stand above other cacti and a variety of shrubs.

Desert tortoise

SETTING THE STAGE

PART ONE

Sonoran Desert Essentials

THERE'S NOTHING AVERAGE ABOUT THE SONORAN DESERT

FROM LOW-LYING COASTAL PLAINS to soaring mountain ranges, the varied geography of the Sonoran Desert sets the stage for its impressive biological diversity. The region sits between two continental-scale mountain ranges—the Rocky Mountains to the north and the Sierra Madre Occidental to the south—and exhibits biological influences from both. The landscape undulates through alternating mountains and valleys, with elevations from sea level to over 10,000 feet (about 3 km). This accounts for a wide variety of climatic conditions in close proximity to each other and the occurrence of plants and animals that are highly adapted to these conditions. Within a couple of hours, you can travel from arid desert plains through scrublands and grasslands to oak woodlands and evergreen forests. A one-hour drive from the Tucson valley to the top of neighboring mountains traverses a sweep of climate zones and biodiversity akin to driving from Mexico to Canada.

From any street corner in Tucson, you'll see mountains in every direction. Before long, the distinctive contours of each range become so identifiable that you can readily navigate by them. From higher elevations, the repeating pattern of alternating mountains and valleys is evident, stretching as far as the eye can see. One

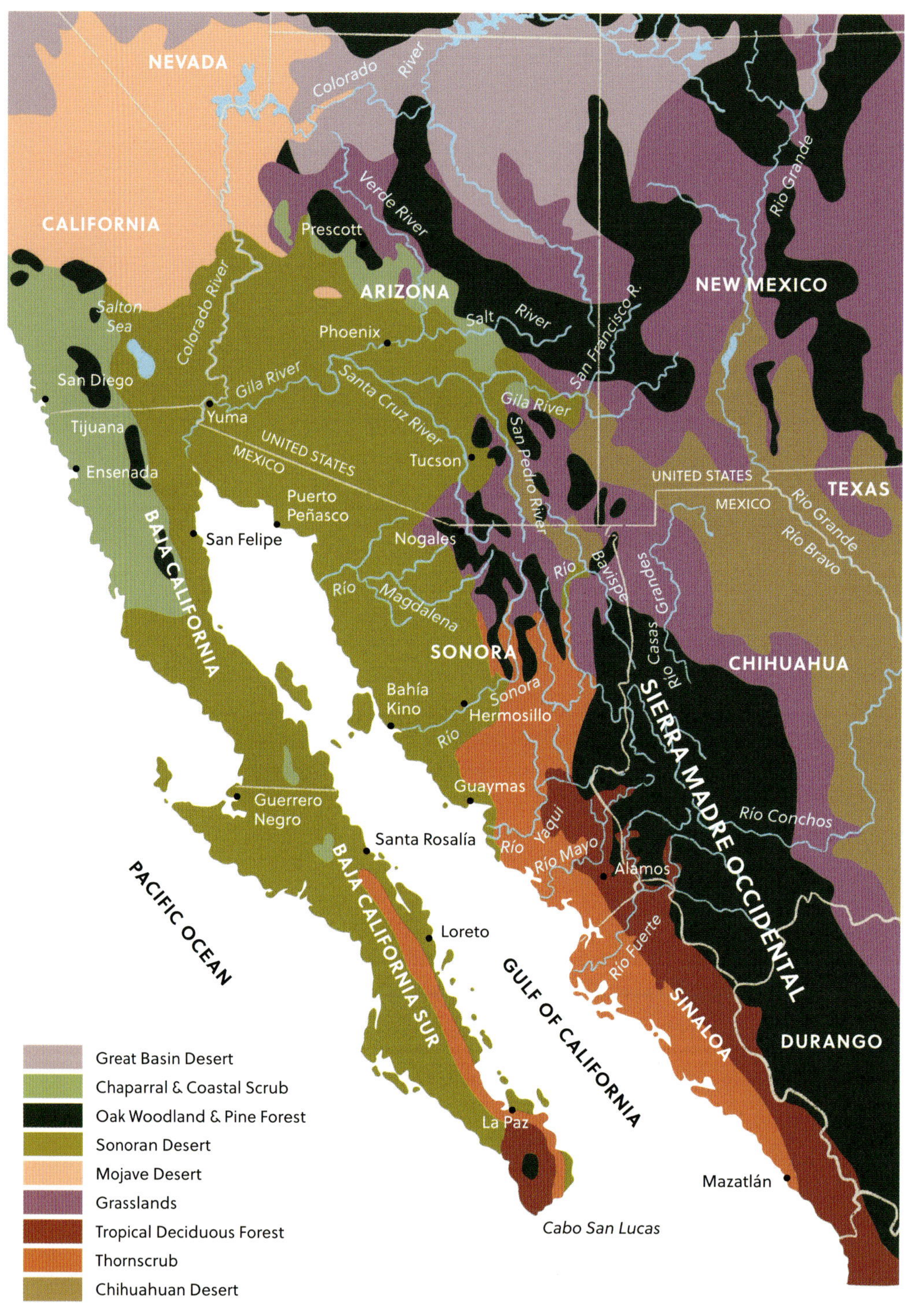
NEVADA
CALIFORNIA
ARIZONA
NEW MEXICO
TEXAS
SONORA
CHIHUAHUA
BAJA CALIFORNIA
BAJA CALIFORNIA SUR
SINALOA
DURANGO
SIERRA MADRE OCCIDENTAL
PACIFIC OCEAN
GULF OF CALIFORNIA
UNITED STATES
MEXICO
Colorado River
Verde River
Salt River
Gila River
Santa Cruz River
San Pedro River
San Francisco R.
Rio Grande
Río Bravo
Río Conchos
Río Casas Grandes
Río Bavispe
Río Magdalena
Río Sonora
Río Yaqui
Río Mayo
Río Fuerte
Salton Sea
Prescott
Phoenix
Yuma
Tucson
Nogales
San Diego
Tijuana
Ensenada
San Felipe
Puerto Peñasco
Bahía Kino
Hermosillo
Guaymas
Guerrero Negro
Santa Rosalía
Álamos
Loreto
La Paz
Cabo San Lucas
Mazatlán
Great Basin Desert
Chaparral & Coastal Scrub
Oak Woodland & Pine Forest
Sonoran Desert
Mojave Desert
Grasslands
Tropical Deciduous Forest
Thornscrub
Chihuahuan Desert

▲ Tucson viewed from Sentinel Peak ("A" Mountain), with Santa Catalina Mountains in the background

geologist compared an aerial view of the region's topography to "an army of caterpillars crawling northward from Mexico."

Southern Arizona is part of a large geological province known as "Basin and Range," which stretches from southeastern Oregon into northwestern Mexico. The whole region has been stretched and extended by plate tectonic forces, causing the Earth's crust to crack into multiple slivers, like the brittle chocolate coating on a caramel candy as you stretch it apart.

Sky Islands

Southeastern Arizona and northeastern Sonora are crossed by approximately 65 separate mountain ranges. The cooler, wetter, forested mountaintops are isolated from one another by a "sea" of desert and grasslands, hence their designation as "Sky Islands." These mountain ranges provide stepping stones for high-elevation species to "hop" south from the Rocky Mountains or north from the Sierra Madre, thereby creating an especially diverse assortment of plants and animals throughout the Sky Island region. Though wings or wind may carry some species from peak to peak, most rely on grassland and desert corridors for safe passage.

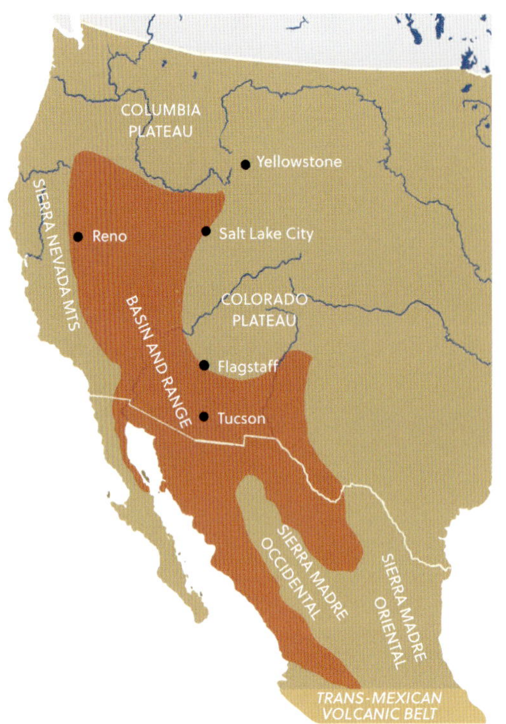

COLUMBIA PLATEAU
Yellowstone
SIERRA NEVADA MTS
Reno
Salt Lake City
BASIN AND RANGE
COLORADO PLATEAU
Flagstaff
Tucson
SIERRA MADRE OCCIDENTAL
SIERRA MADRE ORIENTAL
TRANS-MEXICAN VOLCANIC BELT

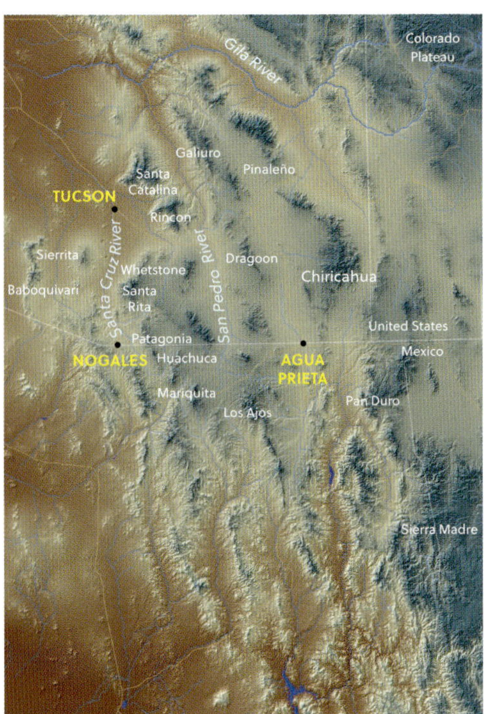

Gila River
Colorado Plateau
Galiuro
Pinaleño
Santa Catalina
TUCSON
Rincon
Santa Cruz River
San Pedro River
Sierrita
Whetstone
Dragoon
Chiricahua
Baboquivari
Santa Rita
Patagonia
United States
Mexico
NOGALES
Huachuca
AGUA PRIETA
Mariquita
Los Ajos
Pan Duro
Sierra Madre

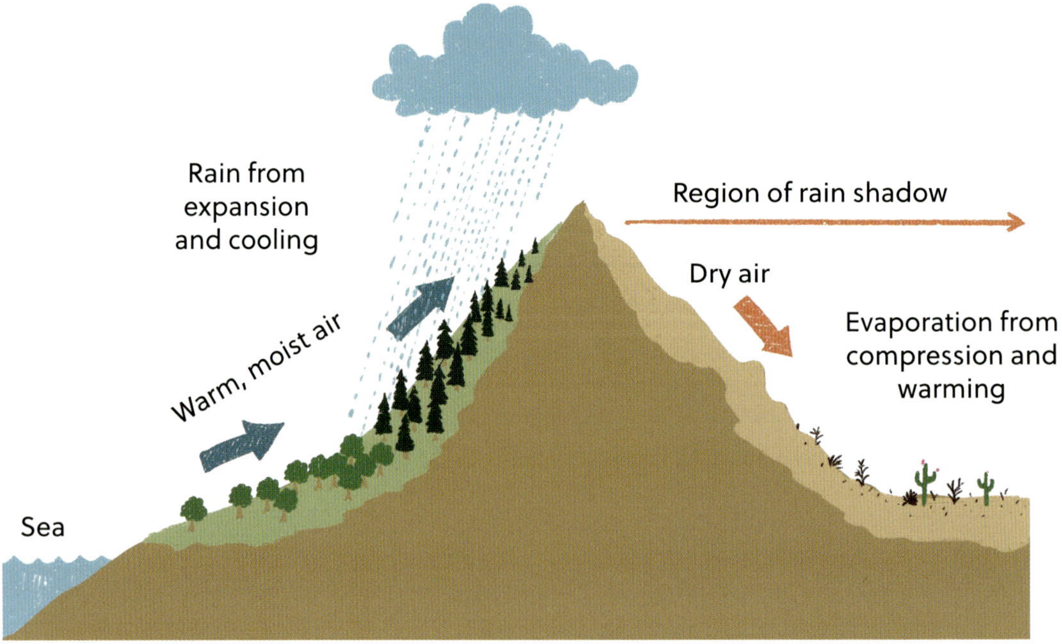

Rain from expansion and cooling
Region of rain shadow
Dry air
Warm, moist air
Evaporation from compression and warming
Sea

▲ Alternating basins and ranges as far as the eye can see

Opposite, clockwise from upper left: Basin and Range Province Map

Mountain ranges of the Sky Islands region

Mountain ranges wring water out of clouds that rise to pass over them, forming a dry zone, or rain shadow, on the far side.

In the northern reaches of the Sonoran Desert, around Tucson, the basins bottom out at about 2500 feet (762 m), and the surrounding mountains soar up to 9500 feet (about 3 km). With increased elevation, temperatures cool considerably—the average temperature difference between central Tucson and the top of the tallest nearby peaks is 30°F (17°C). As air rises over these ranges, it cools, and any atmospheric moisture may condense as dew, rain, or even snow in winter. These mountains help extract water from moist air masses coming from the Gulf of California or Pacific Ocean, forming clouds that bring life-giving rain to their peaks and sometimes the surrounding lowlands. Some of the precipitation runs in streams from the mountains through washes, feeding riparian (streamside) habitats and eventually sinking into the soil to replenish the groundwater.

Cooling temperatures and the associated precipitation establish conditions for distinct communities of plants and animals at different elevations. Biologists recognize about eight distinct biotic communities on the mountainsides of Arizona's highest Sky Islands: desertscrub, desert grassland, oak-grassland, oak woodland, chaparral, pine-oak woodland, pine forest, and mixed conifer (or fir) forest. In the heat of summer, this range of temperatures offers relief for humans who can shift to higher-altitude hikes and picnic spots. On a seasonal basis, many other animals also move up and down the mountains in search of water, food, or favored temperatures.

Over time, this variety of environmental conditions has allowed plants and animals to survive major changes in climate. For example, some species that inhabited the warmer valleys during the last ice age have since relocated to higher elevations as the climate has warmed. This process continues today. In 2013, researchers from the Desert Museum and the University of Arizona showed that the elevational ranges of many plant groups were moving up Mount Lemmon, the mountain north of Tucson, in response to a warming climate.

What is a Desert?

Although many people imagine deserts to be expanses of lifeless sand dunes, the designation actually describes a broad range of landscapes. The Sonoran Desert, in fact, does include some dune fields, but most of it looks more like a sparse shrubland with a profusion of cacti and shrubs providing food and shelter for a great variety of animal life. A common definition of desert is a place that receives fewer than 10 inches (25.4 cm) of rainfall per year, which is true for most of the Sonoran Desert. In the northernmost stretch near Tucson, the average rainfall is a bit higher, between 11 and 12 inches (about 28 to 30.5 cm) annually. However, rainfall alone is not enough to make this determination. For example, the north slope of Alaska receives less than 10 inches of rain, but this tundra is definitely not a desert.

A better definition of desert takes into account the water lost to the air by evaporation and transpiration (water loss through plants). Using this measure, the climate of Tucson can evaporate about five times more water than falls in rain every year (an aridity ratio of 5:1), right on the boundary between arid and semiarid climates. Farther south and west in the Sonoran Desert, near Yuma, Arizona, where rainfall is only 3 inches (7.6 cm) per year, this ratio is about 30:1. For comparison, in the interior of the Sahara Desert, the ratio is 600:1.

The common denominator of all deserts is extreme aridity where water is only freely available for short periods after rains; most of the time, lack of water is the primary limiting factor to the proliferation and nourishment of life. This might lead to the assumption that desert plants and animals struggle to survive. However, this couldn't be further from the truth. Most of the species found in deserts *require* an arid environment for their survival. They are so well-adapted to their environs that they would not do well if water was suddenly abundant—as many cactus gardeners have inadvertently discovered. Deserts are also lands of extremes, where daily temperatures can fluctuate 40 degrees F (22 degrees C), and long dry periods are punctuated by rare storms that bring flash flooding. The plants and animals that live here all have strategies to cope with these highs and lows.

▲ This elf owl finds relief from the heat or cold in its saguaro cavity nest.

North American Deserts

The Sonoran Desert is one of four deserts in North America, clustered in the southwest United States and northwest Mexico. Northernmost and at the highest elevation is the Great Basin Desert. It has very cold winters, restricting the growing season to summer. Vegetation here is dominated by low, small-leafed shrubs, such as big sagebrush. The Mojave Desert is shaped mostly by its winter rainy season. The dominant perennial plants are low shrubs, though annual wildflowers unfurl carpets of color after a rainy winter. Few trees and succulents are found here, with the exception of the Joshua tree, a tall, branched yucca that forms extensive woodlands above 3000 feet (914 m) in elevation. The Chihuahuan Desert is the southernmost North American desert, but its relatively high elevation keeps it cooler than the Sonoran Desert and hard freezes are common. Its plant community is made of many species of low shrubs, succulents, and small cacti, with occasional trees. Most of its rainfall occurs in the summer months.

In comparison to its neighbors, the Sonoran Desert is lush. Small trees (such as ironwood, palo verde, and mesquite) and large columnar cacti (such as saguaros and organ pipe) dominate the visual landscape and differentiate it from the other three deserts. The amount and seasonality of rainfall as well as the rarity of hard freezes make this interesting assembly of plant types possible. Much of the area gets both winter and summer rains. From December to March, storms originating in the North Pacific Ocean bring occasional gentle and widespread rains. From July to mid-September, moist air surges northward from the Gulf of California, helping fuel intense thunderstorms accompanied by localized deluges and flooding. The two rainy seasons are so distinct that residents of Sonora, Mexico have different names for them—the winter rains are *equipatas* (derived from *quepa*, the Yaqui-Mayo word for rain) and the summer rains are *las aguas* (Spanish for "the waters").

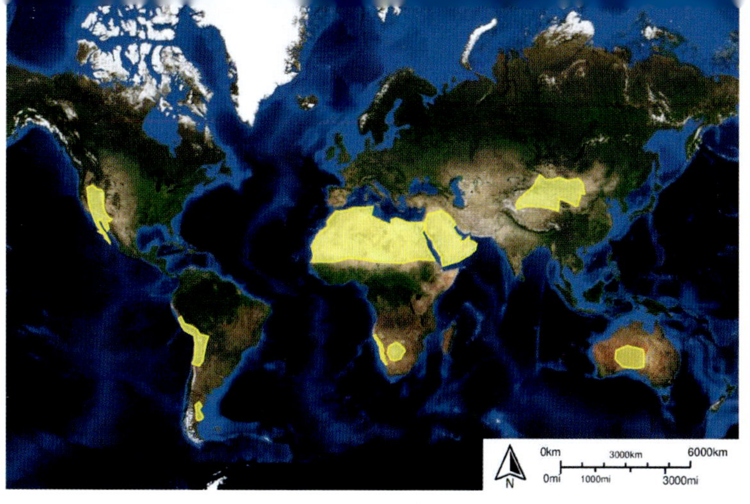

◂ Global map of the world's desert regions

◂◂ Yellow brittlebush blooms cover a hillside in spring.

◂◂ Brittlebush and penstemon dominate this spring wildflower display.

Like most deserts in the world, the Sonoran, Mojave, and Chihuahuan Deserts are located at or around 30 degrees latitude. This is a zone where global atmospheric circulation drops dry air that has already lost its moisture in tropical and polar storms. In addition, these deserts are near the west coast of the continent, where cold ocean currents keep the air above them relatively dry and cool. Finally, with the exception of some of the Sonoran Desert, most of these deserts are inland and separated from the ocean by both distance and mountain ranges. Storms traveling eastward from the Pacific are forced up and over coastal ranges where air masses cool and drop most of their water before getting to the deserts. Most of the North American deserts are in a rain shadow, a dry area caused by coastal mountain ranges obstructing rainy weather. However, this is only true for part of the Sonoran Desert.

In addition to the planetary wind patterns that helped create and sustain the Sonoran Desert, an important regional climate feature is the North American monsoon. Like its more famous cousin, the South Asian monsoon, it is a seasonal shift in winds that brings heavy rains or extreme dryness. During most of the year, the prevailing winds over the Sonoran Desert come from the west and are dry. However, in early summer (May–June), the land surface in this region heats up, forming a dome of high pressure and causing the wind patterns to shift to a more southerly source. These winds pick up moisture from the Gulf of California that feeds summer thunderstorms over much of the Sonoran Desert from about July until mid-September. During this season, Northwest Mexico receives about 75 percent of its annual precipitation; in Arizona and New Mexico, it's about 50 percent. The proximity of the warm surface waters of the Gulf of California is a key factor in bringing summer rains to the region.

DEEP HISTORY OF THE SONORAN DESERT

PEOPLE TEND TO THINK OF HISTORY in terms of human lifetimes or, in textbooks, centuries. It's difficult to fathom the deep history of geologic time, measured in millions and even billions of years. However, this time frame encompasses the geological events that explain why our landscapes are the way they are today and have shaped the features and resources that impact our daily lives. It also gives us important clues about how our environments may respond to the changes we are making to our planet today.

We have seen how the presence of mountain ranges and the Gulf of California have influenced the development of the Sonoran Desert climate and its biodiversity. How did they come to be? How have they changed over time? What other factors have influenced the development of this unique assembly of plants and animals?

Making and Moving Mountains

We'll begin our story about 75 million years ago, when the region we now call the Sonoran Desert was part of a large mountain belt system. The entire region sat much higher than it does now, perhaps at 13,000 feet (about 4 km) or more, like the Altiplano of the Andes mountains of South America today. The collision of the western edge of North America with an ancient ocean plate dramatically compressed the region, creating a broad, high mountain range. To visualize this, imagine North America as a mass of cookie dough and your hands compressing it from the sides into a tall, wide, ridged form. About 45 million years ago, North America began overtaking a zone of hot rising magma that heated the whole region and fed volcanoes throughout the landscape. The Chiricahua Mountains are the remnants of one of these volcanic explosions.

Then about 25 million years ago, the ancient ocean plate was completely subsumed under the North American continent, and the pressure from the west eased. The intense pressure was replaced by a slippery fault zone, which evolved to be what we now know as the San Andreas Fault. Over millions of years, the high mountains collapsed and spread out under their own weight, heated from below, much like a scoop of cookie dough spreading flat in the oven. Thankfully cookies don't take that long to bake!

Finally, about 12 to 4 million years ago, the land mass cooled and, as it continued flattening, the upper layers of the crust cracked into the basins and ranges that formed the Sky Island mountains. This happened gradually, earthquake by earthquake, stretching the land surface to double its length. If Los Angeles and Tucson existed 30 million years ago, they would have only been a four-hour rather than an eight-hour drive apart. Today's mountains are not quite as tall as they once were. However, the deep basins between them offer a greater variety of elevations and habitat diversity than 30 million years ago.

Over that period, the mountain peaks have slowly eroded, shedding sediment into the basins. Many valleys in the Sonoran Desert region are filled with more than 10,000 feet (3048 meters) of sediment. These huge basins of unconsolidated sand, clay, pebbles, and other debris provide another critical resource for life in the Sonoran Desert—groundwater. Inch by inch, rain and snow that was not immediately used by plants or evaporated seeped into the spaces within the accumulated sand and debris, forming aquifers that could

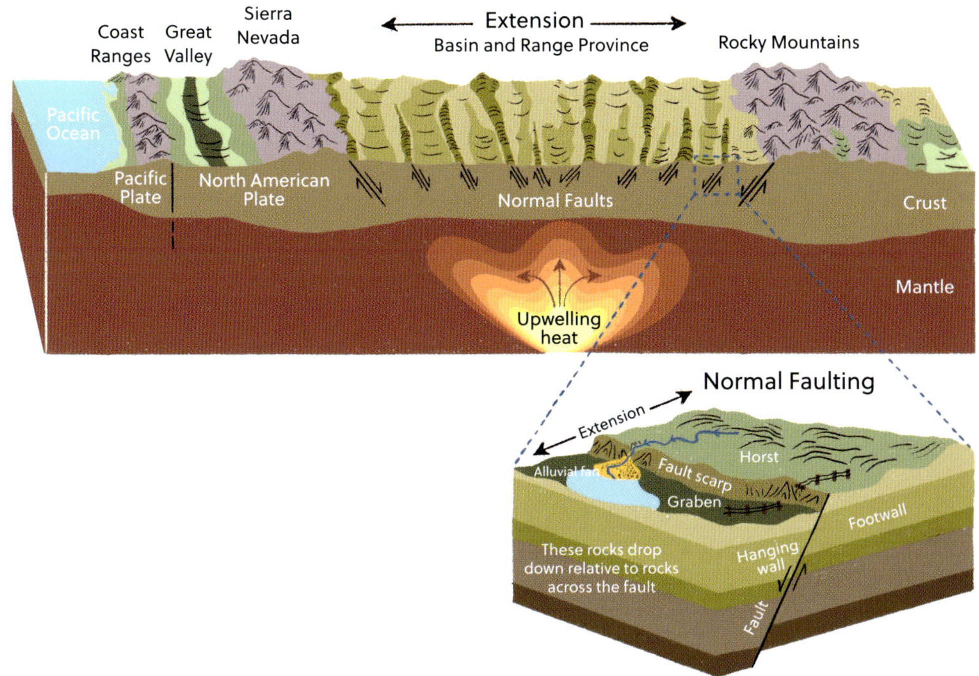

nourish deep tree roots and feed rare but important streams. These aquifers have been especially important for supporting human life in the region, providing groundwater that could be mined or retrieved from sunk wells to support our settlements, agriculture, and industry.

▲ The Basin and Range formed as upwelling heat caused the Earth's crust to stretch thin, and crack, like cookie dough in a hot oven.

Opening of the Gulf of California

Around 6 million years ago, the tectonic forces tugging the crust apart managed to pull a sliver of North America onto the Pacific Plate. A crustal spreading center known as the East Pacific Rise slipped under the continent and "stole" (essentially, repositioned) the land, creating what is now the Baja California peninsula and much of western California. On many maps, this land is depicted as part of North America, but on a geological map, it is shown to be part of an entirely different plate, moving northwest with respect to the rest of the continent at about 2 inches (5 cm) per year, or about as fast as your fingernails grow.

The San Andreas Fault, 800 miles (1288 km) long, separates the Pacific and North American plates here. At the south end of this fault, in the Gulf of California, new ocean crust is forming and slowly pushing the Baja California peninsula away from mainland Mexico. This new ocean basin is one of the youngest in the world and brings life-giving water vapor to much of the Sonoran Desert through monsoon rains. Without it, the Sonoran Desert would be very different.

Earthquakes

Except for the major influence of San Andreas Fault activity, the Sonoran Desert is seismically quiet, with discernable earthquakes only once every few decades. The last major earthquake in the Tucson area occurred on May 3, 1887 at 2:15 p.m. That afternoon, the earth's surface ruptured with an estimated magnitude of 7.2 on the Richter scale about 20 miles (32 km) south of Douglas, Arizona, near the village of Bavispe, Sonora. It cracked plaster walls in Tucson and El Paso, Texas; knocked over an adobe wall at the Spanish cemetery at Mission San Xavier del Bac near Tucson; and stopped large pendulum clocks in Phoenix. More tragically, it was responsible for 51 deaths in Mexico.

Tucson residents first thought the large clouds of dust and forest fire smoke rising above the crest of the Santa Catalina Mountains were due to an erupting volcano, but the fires were ignited by falling boulders crashing together and causing sparks on the dry hillsides. Tohono O'odham residents in the village of Pan Tak below Kitt Peak reported a massive rock fall. Geysers of water shot up from the flood plain of the San Pedro River while other streams and springs throughout the region either dried up or initiated flow. An estimated 50,000 cattle died that year in the San Pedro River valley as a direct result of wildfires or later starvation.

Volcanoes

There have been two contrasting styles of volcanism in the Sonoran Desert in recent geologic time. An intense volcanic episode from about 40 to 20 million years ago produced thick, viscous magmas, exploding from the Earth's surface in large eruptions of gas and ash (as in the 1980 Mount St. Helens eruption in Washington State). In contrast, volcanic activity during the last 10 million years or so initiated thinner, more syrupy lavas that rose up along deep cracks in the earth and formed basalt flows on the surface.

One of these basaltic eruptions formed the Pinacate field, just north of Rocky Point, Sonora, Mexico, and has become an international showcase of natural history. The field contains a central 4000-foot (1219 m) stratified volcano composed of multiple lava flows and ash layers, surrounded by approximately 400 outlying single-eruption basalt cinder cones and flows and 10 unusual steam-blast explosion craters, some with diameters greater than a mile (1.6 km). These unusual craters owe their explosive origin to the rising magma contacting water-saturated sediments, which adds the force of steam blasts to the normal volcanic fountain.

Life History: The Fossil Record

The tumultuous geological spectacle—mountains building, ripping apart, and eroding; a new ocean opening; volcanoes erupting—merely sets the stage for the evolution of the modern Sonoran Desert. Climate events and the expansion of the biosphere advance the drama into the present day. When we started our story 75 million years ago, near the end of the age of dinosaurs, the Earth was much warmer than it is today, and humid temperate evergreen and tropical rainforests covered most of North America. The fossil record reveals that primitive ferns, cycads, and palms grew as far north as Alaska.

During the next 25 million years, the area that would become the Sonoran Desert dried out somewhat, and tropical deciduous forests (comprised of trees that shed their leaves annually) appeared. During dry seasons, leafless trees allowed sunlight to reach the forest floor. This introduced new habitat conditions and supported the evolution of new species, such as cacti and succulents. Global temperatures were more than 23°F (13°C) higher than today, encouraging the dispersion of tropical plants and animals throughout North America. Something like today's Sonoran Desert came into being 8 to 15 million years ago during a dry period, and the region continued to be warm and tropical until the start of the Ice Age, 2.6 million years ago. This tropical heritage is still evident in the mix of Sonoran Desert species today—consider the columnar cacti (saguaro, organ pipe, senita) and small trees (desert ironwood, palo verde) surrounding you on a desert walk.

During the Ice Age (or the Pleistocene Epoch, occurring 2.6 million to 11,000 years ago), the Earth cooled dramatically. There were approximately 20 periods of glaciation in which polar ice expanded toward the equator and global temperatures were 10°F (5.5°C) cooler than today. At its maximum extent, ice covered about 30 percent of the globe. Mountain glaciers covered the peaks of the Rocky Mountains and Sierra Nevada in the Western United States, extending as far south as the Sierra Madre del Sur in southern Mexico. Lakes that are now dry were full.

Thanks to the humble packrat (or white-throated woodrat), we know a fair bit about plant communities during the last glacial cycle, about 45,000 to 11,000 years ago. These rodents collect all sorts of plant material from their environment, not only for food but also to build elaborate shelters that protect them from predators and the elements. Some of these materials get cemented together in their middens (waste piles of urine and fecal matter). Their sticky urine coats their refuse, preserving the waste into hardened blocks of leaves, sticks, pollen, bones, rocks, and anything else the packrat left on the trash pile, leaving a record of the plants and animals that lived in these areas 40,000 years ago.

Examining middens is not for the squeamish, and today's committed scientists have learned that about 45,000 to 11,000 years ago, what is now the Sonoran Desert was dominated by woodland trees and shrubs, such as pinyon pines, junipers, and shrub live oaks. Joshua trees, a form of yucca, were also common, while heat-tolerant desert plants were present only at low elevations and farther south, or in rare, protected pockets. The Sonoran Desert as we know it today did not form until about 9000 years ago as woodland plants retreated upslope and northward. About 4500 years ago, palo verdes and desert ironwood trees as well as organ pipe cacti made their way north from their Ice Age retreats. The region cycled back and forth between desert and woodland ecosystems repeatedly throughout the Pleistocene, though it was characterized by cooler climates and vegetation most of the time. The Sonoran Desert only looked as it does today for about 5 percent of the last 2.6 million years.

Throughout North America and in the Sonoran Desert, the Ice Ages were marked by the proliferation and eventual demise of a menagerie of mega-mammals. Animals such as antelope, bear, camels, llamas, saber-toothed cats, dire wolves, bison, and horses were common. Giant anteaters, capybaras, and ground sloths migrated to North America from South America over the

Panamanian land bridge during this time. Mammoths, hyenas, and jaguars arrived via a Eurasian land bridge. Exactly why most of these species became extinct at the end of the last Ice Age, about 11,000 years ago, is still an unresolved scientific question. There are two main hypotheses: (1) hunting by humans, who arrived in the Americas around the same time, or (2) changes in climate and vegetation. Proponents of each idea continue to gather data as new fossils and new dating techniques emerge. It is one of many remaining mysteries in our quest to fully understand how the natural world has changed over time and how humans have impacted that change.

▲ Packrat midden

ALL THE WORLD'S BIOMES

ONE OF THE REMARKABLE THINGS about the Sonoran Desert region is that within little more than a day's drive, you can travel from warm tropical forests to cool coniferous forests, passing though grassland and woodland—you can even stop for a dip in the ocean. These adjacent biological communities all help shape the Sonoran Desert as plants and animals move across porous boundaries among these biomes.

A biome is a large area that is characterized by the plants and animals that live in it; tropical rainforest and tundra are examples. Because plants are the most visible and constant parts of a biological community, ecologists classify biomes based on their vegetation. However, biomes do contain characteristic animal life as well. Several biomes have been described across the globe, and most are represented in the Sonoran Desert region.

‣ Vegetation types change dramatically as temperature drops and moisture availability increases up the mountains.

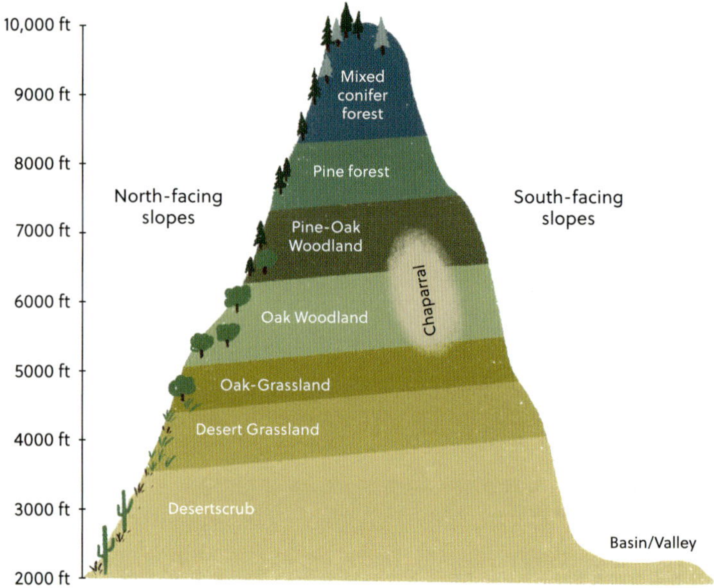

We'll use vegetation types to describe these biomes as well as many of the landscapes in our recommended adventures. Here's a brief primer on plant life forms. Most of these are common terms, but biologists sometimes use them in particular ways.

- **Annual** plants complete their life cycle, from germination to seed production, within one growing season and then die.
- **Coniferous** trees are cone-bearing and keep their needle-shaped leaves throughout the year.
- **Deciduous** trees drop their leaves during the cold and/or dry season.
- **Grasses** have narrow leaves, hollow stems, and clusters of very small, usually wind-pollinated flowers.
- **Herbaceous** plants (herbs) are non-woody plants that have flexible green stems with few or no woody parts.
- **Perennial** plants live for more than two years. They may die back seasonally, but will resprout from roots when conditions are favorable.

- **Shrubs** are woody plants that are typically less than 13 feet (about 4 m) tall and have multiple stems.

- **Succulents** are plants that can store water in their leaves and stems. Cacti, native to the Americas, are succulents with thick fleshy stems and spines instead of leaves.

- **Trees** are woody plants that are generally more than 12 feet (3.7 m) in height and have one central stem.

- **Woody** plants have hard stems and buds that survive above ground in winter.

Tundra

Occurring near the Earth's poles and on some mountaintops, tundra is the coldest biome. Extremely frigid winters limit plant life to ground-hugging woody shrubs and perennial herbaceous plants. Tundra is too cold for trees or succulents, and the growing season is too short for annual plants.

◂ Tundra in the San Francisco Mountains in northern Arizona

▲ Coniferous forest on Mount Lemmon

Where can you find tundra in the Sonoran Desert region? The San Francisco Peaks near Flagstaff, Arizona reach 12,600 feet (about 3840 m). There, only 45 miles (72 km) from the northernmost saguaros, a small area of alpine tundra includes some of the same plant species one can find in the arctic tundra of Alaska.

Coniferous Forest

Coniferous forests are dominated by pines, firs, and spruces. Many conifers can tolerate cold that's just a little less severe than in tundra. In the coldest forests near the tundra boundary, trees may be relatively short, only several feet (a couple of meters) tall. In warmer conditions, these trees may tower over 300 feet (90 m).

In the Sonoran Desert region, coniferous forests grow on higher mountain ranges to the north and east of the Sonoran Desert proper. Most of the trees found in these forests are the same as those found in the Rocky Mountains to the north.

Temperate Deciduous Forest

Temperate deciduous forests are generally characterized by dense stands of broad-leaf trees that lose their leaves in winter. Winters are milder than in conifer-dominated climates, but still too cold for plants to grow. Summers are usually warm and humid. Temperate deciduous forests are home to more species than the two colder biomes. In addition to trees, there are many herbaceous plants and shrubs. Pure temperate deciduous forest is rare in the region and found in scattered groves of aspen and ribbons of riparian trees (such as cottonwood) alongside streams.

◂ Deciduous trees on Mount Lemmon

Mountain slopes in the Sonoran Desert region are wooded with a mix of coniferous and temperate deciduous forest tree types, mostly oaks and pines. These oaks, however, are evergreen species, holding onto their leaves except in the most severe droughts. This mix of species is derived from the temperate forests of the Sierra Madre Occidental in Mexico, where temperate and coniferous forests are confined to Sky Island mountains that rise well above the arid deserts and grasslands of the intervening basins.

Grassland

Grassland is a semiarid biome with warm, humid, moderately rainy summers and cold, dry winters. Not surprisingly, grass is the dominant life form—scores of species form continuous carpets over large areas. Annual plants are also well-represented, including those that grow from bulbs and die back to the ground each year. Trees, shrubs, and succulents are kept to a minimum by periodic fires.

Desert or semi-desert grasslands differ from the true prairies of the American Midwest. They are shorter, less dense, and more frequently interspersed with desert shrubs and succulents. Desert grasslands are mostly found to the east of the Sonoran Desert proper.

▾ Grasslands flanking the Santa Rita Mountains

◂ California chaparral

◂ Sonoran Desert inland chaparral

Chaparral

Chaparral is a semiarid biome that occurs on the west coast of every continent between about 30 and 40 degrees latitude. It is known for mild, moist winters and hot, dry summers, much like a Mediterranean climate. Chaparral plants are woody evergreen shrubs with small leathery leaves. They form impassable thickets 5–8 feet (1.5–2.4 m) tall. During the long summers, resinous leaves and dry woody stems become explosively combustible, and wildfires raze large areas to the ground every few decades. These periodic fires are necessary for maintaining the health of this biological community. After a fire, annual species make a brief showing, but the land is soon reclaimed by the shrubs that sprout from seeds or roots.

The main area of chaparral in the Western United States occurs on the western slopes of the mountains along the Pacific Coast in Southern California and northern Baja California. Within the interior Sonoran Desert, there are small patches of chaparral along the desert's northern edge and on the slopes of Sky Islands where manzanita and shrub live oak grow.

Above from left to right:
Desertscrub in Ironwood Forest

Thornscrub in Baja California

Tropical deciduous forest near Álamos, Sonora

Desert or Desertscrub

Desert/desertscrub is the most arid biome. For most of the year, vegetation is constrained by the lack of water. Temperature and seasonality of rainfall determine the specific types of plants and animals that can survive, but all desert vegetation looks fairly similar. Because leaves increase water loss, plants have few or no leaves. Vegetation is also widely spaced—you can easily walk off-trail through the desert, picking your way between plants. More detailed descriptions of the special features of deserts are provided in "Adaptations to Desert Living" (page 57).

Thornscrub

Thornscrub is an intermediate biome between desert and tropical forest. The vegetation is mostly short trees (10–20 feet/3–6 m tall), shrubs, and, in the Western Hemisphere, abundant cacti. It is generally more dense and taller than desert vegetation, and many species are thorny. A practical definition of thornscrub is an impenetrable thicket that you cannot walk through without scratching your skin or tearing your clothing. Annuals, herbaceous perennials, and vines are also abundant. Most perennial plants will drop their leaves during the dry season but grow lush during the short rainy season. The climate is nearly frost-free, and the seasons are determined more by varying rainfall than temperature. The Sonoran Desert merges gradually into thornscrub to the south in central Sonora.

Tropical Forest

Tropical forest is defined by the absence of freezing temperatures and the occurrence of ample rainfall for at least part of the year. While tropical rainforests are never stressed for water, some tropical forests have a dry season. Tropical deciduous forests, which occur in the southern Sonoran Desert region, have a dry season that lasts from three to nine months, during which time the trees shed their leaves. Many trees flower in the winter–spring dry season, even while leafless, and are shorter than trees in tropical rainforests, where the canopies can be 150 feet (46 m) or higher.

During the rainy season the vegetation is luxuriant, forming closed canopies of foliage 15–35 feet (4.6–10.7 m) above the ground. Almost all plant life forms are present. Flowering epiphytes (plants that grow on other plants or rocks) are a special feature of these habitats. The transition from thornscrub to tropical deciduous forest occurs in the southern part of Sonora. Many of the plants and animals throughout the Sonoran Desert evolved from ancestors in these tropical biomes.

Riparian Communities

Riparian habitats occur where there is water near the surface most of the year. The term riparian strictly refers to the zone along the banks of rivers or streams but is also more loosely applied to shoreline communities along slow or non-flowing waters such as marshes,

▲ Santa Cruz River near Tumacácori National Historical Park

lakes, and ponds. A riparian community of plants and animals can be found within any biome and is not itself considered a biome.

These habitats are critically important to maintaining the diversity of life in arid and semiarid environments like deserts and grasslands. They support a wide variety of plants and animals that could otherwise not survive there. These ribbons of green forest also help augment populations of more arid-adapted species in adjacent habitat. Viewed from above, it's easy to spot them—even a trickle of a stream, if sustained, will support a conspicuous oasis along its banks. Riparian habitats are thought to support 80 percent of all wildlife in the Sonoran Desert at some stage in their life cycles.

Marine Biome in the Desert?

The Sonoran Desert is bisected by the Gulf of California, which helps shape the character of the entire region. This marine biome provides life-giving moisture to summer monsoon storms as well as sustenance to human and other communities along its shores. This long, narrow ocean basin also has extremely high biodiversity due to its shape and location. Twice-daily tides bring nutrient-rich water from the deep Pacific Ocean up to the shallow, narrow northern Gulf with some of the largest tidal ranges in the world—up to 30 vertical feet (9 m). These nutrients feed plankton that serve as the base of the food web for one of the most abundant and diverse marine

▲ Cabo Pulmo in the Gulf of California near the southern tip of the Baja peninsula

communities in the world. More than 6000 animal species have been recorded in the Gulf, and this is likely just 70 percent of the actual number of creatures living in its rich waters.

The Gulf is so productive that it provides about half of Mexico's total fisheries catch and so rich in plankton that groups of finback whales have abandoned their traditional migration routes to take up permanent residence there. With nearly 1000 islands and islets, the Gulf also provides abundant coastlines and diverse habitat for seabirds and marine reptiles, including five threatened or endangered sea turtles, a sea snake, and a crocodile. Although much of the mainland coast has been damaged by urbanization, marina and harbor construction, shrimp aquaculture, and other development, the remoteness of the Baja peninsula and federal protections for the islands have helped to maintain healthy coastal refuges. As in most of the world's oceans, unsustainable fishing is also a major concern in the Gulf, and most areas are overfished. The good news is that the Mexican government has created many new protected areas, including two marine protected areas where no fishing at all is allowed. Additionally, local fishing communities have been working with scientists and government agencies to implement and certify new sustainable practices (see Adventure to Puerto Peñasco, page 363).

DESERT WATERS

DESERT DWELLERS KNOW IT WELL—the seasonal anticipation that comes when the first clouds of the monsoon season gather, and the elation that follows when the skies finally release their precious cargo. Often the first sign that it's raining somewhere is the distinctive scent of desert rain arising from parched soils and desert plants. Recent research has shown that the feeling of euphoria may be due to more than just knowing that your garden is going to get a good soaking. Many of the compounds released by desert plants have been shown to have health benefits, such as stabilizing emotions, improving sleep patterns, enhancing digestion, and reducing depression and anxiety. These same volatile organic oils are produced by plants as protection from intense sun and aridity, and they build up on leaf surfaces during the hot dry months. Even wind and humidity that precedes a storm can start to release these compounds, enhancing the sense of expectation.

Annual rainfall in the Sonoran Desert varies from 3–20 inches (7.6–51 cm), depending on location, and generally increases with elevation. In the northern reaches of the desert, near Tucson, the long-term average is 11–12 inches (28–30.5 cm). Hermosillo, the major city in Sonora, is just slightly wetter, with 13.9 inches (35.3 cm). Rain falls about equally in two rainy seasons, the first from December to March and the second from July to early September. August, September, and December have traditionally been the wettest

▲ Monsoon season rain shower over the Altar Valley. Monsoon rains can be intense but very spotty.

months whereas May and June are generally the driest. Winter rains tend to be widespread and relatively gentle, sinking into the relatively soft ground and feeding thirsty plants; summer, on the other hand, often brings violent thunderstorms that fall hard and fast on ground that has been baked solid in the hot dry oven of May and June. However, rain in both seasons is important for different categories of plants and animals.

Rainfall in the desert is infrequent and also undependable. Sometimes it's distributed throughout the season in small showers; other times it comes in a few large storms. In the driest parts of the desert, such as Yuma, Arizona, a single storm can produce more rain than typically falls in an entire year. Summer storms are typically spotty with widely varying precipitation, even in locations within the same city. In fact, throughout monsoon season, it's not unusual to hear Tucson residents complain that the rain seems to fall everywhere except in their neighborhood.

The region's mountains act as rain collectors, forcing air up, cooling it, and wringing out its water vapor as rain or even snow. After a good rainfall, the normally dry washes and streambeds may flow for a few hours or a few days, sometimes with surprising flash floods.

Some of this water seeps into the soil and becomes groundwater, feeding the rare streams and riparian zones. Although these aquatic sites represent only a tiny percentage of land cover in the desert, they play an outsize role in sustaining the variety of plants and animals that can survive here. Even washes that are dry most of the year may collect enough water to support trees such as ironwoods, mesquites, and palo verdes, which border the water source and stand out as a strand of green against the sparse desert. Intermittent streams carrying water from storms or snowmelt support trees like sycamore and ash in the uplands, and cottonwood and willow at lower elevations. Where the water table intersects the land surface, perennial streams support these tree species in denser profusion. Surface water may also occur in marshy areas called *ciénagas*.

Disappearing Rivers

Riparian areas are the desert's lifeblood. Covering only a few percent of the total land area, these green arteries traverse the surrounding arid land and provide habitat and migration corridors for many species. Nearly 80 percent of Arizona's wildlife species, including most of the threatened or endangered animals, depend on riparian areas for food, water, shelter, or migration during some part of their lives. Birds, such as bald eagles, black hawks, and summer tanagers, nest along them; mammals, including beavers, raccoons, otters, and many others, rely on these areas for food, shelter, and water. Riparian corridors also provide shade and cover for many mountain species to move among forested Sky Islands. Aquatic species, such as fish, leopard frogs, garter snakes, and dragonflies, all depend on these desert waters. For people today, riparian areas offer places for recreation—for hiking, riding, cycling, fishing, boating, birding, and more.

Even so, most regional riparian areas have been degraded or destroyed. In Arizona, all the major rivers have been severely compromised and at least 70 percent of rivers and streams have been altered by dams, diversion, and groundwater pumping. A similar fate has befallen the rivers of Sonora. Where dams have restricted or eliminated water flow downstream or where groundwater pumping has caused the water table to drop deep below the surface, riparian forests have disappeared along with their animal inhabitants. Now, as we begin to understand the importance of maintaining the integrity and function of riparian ecosystems, organizations and communities are working to protect and restore what remains while meeting the needs of an ever-growing human population. Special attention and protections have been granted to the few remaining free-flowing rivers, including the San Pedro in the Sonoran Desert.

Tucson's Water Story

Tucson's water story illustrates the complexity of water issues in a thirsty land. The Tucson Basin is like a large bathtub—the surrounding mountains are the rim; the deep layers of gravel, sediments, and rock beneath form the basin; and the Santa Cruz River, whose surface and subsurface waters flow to the lowest point of the basin, is the drain. Tucson exists where it does because, over millennia, storm runoff from throughout the Santa Cruz watershed percolated into the aquifer and filled the basin. From recent archaeological excavations near Sentinel Peak (or "A" Mountain), we know that Tucson has been continuously inhabited for at least 4000 years, making it one of the oldest settlements in the United States. Why?

◂ Of the major rivers in Arizona, only the Verde and San Pedro are free-flowing. The Gila River watershed is shown in green.

At this spot along the Santa Cruz River, the mountain's bedrock pushed groundwater to the surface, providing year-round flow that supported a lush riparian woodland where Indigenous people gathered wild foods and used the river's water to cultivate corn, beans, squash, and cotton. This permanent water source was essential for human life to thrive. The Tohono O'odham called this place of water flow and human habitation Chuk Shon ("base of the black hill," referring to the foot of "A" Mountain), from which Tucson's name derives.

Today at this site, the Santa Cruz River is a dry channel, flowing only after rainstorms. What happened? Tucson's first inhabitants drew water from the river by scooping it out or directing it through narrow canals to irrigate crops (the first appeared around 1200 BCE). In the late 1600s, the Spanish colonizers continued to utilize water in much the same way; they watered their crops through a communal system of *acequias* (Spanish for irrigation ditches), which directed water from the river through the fields and then rerouted it back to the channel downstream. They also dug shallow wells for municipal use. In the mid-1800s, the population remained small—around 250 people—putting little strain on the water supply, and water was delivered by wagon. What the community used was replaced by rainfall and snowmelt along the watershed.

However, in the 1880s as the population grew and needed more water, people began to pump water from deeper wells and made bigger canals. Larger irrigated farms appeared, undermining the old acequia system. By 1890, a series of drought years were followed by heavy floods that scoured riverbanks, already destabilized by overgrazing and canal building, and deeply eroded the river bottom. This, combined with unregulated groundwater pumping, resulted in the complete disappearance of the Santa Cruz River's surface waters by the late 1940s.

Human demand for water in the basin continued to far exceed what precipitation could replace. Until the 1990s, groundwater pumped from wells throughout the community was the sole source of water for residential delivery. We now know that that much of this groundwater accumulated 8000–9000 years ago, when the region had a much wetter climate, and that it is not quickly renewable. Tucson was the largest municipality in the United States that relied solely on groundwater. By the latter part of the twentieth century, the consequences of this dependence were clear. The water table surrounding central Tucson's wells had dropped 200 feet (61 m). Midtown houses developed large cracks as the ground subsided. In the most affected areas, some wells had to be shut down. Similar impacts were felt in towns and agricultural areas throughout Southern Arizona. To address this, Arizona passed the Groundwater Management Act in 1980, which requires that municipal water recharge (replenishment) must equal pumping by 2025. This required Arizona cities to find a new source of water, and they turned their attention to the region's major river, the Colorado.

Colorado River and the Central Arizona Project

The Colorado River provides water to seven US and two Mexican states in the arid West. It is the most dammed and diverted river in the world, serving some 40 million people and thousands of acres of farmland throughout its watershed. It is so overdrawn by its consumers that it no longer reaches its outflow point in the Gulf of California.

▲ Central Arizona Project Canal

Tucson receives Colorado River water pumped along a 336-mile-long canal called the Central Arizona Project (CAP), which was started in 1973 and completed in 1994. The CAP provides Southern Arizona with about 1.5 million acre-feet of Colorado River water per year. An acre-foot is enough water to cover an acre of land with one foot of water, or about 320,600 gallons (1.2 million liters). This system of aqueducts, tunnels, pumping plants, and pipelines begins at Lake Havasu on the Colorado River and ends at the southern boundary of the San Xavier District of the Tohono O'odham Nation southwest of Tucson.

CAP water is allocated to cities and towns, Native American nations, and agricultural users. In drought years, some of the water is left in the river to maintain safe reservoir levels, and other users take varying cuts based on intensely negotiated rules. At its recharge facility west of the city, Tucson Water has been banking Colorado River water underground since 1996. This helps meet demand when the Colorado River cannot provide sufficient water due to drought years or increasing numbers of users.

For decades, the Colorado River has been overallocated (more demand for water than supply). Until recent years, large dams on the river have held enough water to meet regional demands and

▲ Lake Mead behind Hoover Dam. The white "bathtub ring" marks the distance the water level has dropped.

mitigate the impact of a shortage. However, since about 2000, the Colorado River basin has been in a long-term drought, significantly reducing river flows and forcing cutbacks in water delivery to states. Tucson is in a good position to weather these cuts and deliver water to residents due to stored groundwater, but some regional farmers have had to contend with cutbacks.

Reclaimed Water

Tucson Water has also operated a reclaimed water production, storage, and delivery system since the mid-1980s. Wastewater from the sewage treatment facility is further filtered and disinfected for use in irrigation and other non-potable applications at golf courses, parks, schools, and homes. Reclaimed water treated to a higher level of purity will soon be part of the potable water system in Tucson and other Arizona cities as well.

Riparian Ecosystem Restoration and Protection

Healthy riparian ecosystems improve quality of life for all residents. Tucson has been using treated wastewater to restore an area along the Santa Cruz River called Sweetwater Wetlands (see Adventure to Sweetwater Wetlands, page 281). Treated wastewater filters into recharge basins at the site in the riverbed. As the water infiltrates, it is further cleaned by the soil sediments. Wells beneath these recharge basins capture this cleaned water and distribute it through the reclaimed water delivery system. These wetlands provide habitat for urban wildlife, including residential and migratory birds, raccoons, and bobcats, and Sweetwater Wetlands Park is a wonderful space to enjoy nature. Several other projects throughout the region also restore and revitalize these important habitats, utilizing partnerships among private landholders and US and Mexican federal refuges and protected areas. Biological surveys have shown that many species, some of which are threatened by loss of habitat in their range, now utilize these sites.

Water for the Future

Animals, plants, and Indigenous people here all adapted to our desert's water scarcity, getting by with very little. When human newcomers came to the area, they didn't follow this example very well, and much wisdom about water conservation has been lost. Human populations continue to grow in the region faster than national averages and, according to climate projections, the drought-stricken Colorado River is not likely to recover. These demands require conservation on a whole new scale, and municipal and agricultural entities are working quickly to address likely shortages. About 70 percent of water in the region is used for agriculture, and this sector has been adapting by utilizing drip irrigation systems, switching to less water-thirsty crops, and when necessary, reducing the amount of land farmed. Cities and towns are investigating ways to augment their water supplies in the future by treating wastewater to meet drinking-water quality standards. Municipalities in Mexico already rely to some degree on desalinated water from the Gulf of California, and Arizona is also eyeing this sea as a potential future source. However, with current technologies, the economic and environmental costs of desalinated water are very high. For the coming decades, conservation and restoration efforts are the most powerful and economically viable tools for protecting the water needed to supply all Sonoran Desert residents—human, plant, and wildlife alike.

ADAPTATIONS TO DESERT LIVING

PLANTS AND ANIMALS IN the Sonoran Desert have some superpowers that allow them to endure very hot summer days, cold winter nights, and months with little rain. Organisms here have evolved to thrive in this environment. In fact, many are so well adapted to the desert that they could not survive anywhere else.

Desert Plants

Imagine yourself stuck in one place in the middle of the desert, unable to move. You have to make your own food, drink water, protect yourself from the heat of summer and cold of winter, deal with drought, and avoid becoming someone's lunch—all without moving from your designated spot. This is what it's like to be a desert plant. For humans, this would be an insurmountable challenge, because we are not as well-adapted to desert life. However, desert plants have evolved many adaptations that help them flourish here.

◂ Desert Museum mountain lion

▲ Field of spring poppies at Tumacácori National Historical Park

ROOT STRUCTURES

Desert plants have highly adapted root systems. Most cacti have huge masses of shallow, wide-spreading roots that can soak up large amounts of water very quickly. This is useful, because most desert rains don't infiltrate very deeply into the soil. In contrast, mesquite and ironwood trees as well as creosote bushes have far-reaching roots that can tap into water deep under the ground.

SEEDS THAT SLEEP

Most desert wildflowers have developed another strategy—they avoid the drought altogether. During dry periods, they exist as seeds in the soil, sometimes for years. When a sufficient amount of rain soaks into the soil and the temperatures are just right, these seeds sprout. The young plants grow very fast, bloom, make seeds, and then die. This cycle repeats itself over and over in the desert.

LEAVES AND STEMS

All plants lose water from their leaf and stem surfaces to the air through a process called transpiration. Transpiration occurs mainly through a plant's stomates, tiny openings in the "skin" of a plant similar to the pores on your skin. The stomates of desert plants have special adaptations to cut down on water loss—they are smaller than those in non-desert plants, and there are fewer of them; in many

▸ Small leaves on palo verde

▴ Palo verdes have green bark.

cacti, the stomates lie deep in the plant's tissue; and in many desert plants, the stomates open only at night when cooler temperatures reduce water loss.

Desert plants also have smaller leaves than non-desert plants. Due to the reduced surface area, less water evaporates from smaller leaves than larger ones. Some plants, such as ocotillos and palo verdes, drop their leaves during times of drought to further reduce water loss. And cacti have no leaves at all.

GREEN BARK

Palo Verde trees exhibit an unusual adaptation that can be gleaned from the meaning of their name—*palo verde* means "green stick" in Spanish. The green bark contains chlorophyll, which does most of the job of photosynthesis for these trees. Photosynthesis is the process of transforming sunlight, carbon dioxide, and water into nourishing sugar and oxygen. This compensates for their very small and sometimes sparsely distributed leaves. Cacti are green for the same reason.

SUCCULENCE

Plants such as cacti and agaves soak up water when it is available and store it in the soft, juicy tissues of their leaves or stems. This ability is called succulence, and plants with this ability are called succulents. They use the stored water to survive periods of drought. Some plants, like saguaros and barrel cacti, have pleats or folds that expand to take in water and contract as the stored water is used up.

▲ Pleated exterior of a saguaro

◄ A seriously spiny teddy bear cholla

SPINES

One of the most noticeable characteristics of many desert plants is their prickly appearance. Spines protect cacti from predators who might want to munch them for food or water. They also provide some shade from the unrelenting sun. Spines evolved from leaves over time to provide protection and reduce water loss associated with leaves.

WAXY COATINGS

The stems of cacti and other succulents are coated with a waxy substance to help prevent water loss through evaporation.

Animals

Like plants, desert animals have plenty of adaptations that help them deal with scarce water supplies and high temperatures. These adaptations are both physical and behavioral.

SURVIVING THE HEAT

Nocturnal living is the most common heat-avoidance method for desert animals. The desert comes to life at night—kangaroo rats seeking out seeds; great horned owls looking for rats and other rodents; banded geckos (lizards) hunting for insects; kit foxes searching for prey; and many other animals moving about. During the hot days, these desert animals sleep in cool hidden places such as underground burrows, rock crevices, or cactus holes.

Some animals remain active during parts of the hot day. They've developed adaptations to cope with the heat. A jackrabbit's long ears, thin and full of blood vessels, release extra body heat into the

surrounding air, cooling the animal down. Similarly, a lizard cools itself by raising its body high above the ground, which can be 40°F (22°C) warmer than the surrounding air.

Clockwise from above left:
Jackrabbit

Kangaroo rat

Spade on the hind foot of a Couch's spadefoot

SURVIVING THE DROUGHT

Some desert animals are able to get all the water they need from the food they eat. Packrats eat cacti and other water-rich, "juicy" plants. Kangaroo rats, experts at water conservation, don't have to drink water or eat juicy plants—instead, their unique digestive system draws water from the seeds they eat. Large desert mammals, such as coyotes, bobcats, and foxes, need to drink water. Although they get moisture from the bodies of the mice and other small animals they eat, this is not enough, and they are rarely farther than a day's traveling distance from a water source.

One of the most dramatic examples of desert adaptation is found in the Couch's spadefoot. For most of the year, this small amphibian lies hidden beneath the surface of the desert. When the summer rains arrive, the vibrations of the falling raindrops wake the spadefoot, spurring it to surface in search of a rainpool and a mate. Time is short—the entire cycle from egg to tadpole to toadlet takes as little as 10 days and must occur before the rainpool dries up. Then the young toadlets leave the pool to dig their own burrows and wait through fall, winter, and spring for the next season of summer rains.

The next page shows some other examples of desert animals and their unusual adaptations.

▸ Desert tortoises store water in their bladders, where it can be reabsorbed for use during dry times.

▸ Bighorn sheep have enlarged stomach compartments that can store enough water to last for several days.

▸ Gambel's quail have body temperatures of 107°F (42°C), allowing them to be active during the heat of the day while releasing heat—as long as the air temperature is under 107°F.

◂ Round-tailed ground squirrels depend on succulent vegetation for moisture and, during the hottest, driest part of summer, pass several weeks dormant in underground burrows until summer rains bring new growth. This is called estivation and is like hibernation, except that it's brought on by summer heat and dryness.

◂ Gila monsters can store fat in their tails and survive for several years on the energy stored there.

Humans have also adapted to aridity and heat, although not always in ways that are sustainable for the long term. The wide variety of behavioral and social adaptations adopted by different cultures include different types of clothing, shelter, foods, and cooling methods.

During the summer heat, people mostly stay indoors with air-conditioning or evaporative cooling if possible. Outdoors, water bottles, sunscreen, and hats are omnipresent accessories. To mitigate the effects of the desert climate, modern societies have turned to the lessons and traditions of Indigenous people in adopting more water- and energy-saving practices, such as water harvesting, landscaping with desert plants, adding shade trees, building with insulating materials, and using passive heating and cooling.

PEOPLE AND NATURE IN THE SONORAN DESERT

THE IMPACT OF MODERN HUMANS on the Sonoran Desert is evident everywhere. Desert vegetation has been transformed into farms and housing; roads and canals crisscross the landscape; mining pits expose deep layers of bedrock; and former rivers are now mostly dry channels. Because recent change is so dramatic, it's harder to see how people have actually been shaping the Sonoran Desert landscape for thousands of years.

First People

People arrived in the region at least 13,000 years ago. Believed to have traveled from Asia across the Bering Strait land bridge and perhaps by boat along the coastline, they hunted large, now-extinct animals, such as mammoths and North American horses, tapirs, and camels, as well as extant animals such as rabbits, bison, bears, and rodents. Overhunting by these first people is one of the leading explanations for the demise of large mammals that once roamed the area. If true, this would be one of the most significant impacts people have had on this landscape over time.

From about 7000 to 2000 years ago, people hunted small game and gathered a variety of plants for sustenance. With evidence of human habitation going back 4000 years, Tucson is thought to be one of the oldest continuously inhabited settlements in North America. During this period, people started to select, plant, and move seeds around in early agriculture. Around 3000 years ago, they introduced new plants, like corn from Mesoamerica.

Hohokam Period (300–1450)

Starting around 2000 years ago, during the Hohokam period, people began to develop highly sophisticated farming systems. These systems included irrigation canals that collected water from rivers and mountain runoff. During this time, people built ball courts, platform mounds, and the largest network of irrigation canals in North America before the arrival of Europeans. The word "Hohokam" comes from "Huhugam," which translates to "ancestors," among other meanings, in Tohono O'odham.

The agricultural practices of that time brought about considerable changes to the land and its biodiversity. Cultivation began where surface water was available, such as along the Santa Cruz River in what is now downtown Tucson. Archaeologists have discovered that people grew corn (maize) there 3000 years ago. Pinto and tepary beans followed, along with gourds, squash, cotton, amaranth, devil's claw (a medicinal and basket material), and other crops.

▾ Devil's claw seed pods are used in basketry and for food.

◢ Amaranth at Mission Garden, Tucson. Both the greens and seeds of amaranth are edible and nutritious.

People of the Hohokam period dug hundreds of miles of canals to bring water from rivers to their fields. The canals serviced between 30,000–60,000 acres (12,000–24,000 hectares) in the Phoenix Basin alone. They also engineered ditches and brush structures to divert water flowing over the alluvial fans (deposits made of mud, silt, and sand) at the bases of mountains after large rainstorms. Around what is now Tucson, they farmed agave in contoured terraces. Check dams, known as *trincheras* (Spanish for trenches), were constructed of rocks piled across drainage slopes. The rock piles slowed the flow

▲ Trincheras with agave near Mission Garden, Tucson

▲ Hohokam canals

of water downhill, allowing time for agave roots to soak it up. People favored *Agave murpheyi* for its food and fiber and, during the 12th and 13th centuries, more than 100,000 agaves may have been growing in fields around Southern Arizona. You can still see some of these trincheras at Tumamoc Hill (see Tumamoc Hill Adventure, page 269) in Tucson and Los Morteros Conservation Area in Marana, among other places.

Other Indigenous cultures also transformed their environments. In the Colorado River Delta, the Cocopah cultivated panic grass (a grain); they planted their crops as floodwaters receded each year, a practice also adopted by other Indigenous people in Sonora. The Comcáac (or Seri) live on the coast of Sonora in one of the driest areas of the desert; they carried species of wild plants and animals with them as they moved around the mainland and to islands in the Gulf of California. Their journeys are thought to have expanded the ranges of at least five of the 49 species of reptiles in their lands. Some of these animals interbred to create new hybrids, such as the piebald chuckwallas of Isla Alcatraz in Kino Bay.

Colonial Period (early 1600s to 1821)

By the time the first Europeans settled in the region in the 1600s, Hohokam civilization had collapsed, perhaps weakened by massive floods in 1358–59, followed by 20 years of drought and more massive floods in the 1380s. Other factors that may have played a role were salt accumulation in the fields from years of irrigation with relatively salty water, and regional political conflicts. The arrival of Europeans unleashed one of the greatest ecological revolutions in the history of the world. European diseases, such as measles, influenza, and smallpox, spread death and devastation among the people of the Sonoran Desert who had no resistance to these microbes. Like Native populations all over the Americas, the Sonoran Desert's Indigenous population plummeted by as much as 95 percent from about 1600–1800.

Europeans brought many other organisms to the Americas as well, changing Indigenous lifeways forever. Jesuit Padre Eusebio Francisco Kino and his entourage came to the region in the 1680s, founding 24 missions and chapels in Sonora, Southern Arizona, and the Baja peninsula. Each of these missions needed to be

◂ White Sonora wheat

◂ Kino heritage orchard at Tumacácori National Historical Park

self-sufficient, with crops, orchards, and cattle to support its inhabitants. Winter wheat helped fill a gap in the agricultural cycle when it was too cold for corn, beans, or squash. The colonists also brought a variety of fruits, including pomegranates, figs, citrus, quince, apricots, loquats, plums, mulberries, peaches, grapes, and olives. Other European crops, such as spinach, cabbage, artichoke, fava beans, leeks, peas, carrots, and herbs—including chamomile, basil, dill, and parsley—were grown in mission gardens. You can see and taste a little bit of this history today in Tucson's Mission Garden (see Mission Garden Adventure, page 263).

During early European settlement, ranching was the most extensive land-transforming activity in the Sonoran Desert. The use of mules and oxen expanded and intensified the spread of cultivated agriculture. Cows, sheep, and goats grazed plants that were inedible to people, converting these to meat and milk as well as hides and tallow. Horses greatly extended the range people could travel. Cows,

▲ Native (pure) silver often forms wires and ribbons, as in this specimen.

▼ Copper is sometimes found in its native (pure) form, as in this specimen, but more often in colorful combinations with other elements.

horses, sheep, and goats foraged from floodplains to mountaintops. During the Spanish colonial period, overgrazing became prevalent in Sonora, but Apache resistance in what is now Arizona kept ranching in check in the northern Sonoran Desert until the later 1800s.

Impacts of Mining

Well before the arrival of the Spanish, Indigenous people were mining the surface and near-surface of the region for useful materials, such as coal, clay, hematite, salt, copper, gold, silver, turquoise, quartz, and other minerals. Though they established trade routes between distant tribes to swap materials, environmental impact was minimal. Europeans took mining to a whole new level and, starting in the late 1600s, it became the most intensive land-altering activity in Sonora.

In addition to the direct impacts of digging pits and tunnels, denuding hillsides, dumping waste, and treating it with chemicals, this type of mining required water, charcoal, timber, firewood, tallow, salt, food, and shelter for the miners. Towns and transportation routes grew. Streams were diverted and groundwater polluted. Cattle ranches proliferated to supply these mining districts as well.

The need for labor in a variety of skilled/paid and unpaid jobs attracted people from all around the region and the world. Indigenous people were forced to work in the mines through a variety of mechanisms (Indigenous slavery was officially outlawed in the mid-sixteenth century) and worked alongside slaves from Africa and the Philippines. In the early days, there was no mechanization, and the work, including handling a toxic sludge of ore and mercury to extract silver, was backbreaking and dangerous.

The silver deposits were mostly near the surface and, after they were exhausted, US companies moved in during the 1800s to begin mining the copper that lay below. Some of the original copper mines are still producing, and Sonora is now the top-ranking state in Mexico for mineral extraction. Mining in the north, in what is now Arizona, did not take hold until later in the 1800s and 1900s due to resistance by Apache groups. Once the industry got going, Arizona's similar geology has made this state the top producer in the United States.

Anglo-Americans

After the United States annexed half of Mexico's national territory in the Mexican-American War of 1846-48, Anglo-Americans and Europeans were drawn to the region by potential wealth to be gained from gold and silver mining despite the dangers and difficulties of this part of the country. The first mini-rushes were driven by placer deposits along the Colorado River, then in the mountains along the Hassayampa River where the town of Wickenburg was established primarily to process silver ore.

From the arrival of the Europeans until the 1880s, the Arizona-Sonora borderlands were contested ground, where no single tribe, empire, or nation held all the power. The Apaches and River Yumans fought European and Euro-American conquest for two centuries, limiting the impact of Euro-Americans on the land throughout this period. In the 1880s, however, when mining in Arizona began in earnest, this all changed. In 1880, the railroad came to Tucson, built largely by Chinese crews. Six years later, Geronimo surrendered, effectively ending the Apache resistance and signaling that Arizona and Sonora were safe for business. Capital poured in from the Eastern United States, California, and the British Isles as Arizona and Sonora became extractive colonies for the industrial world, their resources wrested from the ground and shipped out for processing and consumption. This was the era when the Three Cs were dominant—cattle, copper, and cotton.

Cattle ranching took off on both sides of the border. When the Comcáac (Seri) resisted the incursion of cattle on their traditional lands, they were decimated by the superior weapons of the cowboys. Copper mining was the second industry to expand. As extractive techniques improved, it became economically viable to mine ores of lower and lower grade. Eventually, the copper constituted less than 1 percent of the ore rock. This meant that huge amounts of earth were moved. In Bisbee alone, thousands of miles of shafts and tunnels were dug underground, and ores were transported from mine to smelter by rail. After open-pit mining was developed, the region was pockmarked by huge holes and equally large tailings (mining waste) piles rising above the desert floor like pyramids. These are still visible across the region today, including south of Tucson.

The third major extractive industry—agriculture—was ultimately the most transformational. After Mexico won its independence from Spain in 1821, agricultural interests turned an eye to the rich coastal floodplains of western and southern Sonora. The Yaqui (Yoeme) fought several wars with the Mexican army to maintain control of their land, but by the late 1800s, most Yaquis had fled the violence or were forcibly relocated. The Rio Yaqui was eventually dammed and controlled to serve nearly 600,000 acres of irrigated agriculture and the communities that sprung up around it. North of the Yaqui Valley, advances in pump technology in the mid-twentieth century supported wheat and cotton fields in what was previously desert or riparian habitat. Great mesquite riparian forests and plains of desert ironwoods disappeared under plows.

In Arizona, the US Reclamation Service built Roosevelt Dam in 1903 on the Salt River east of Phoenix and turned the Salt River Valley into one of the largest agricultural areas in the southwestern United States. It was a British embargo on industrial cotton during World War I that prompted the growth of Arizona's cotton industry across the former saltbush and creosote flats of the desert, making the state one of the leading cotton producers in the world.

Urban development followed agriculture, and the availability of affordable air-conditioning starting in the 1950s hastened this trend. Water development projects, such as the Central Arizona Project, helped encourage more urban and suburban growth. Today, agricultural and municipal interests fight for limited water—the ultimate restriction on growth in the region—through political, legal, and economic channels.

As suburban sprawl continues, more non-native species have taken up residence as well. The number of non-native plants in Arizona alone went from about 190 in 1942 to about 330 species today. Many of these are grasses introduced by the US Soil Conservation Service to control erosion and provide forage for cattle. Some of these species, like Lehmann lovegrass and buffelgrass, became invasive, crowding out a diverse mix of native grasses and converting desert landscapes to grasslands. In Sonora, millions of acres of desert and thornscrub have been bulldozed to make way for buffelgrass pastures.

Indigenous Peoples and Nations Today

Numerous groups of Indigenous people inhabit the Southwestern United States and northwestern Mexico. Several are original inhabitants of the Sonoran Desert, including the Tohono O'odham, Hia-Ced O'odham, Akimel O'odham, Pima, Yaqui (Yoeme), Cocopah, Yuma, and Seri. The neighboring highlands of the Sierra Madre in Sonora, Mexico are also home to the Opata, Warihio, Jova, Mayo, and Lower Pima while nearby highlands in the United States are home to the Nde (Apache) people. Here we'll provide a little bit of background about a few of these cultures—Tohono O'odham, Yaqui (Yoeme), and Comcáac (Seri).

TOHONO O'ODHAM

For thousands of years—or as the O'odham relate their history, "since time immemorial"—the ancestral O'odham homelands encompassed a vast area of the Sonoran Desert region, from northern Sonora west to the Gulf of California, north to central Arizona near present-day Phoenix, and east to the San Pedro River basin. In historic times, these lands and their residents have had many designations imposed upon them by foreign governments, including Spain, Mexico, and the United States. Today O'odham peoples are federally recognized in the United States as four geographically and politically distinct tribes: the Tohono O'odham Nation, the Gila River Indian Community, the Ak-Chin Indian Community, and the Salt River Pima-Maricopa Indian Community. A fifth, the Hia-Ced O'odham, are not federally recognized but reside throughout southwestern Arizona. All groups speak various dialects of the O'odham language, derived from the Uto-Aztecan language group. The name Tohono O'odham (Toe-HO-no AH-tum) means "desert people."

The Tohono O'odham Nation is the second-largest reservation in the United States, covering 2.8 million acres or 4460 square miles (11,550 sq km), an area about the size of Connecticut, distributed in four noncontiguous parcels within the Sonoran Desert. In Sonora, approximately nine O'odham communities are found along the US-Mexico border. Formerly, residents of these communities crossed the border freely, but today tighter US immigration policies have made this more difficult, dividing families and communities and complicating easy access to services across the border.

The Tohono O'odham consider themselves to be descendants of the early farmers and the Huhugam people who inhabited the Tucson area from around 300 until around 1450. Written records of the Tohono O'odham in the region began with the arrival of the Spanish around 1690. In 1691, Father Kino made contact with the Tohono O'odham living at Bac and Chuk Shon (which became Tucson). In 1700, he established the Mission San Xavier del Bac and introduced Christianity, wheat, livestock, fruit, and metal tools to the region. The San Xavier Reservation was established in 1874, and the main Tohono O'odham reservation to the west was established in 1917.

Today's Tohono O'odham Nation includes approximately 30,000 enrolled members. The tribal government runs health care, education, and other services. The Tohono O'odham language is still spoken and taught in schools, but fluency has declined markedly with younger generations. Entities such as the Tohono O'odham Nation Cultural Center and Museum (see Adventure 19, p. 350), Tohono O'odham Community College, and the University of Arizona's American Indian Language Development Institute are making great efforts to keep the language and traditions of the people alive and pertinent to tribal life today.

YAQUI (YOEME)

The Yaqui homeland is centered along the rich floodplain of the Yaqui River Valley in Sonora, Mexico, where throughout history they farmed and fished. By 552 CE, Yaqui family groups ranged and settled throughout the Sonoran Desert region as far north as the Gila River. The Yaqui traded native foods, furs, shells, salt, and more with other tribes, including the Shoshone, Comanche, Pueblos, Pimas, Aztecs, and Toltecs.

In 1533, the Yaquis encountered the first white people in their region, a Spanish military expedition, which heralded a 400-year period of conflict and struggle against successive waves of Spanish and Mexican settlers seeking to subjugate them and take their lands. Between 1608 and 1610, the Spanish attacked violently and repeatedly, but the Yaquis successfully raised an army to defeat them. To secure peace, the Yaquis asked the Jesuit missionaries to establish churches, and most of the 60,000 Yaquis settled in the eight sacred pueblos (or towns) where these churches were established.

Peace was elusive, however. The Yaquis continued to resist domination despite massacres, deportation, and disease that diminished their population. Many Yaquis left Sonora to join family groups in Arizona living along the Santa Cruz and Gila Rivers in communities such as Old Pascua and Barrio Libre in Tucson, Yoem Pueblo in Marana, and Guadalupe near Tempe.

Today, the Yaqui have lands in both Mexico and the United States, formally recognized by both governments. In 1939, the Yaqui of Sonora received official recognition and title to their land, yet the loss of culture continued as large dams along the Yaqui River forced Yaqui farmers to buy water, further reducing their self-sufficiency. In 1964, the Pascua Yaqui Association received 200 acres southwest of Tucson where New Pascua was built. In 1978, New Pascua received formal recognition as a US Native American tribe.

Yaqui cultural traditions, with their unique blend of Indigenous and Christian beliefs, flourish in Southern Arizona. Yaqui Easter ceremonies, held in Old Pascua (*Pascua* is Spanish for Easter), are open to the public and include a week of traditional music and masked dancers depicting events of Holy Week. Central to the Easter observances is the Deer Dancer, a highly respected and important symbol of ancient Yaqui cultural and spiritual belief.

SERI

The Seri, or Comcáac, as they call themselves, live along the central Gulf of California coast of Sonora, Mexico, across from Tiburón Island. They are hunter-gatherers and seafarers who endure some of the harshest conditions in the Sonoran Desert region, with annual rainfall rarely exceeding 2 inches (5 cm). Drinking water here is a scarce commodity, limiting the size of communities to extended family groups. In earlier times, these groups were small and nomadic—they migrated over large areas and dwelled in temporary camps to find resources to survive.

Upon the arrival of Coronado's Spain-financed expedition in the 16th century, the population of Seri groups was probably around 5000 people. Like other Indigenous groups, their territory and numbers dwindled because of persecution and disease. By the 1930s, only about 300 Seri remained, most of them concentrated on Tiburón Island. The strait that separates the island from the mainland is one of the most perilous in the world, but the Seri navigated it expertly on balsa rafts made of *carrizo* (Spanish for "reedgrass") lashed together with mesquite root twine.

In the 1960s, many Seri returned to the mainland, participating in the fishing economy of the region. They also became known for their ironwood carvings and basketry. Today the population is close to 1000 people living in the two villages of Punta Chueca and El Desemboque north of Kino Bay, Sonora.

▲ San Xavier del Bac Mission

Tucson: A Long History of Settlement

Tucson's name is derived from the Tohono O'odham phrase *chuk shon*, meaning "base of the black hill," the name given to the foot of Sentinel Peak or "A" Mountain. Here, the bedrock at the base of the mountain pushed the Santa Cruz River to the surface, providing life-giving perennial flow until overpumping in the last century depleted it completely. What we see today as a dry, channelized ditch, flowing only after rainstorms, was once a lush riparian forest where Native communities lived, subsisting off wild foods and using the river's water to cultivate corn, beans, squash, and possibly cotton. Recent archaeological excavations near "A" Mountain have revealed that Tucson has been inhabited by people for at least 4000 years, making it one of the oldest continuously inhabited settlements in the United States.

Beyond the permanent water in the Santa Cruz River, other factors also made this setting ideal for survival. Mild winter temperatures and two distinct rainy seasons provide for a nearly year-round growing season with two distinct periods of plant growth. Gentle winter rains allow for the harvest of wild greens and herbs from February through April; they also provide moisture for perennial plants like legume trees and cacti, which produce fruit and seed in late spring or early summer, awaiting germination with summer monsoon storms. Wild foods, supplemented with crops of squash, beans, and corn, are available throughout an annual succession of harvests; one food often ripens just as another becomes scarce. For example, cholla buds are collected in early spring, saguaro cactus fruits in early summer, and prickly pear cactus fruits in midsummer. Mesquite pods are ready to harvest in late summer and early fall as cactus fruits become scarce. Knowledge of when and where shoots appear, fruits ripen, and roots or bulbs are ready for harvest as well as how to store and preserve them requires an intimate awareness of the Sonoran Desert environment. During the lean times between harvests, food storage protected communities from starvation.

Native knowledge is still alive in our region and useful, even vital, today. Indigenous people have been technological innovators, constantly observing and experimenting with materials to make life

◂ The outer pod (not the seeds) of mesquite trees can be eaten whole when ripe or ground into a meal when dry.

easier. Through observation of the natural world, these communities learned about the relationships and interactions between living things and their environment to improve their quality of life and preserve their cultures from generation to generation. Today these traditional practices are instructive in adapting modern lifestyles to limited water, increasing temperatures, and evolving health threats.

The Tohono O'odham, for example, suffer some of the highest rates of diabetes in the United States, due largely to the adoption of a modern diet of processed carbohydrates and sugary foods. Many of the native foods they traditionally consumed, however, have been proven to be highly effective in managing blood sugar. Community groups and health professionals are calling for a return to the use of these native foods to keep their people healthy. Additionally, these foods grow in many Tucson backyards as landscape plants and can provide a fun and healthful way to forge a deeper sense of place that is connected to the long history of native plant use in this region.

◂◂ Prickly pear fruit, also known as *tuna* in Spanish and *i:bhai* in Tohono O'odham

◂▴ Cholla cactus flower buds (*ciolim* in Tohono O'odham) can be cooked into a variety of nutritious preparations.

TUCSON: UNESCO CITY OF GASTRONOMY

Tucson has the distinction of being the first City of Gastronomy in the United States, recognized by the United Nations Educational, Scientific and Cultural Organization (UNESCO). This designation was based on Tucson's deep and multicultural food history, stretching back thousands of years, and the current ingenuity of local farmers, ranchers, markets, and chefs in pushing the boundaries of sustainability and culinary creativity.

SEASONS IN THE SONORAN DESERT

THERE ARE FIVE SEASONS in the Sonoran Desert. It exhibits two distinct summer seasons: an especially dry period between spring and summer called the foresummer drought and a rainy season called the monsoon. Temperatures throughout the year can vary widely, even over the course of a day, with swings of 40°F (22°C) or so. Average temperatures and rainfalls provided here are from the National Weather Service from 1991 to 2020. Once you're familiar with seasonal averages, you can prepare for outdoor explorations in any season.

WINTER
(December, January, Early February)

DECEMBER

Average high: 66°F (19°C)
Average low: 41°F (5°C)
Normal rainfall: 0.96 inches (24 mm)

December is a mild month—mostly cool but sunny days and only a few nights when temperatures drop below freezing, and sometimes a few days of light winter rains.

PLANTS

Fruits of desert mistletoe, Christmas cactus, and netleaf hackberry trees ripen at this time, providing food for many birds and mammals. If winter rains begin, many shrubs (such as brittlebush, creosote, and ocotillos) sprout bright new leaves, but many trees (such as mesquites, palo verdes, and sycamores) drop their leaves as the temperatures dip below freezing.

ANIMALS

Birds in the mimic-thrush family, such as mockingbirds and curve-billed thrashers, map their mating territories by singing their well-known copycat songs from the tops of trees, poles, or fences. Cactus wrens build their breeding nests as well as separate roosting nests; some pairs build three or more nests. Anna's hummingbirds may also breed this month—the males can be heard singing their squeaky songs around feeders.

Clockwise, from top: Desert mistletoe, northern mockingbird, curve-billed thrasher

Above, left to right:
Male phainopepla

Fairy duster

Anna's hummingbird

Gila woodpecker

JANUARY

Average high: 67°F (19°C)
Average low: 41°F (5°C)
Normal rain: 0.84 inches (21 mm)

In January, deserts experience freezing temperatures perhaps half a dozen times. However, up in the mountains, it freezes nearly every night and a foot of snow may fall. Desert days are mostly clear and pleasant, ranging from cool to warm; sometimes cold rains sweep in from the northwest.

PLANTS

At lower elevations, Fremont cottonwoods sprout new leaves and open blossoms. With sufficient rainfall, many annuals and grasses sprout new green growth.

ANIMALS

January kicks off the breeding seasons for mockingbirds, curve-billed thrashers, cactus wrens, and packrats (white-throated woodrats). Male phainopeplas (glossy black-crested birds with white patches on their wings) perch conspicuously in palo verde or mesquite trees that host desert mistletoe—the berries are an important food source—and perform fluttery flight displays to attract females. Mule deer breeding season, called "the rut" and lasting three to four weeks, is in full swing. Males engage in aggressive but seldom injurious sparring with their antlers. Mountain lions feed well this month in the mountain foothills, where distracted male deer make easier prey.

FEBRUARY

Average high: 69°F (21°C)
Average low: 43°F (6°C)
Normal rainfall: 0.84 inches (21 mm)

By February, winter loosens its grip on the desert—only a couple of nights may dip below freezing. Later in the month, occasional warm days conjure thoughts of spring, but cold snaps are still probable.

PLANTS

Blooming shrubs may include chuparosas, baby bonnets, and fairy dusters. Later in the month, if the fall and winter rains were generous, desert wildflowers—Mexican gold poppies, lupines, and owl's clover—may blossom. In mountain canyons, deciduous trees, such as alders and walnuts, may bloom before sprouting new leaves.

ANIMALS

Costa's hummingbirds join Anna's hummingbirds in establishing breeding territories around backyard feeders and blooming shrubs. Male Costa's hummingbirds display for females and mark their territories with a distinctive zing-sounding call. Around mid-month, rust-colored hummers—rufous hummingbirds migrating through the Southwest—show up at feeders. Gila woodpeckers hammer away at tree trunks and even metal pipes around buildings; they are marking their territories using sound. In the cool evenings or predawn mornings, great horned owls can be heard calling softly, usually in duos, as they begin their breeding season. Pipevine swallowtail butterflies are common fliers this month.

SPRING
(Late February, March, April)

MARCH

Average high: 76°F (24°C)
Average low: 48°F (9°C)
Normal rainfall: 0.56 inches (14 mm)

Spring begins in earnest in the desert, with warm sunny days and cool nights. The days get warm enough in the high country to begin melting snow and filling creeks and are marked by the magical sound of running water.

PLANTS

March is wildflower month. Look for dozens of wildflower species, including California poppies, globe mallows, penstemons, evening primroses, desert marigolds, blue dicks, gilias, bladderpods, dock, chia, desert hyacinths, and many more. Many shrubs bloom as well, including desert lavender, hop bush, brittlebush, and Mormon tea.

ANIMALS

Many animals are breeding or preparing to breed. Elf owls arrive from wintering grounds in Mexico to breed in saguaro-mesquite desert; males arrive first and try to win females with their distinctive barking call as they perch in the cavities of saguaro cacti or other trees. Burrowing owls and barn owls, which are also found in desert or even urban areas, also breed this month. Migratory songbirds arrive, either to breed or to rest on their way to northern breeding grounds; riparian areas are especially good places to see them. Desert tortoises and desert box turtles emerge from their burrows and begin to mate. Turkey vultures move back to Southern Arizona for the summer.

Clockwise, from upper left: Parry's penstemon, burrowing owl, California poppies with purple lupines

Opposite, clockwise from upper left: Palo verde trees in full bloom

Brittlebush

White-winged dove

Desert spiny lizard

Gray fox

Prickly pear cactus flower

APRIL

Average high: 83°F (28°C)
Average low: 53°F (12°C)
Normal rainfall: 0.24 inches (6 mm)

Dryness begins to settle in the desert, with just a few days of possible sprinkles. Spring weather arrives in the mountains, with days in the 60s°F (>15°C) and nights rarely dropping below freezing. April is known as the "yellow month" in the Tohono O'odham calendar, as trees and shrubs explode with golden hues throughout the month.

PLANTS

Many shrubs—brittlebush, desert lavender, hop bush, and all the desert bean trees (palo verdes, catclaws, and mesquites)—begin to produce yellow to creamy white blooms. As the temperatures rise toward 100°F (38°C), many cacti, such as prickly pear, chollas, and hedgehogs, start to bloom as well. By the end of the month, some big, white saguaro flowers open. Brittlebush may still bloom—look for iron-cross blister beetles (identified by yellow-and-red with black cross patterns on their backs) feeding on the blossoms.

ANIMALS

Bird migration continues. Summer's hawks, including Swainson's, zone-tailed, and black hawks, arrive and get busy finding mates for the summer breeding season. In mountain canyons around Tucson, many hummingbirds, including broad-billed, black-chinned, and Rivoli's, arrive and breed. White-winged doves also return and fill the late spring air with their signature summer calls—"Who-cooks-for-you?" As the days lengthen and warm up, reptiles become more visible—time to watch for rattlesnakes (although they can be out any time of the year). Clark's spiny lizards and western whiptail lizards begin breeding. Bobcats, coyotes, and foxes are having litters. And butterfly activity picks up—look for great blue hairstreak, hackberry, skipper, blue, and queen butterflies.

FORESUMMER DROUGHT
(May, June)

MAY

Average high: 92°F (33°C)
Average low: 62°F (17°C)
Normal rainfall: 0.20 inches (5 mm)

In the desert, the first day over 100°F (38°C) often occurs in May, and most days will be clear, dry, and hot. Many animals—humans included—retreat to the mountains where balmy days and cold, though not freezing, nights beckon.

PLANTS

Many cactus species, including saguaros, senitas, organ pipes, and queens-of-the-night (also known as night-blooming cereus), bloom nocturnally. Delicate lavender blossoms open on desert ironwood and smoke trees. Desert spoon and soaptree yuccas put up tall, woody bloom stalks with white flowerettes; desert spoon is dioecious, with male or female flowers occurring on separate plants. Many red, trumpet-shaped flowers bloom in mountain canyons as hummingbirds become more numerous and continue breeding; among the most spectacular blossoms are those of the coral bean.

ANIMALS

Female nectar-feeding bats, many of which are pregnant, migrate from Mexico into desert areas where nocturnally blooming plants are flowering and give birth in maternity colonies located in buildings, mine shafts, or caves. The two species are Mexican long-tongued and lesser long-nosed; the latter is the first bat species to be removed from the endangered list due to conservation efforts. Gila monster eggs, laid 10 months ago, start hatching—the young lizards are perfectly formed miniature versions of their venomous parents and immediately fend for themselves. In mountain canyons, red-spotted toads are mating, filling the nights with their loud trills.

⇞ Saguaro cactus flowers
▲ Lesser long-nosed bat drinking from a hummingbird feeder

▸▸ Cactus wren with saguaro fruit

▴ Coiled western diamondback rattlesnake

JUNE

Average high: 101°F (38°C)
Average low: 71°F (22°C)
Normal rainfall: 0.23 inches (6 mm)

Famously hot and dry weather characterizes June in the desert, with lots of days over 100°F (38°C) and several as high as 110°F (43°C) or more, often with low or no humidity. The high country remains relatively cool, even while the mercury can climb over 100°F (38°C) down below. This is the start of the Tohono O'odham calendar, marked by the sacred saguaro fruit harvest and celebrations.

PLANTS

Saguaro cactus fruits ripen, split open, and fall to the ground—food for many birds, insects, mammals, and humans. Bean pods on mesquites, palo verdes, and catclaw acacias also ripen as do jojoba seeds. If winter or early spring rains were plentiful, sacred datura may bloom. Organ pipe cactus continue to open their pale lavender blooms.

ANIMALS

June days are filled with the buzzing of male cicadas, also called cactus dodgers, as the insects try to attract mates. Many snakes spend much of the month in their dens, due to the extreme heat and dryness. Lesser nighthawks fill the warm nights with their unique trilling calls. This is a good month to spot hawks that breed in riparian areas among tall cottonwoods or sycamore trees—look for gray, black, and zone-tailed hawks.

SUMMER MONSOON (July, August, Early September)

JULY

Average high: 100°F (38°C)
Average low: 76°F (24°C)
Normal rainfall: 2.21 inches (56 mm)

Summer rains arrive, bringing welcome relief from the hot dry days of May and June. Locally we call them monsoons, which is a slight misnomer since the term refers to a seasonal shift in winds, bringing wet *and* dry periods to a region. Creeks run again, and a second "springtime" begins with the abundant showers.

PLANTS

These rains produce a second round of wildflowers, including summer poppies, devil's claw, and morning glories, as well as blooms of woody plants and some of the agaves. Riparian canyons, especially those close to the Mexican border, are lush, hot, humid, and full of life.

ANIMALS

The rainfalls also trigger a second breeding season for many animals, from insects to the birds and mammals that feed on them. Many butterflies emerge or arrive with the rains—look for monarchs, sulphurs, queens, fritillaries, and two-tailed swallowtails. Giant 4-inch (10-cm) palo verde beetles, which as nymphs feed on the roots of their namesake host plants, emerge to mate and lay eggs. Amphibians, such as spadefoots, Sonoran Desert toads, and red-spotted toads, begin their short and frenzied reproductive cycles in the shallow rain puddles throughout the region. Look for swirling swarms of winged leaf-cutter and harvester ants the morning after heavy rain—these are new queens and males that will mate and establish new colonies.

⏶ Sonoran Desert toad
⏶ Sulphur butterfly

Above, left to right:
Horned lizard

Rufous hummingbird

Canyon ragweed

Monarch butterfly

AUGUST

Average high: 99°F (37°C)
Average low: 75°F (24°C)
Normal rainfall: 1.98 inches (50 mm)

Summer rains continue throughout the month with dramatic lightning and thunderstorms. Temperatures remain high, although they are a little less hot than in July. Mornings tend to be clear while the storms build and break sometime after noon.

PLANTS

Prickly pear cactus fruit begins to ripen; many birds, mammals, and insects feed on them. Blooms continue to burst forth on plants such as barrel cacti, asters, four o'clocks, buffalo gourds, and ground cherries. The little orange fruits of desert hackberry shrubs ripen this month—look for Empress Leilia hackberry butterflies in the foliage. With sufficient rainfall, a good crop of prickly pear cactus fruit becomes very ripe, and bright pink piles of coyote scat on back roads and trails are dead giveaways to the diet of these desert canines.

ANIMALS

Young regal horned lizards continue to hatch this month. Late summer through fall, bird migrations get underway, with species that spent the summer in the north arriving here for the winter or passing through on their way farther south. Hummingbirds, such as rufous and Allen's, migrate through, feeding on summer-season blossoms. In some years, snout butterflies become so numerous that they can clog automobile radiators on rural roads.

SEPTEMBER

Average high: 95°F (35°C)
Average low: 70°F (21°C)
Normal rainfall: 1.32 inches (34 mm)

Rains continue in the first few days of September, but by the end of the month it will seem like a repeat of May—dry and hot. Fall may creep into mountain canyons and the higher elevations as nighttime temperatures drop closer and closer to freezing.

PLANTS

Blooming continues in the deserts and desert grasslands; asters and sunflowers are especially lush. Also, look for the golden yellow blooms of snakeweed, turpentine bush, goldeneyes, and telegraph plants. Sticker and burr season begins as plants put out their seeds in ways that ensure good transportation away from the parents; canyon ragweed, with its almond-sized, fishhook-spined fruits, are a particularly noticeable fruiting plant for hikers. Seep-willow shrubs bloom in washes and rocky canyon bottoms.

ANIMALS

Fall bird migrations reach their peak; ponds in parks, golf course hazards, or wastewater treatment plants are excellent stopovers for waterfowl, some staying for the winter. Turkey vultures, western kingbirds, and many species of hawks congregate as they prepare to move south. Desert bighorn sheep are breeding. Common butterflies include gray hairstreaks, funereal duskywings, and painted ladies. If the summer rains were good, yielding abundant blooms of milkweed, beautiful monarch butterflies may be seen in low- to mid-elevation canyons.

FALL

(Late September, October, November)

OCTOBER

Average high: 86°F (30°C)
Average low: 59°F (15°C)
Normal rainfall: 0.67 inches (17 mm)

Summer hangs on, with warm-to-hot days but cooling nights. In the higher elevations, snowfall and freezes occur. Some years may see heavy rains this month, although this is uncommon.

PLANTS

Allergy sufferers bemoan the blooming of desert broom, a shrub that colonizes disturbed areas. However, broom flowers are a favorite of hundreds of butterflies, bees, wasps, and beetles. Many plants are fruiting, including barrel cacti, soapberry trees, desert hackberries, and wolfberries. Fall colors splash through canyons.

ANIMALS

Resident desert birds and those that spend their winters here gorge on the many plant fruits. Most snakes head to winter burrows this month. One exception is the rosy boa, which lives in the warmer western deserts and gives birth this month and next. (Although most snakes remain fairly inactive in the colder months, keep in mind that they can emerge at any time of year if an accumulation of warm days rouses them.) Wintering hawks arrive—common raptors include northern harriers, rough-legged and ferruginous hawks, kestrels, merlins, and prairie falcons. Turkey vultures are mostly gone, but loud groups of common ravens replace them on carrion patrol.

▲ Desert broom

▲ Fall color in Sabino Canyon

NOVEMBER

Average high: 75°F (24°C)
Average low: 48°F (9°C)
Normal rainfall: 0.56 inches (14 mm)

Balmy weather finally begins to settle on the desert lowlands while winter grips the mountains. Expect mostly dry weather, although well over a half-foot (15 cm) of snow may fall up high. Storms from the northwest may bring cold, even freezing, temperatures to the desert areas as well.

PLANTS

Fall colors meander through low- and mid-elevation canyons where sycamores, cottonwoods, ashes, and walnuts are shedding their leaves. Desert broom seeds take to the air in cloudy puffs that look like snow. Desert mistletoe berries start to form. If clusters of mesquite branch ends begin to brown up and die, chances are mesquite girdler beetles have been at work; the females bore a trough around a twig, creating a "girdle," and then lay their eggs in the soon-to-die tips.

ANIMALS

Anna's and Costa's hummingbirds are the most common hummingbirds at feeders now; both breed in winter. Some Costa's hummingbirds leave Southern Arizona for the winter, returning in early spring to breed before the foresummer drought sets in. Although reptiles are mostly inactive, larger desert mammals such as bobcats, coyotes, badgers, and gray and kit foxes will remain active throughout winter. Male desert mule deer rub the velvet off their antlers, acquired throughout the summer; soon they will begin sparring with each other as they prepare for breeding competitions in the winter months.

BEYOND WATER WOES: OTHER THREATS TO SONORAN DESERT BIODIVERSITY

THE MORE TIME YOU spend in the Sonoran Desert, the more diversity you will encounter. Each mountain, canyon, riparian corridor, and valley has unique plants, animals, rocks, and minerals. The traces of ancient and historical cultures are visible under the mantle of modern society. However, like everywhere in the world today, human activities are accelerating the pace of change in the desert, and many of these changes are threatening the desert's bountiful biodiversity. In addition to our impacts on water resources, people are introducing new species, changing the climate, and transforming the landscape in unprecedented ways.

Invasive Species

An invasive species is defined as a non-native species whose introduction causes economic or environmental harm, or harm to human health. In the absence of natural predators and diseases that kept them in check in their native habitats, invasive species thrive and multiply in their new environments. Some spread so aggressively that they displace native species and can transform the biological communities they invade.

Most of the invasive plants in the Sonoran Desert are grasses from Africa and the Mediterranean region that have replaced native species over vast areas of the region. Some, like buffelgrass and fountain grass, grow large enough to compete with desert trees, shrubs, and cacti. Whereas desert vegetation does not spread fire effectively, these invasive grasses support very hot fires that advance over large areas and kill most native plants and many animals. Repeated fires lead to conversion of the diverse desert landscape to a grassland with just one or a few species.

We don't usually think of grasses as dangerous organisms, but one of the greatest threats to the Sonoran Desert is buffelgrass, which fills in bare ground among desert plants, outcompeting them for water and nutrients, and eventually killing them through repeated fires. It was brought to the region by the US Soil Conservation Service in the 1930s for livestock forage and erosion control and started to spread out of control in the 1980s.

Abundant in the wildland-urban interface, buffelgrass creates pathways for wildland fires to enter residential areas. Buffelgrass can also be found in yards, alleyways, and utility corridors. There is a concerted, multi-agency, years-long campaign to remove buffelgrass

▾ Hillside invaded with buffelgrass (light tan grass)

◢ Buffelgrass plant

from high-value natural areas and from around human property, currently coordinated by the Arizona-Sonora Desert Museum and assisted by the labor of numerous community volunteers. Communities in Sonora are starting to focus on the dangers of this grass as well. Although buffelgrass is still planted for cattle forage in Sonora, conservation organizations are working to protect cities, towns, and native desert from fire.

A newcomer on the invasive front in central and southern Arizona is stinknet, a noxious winter annual that displaces native vegetation and is highly flammable. In the lower-elevation desert areas, another plant, Sahara mustard, a large, fast-growing winter annual, may be more of a threat than buffelgrass. Most native animals will not eat it, and it is immune to most plant diseases. In some places it is already replacing many of the native plants that give the desert its famous carpets of colorful late-winter wildflowers. Native riparian communities are also under threat by invasive plants. Saltcedar (or tamarisk), a tree native to Europe and Asia, has nearly replaced native riparian trees over large areas. Land managers are working to control it using the tamarisk leaf beetle and to restore native trees to these habitats.

Unfortunately, there are also invasive animals. To qualify as invasive, plants and animals need to be able to survive without the assistance of people, so animals like cows and sheep are not invasive, even though they have had transformative impacts on the landscape. For example, overgrazing and drought in the late nineteenth and early twentieth centuries caused conversion of woodlands to grassland and grasslands to desertscrub. Some insects that are invasive in other parts of the country, such as red imported fire ants and Argentine cactus moths, have the potential to invade this region and are being closely monitored. Aquatic habitats have been seriously impacted by non-native fish, crayfish, bullfrogs, and salamanders, many introduced as bait. Other invasive animals, like red-eared slider turtles, are popular pets that people release to the wild. Native fish and amphibians have been extirpated (completely removed from an area) from streams and springs by these introduced aquatic animals. Wildlife managers use a range of strategies to remove invasive species and educate the public to help avoid introductions in the first place.

From top to bottom:
Stinknet in flower

Sahara mustard

Saltcedar (tamarisk)

Habitat Fragmentation

Fragmentation occurs when patches of habitat become isolated from each other by human infrastructure, such as cities, farms, mines, highways, canals, solar and wind farms, fences, walls, and other developments. Over time, species become separated into smaller populations that are more vulnerable to extinction and have lower genetic diversity. Small nature reserves surrounded by unsuitable habitat are likely to decline in biodiversity. To keep ecosystems viable, it is important that healthy natural areas and reserves be as large as possible and connected to one another with protected wildlife corridors. This is one of the main goals of the Sonoran Desert Conservation Plan, which guides development in Pima County in Southern Arizona. As the wall at the US-Mexico border becomes more solid, taller, and longer, it cuts off important north-south exchanges of animals and the genetic diversity they bring. Conservation organizations are documenting the impacts of the existing sections of wall on animals and working to identify primary migration pathways and solutions that allow animals through.

Toward Sustainability

Individuals as well as governmental and nongovernmental organizations throughout the region have recognized and taken action to balance the needs of the environment with a growing human population. Government agencies in both the United States and Mexico have set aside protected areas to conserve some of the region's most biodiverse and unique places as well as threatened and endangered species. In 1998, Pima County, home to Tucson, adopted a forward-thinking, science-based land use planning approach that prioritizes conservation of historical ranches, riparian areas, wildlife corridors, and critical habitat for endangered and threatened species. The Sonoran Desert Conservation Plan has become a model for other communities.

On a smaller scale, individual farmers and ranchers as well as farming and ranching cooperatives are adopting practices that will use less water, slow down rainwater runoff to allow deeper infiltration, conserve topsoil, and protect native biodiversity. They are trying out new crops and breeds of cattle, grazing and planting patterns, moving rocks and earth to slow runoff and direct water, removing invasive weeds, and restoring native plants. Agencies, organizations,

and community volunteers are also coordinating their efforts to control the spread of invasive plants on other public and private lands. Cities, like Tucson, are working with neighborhoods to increase shade through massive tree-planting campaigns, accompanied by infrastructure changes to bring rainwater runoff or recycled water to where the trees need it.

▲ Wildlife overpass under construction north of Tucson will help reconnect a wildlife corridor

On the US side of the border, where relative wealth and government policies have made water cheap and abundant, residents and municipalities are learning water conservation practices from their Mexican and Indigenous neighbors—contouring land and streets to direct water, capturing rainwater in cisterns, and using gray water for irrigation. Newer technologies are also allowing for more efficient and effective wastewater recycling for reuse. These are just a few of the ways in which local communities are adapting to a hotter, drier climate and trying to live in greater harmony with nature.

EXPLORING THE DESERT SAFELY

To avoid unexpected pokes, bites, or stings, be aware of where you are putting your hands and feet.

- Scan the area and the ground when you're walking.
- Use a flashlight in the dark.
- Wear closed-toe shoes.
- Don't reach under, into, or around objects where you can't see. Turn over rocks with a boot or a stick before picking them up.
- Shake out your shoes and other clothing or bedding items left on the ground when camping or hiking.

▸ Going for a hike in Saguaro National Park

Stay hydrated.

- Always bring and drink lots of water. On summer days, this should be 1 quart (1 liter) of water per hour of hiking.
- Drink *before* you are thirsty.
- Carry electrolyte powder or gel on long or hot hikes to aid rehydration if needed. Signs of dehydration are headache, extreme thirst, fatigue, and dizziness.
- Turn back when half of your water is gone.

Stay cool.

- Wear a hat.
- Wear light colors.
- Avoid hiking between 10 a.m. and 4 p.m. in summer.
- Rest often.
- Find shade and slow down if you start to have any signs of heat exhaustion—heavy sweating; cold, pale, clammy skin; fast, weak pulse; nausea; muscle cramps; weakness; dizziness; and headache.

Wear sunscreen and protective clothing to avoid sunburn.

Bring or download a map—your phone won't have service everywhere.

Bring a buddy.

- It's best not to hike alone, but if you do, let someone know where you are going and when you expect to be back.

Avoid flash floods.

- Avoid hiking in washes when it's raining nearby.
- Do not try to cross a flooded roadway in your vehicle.

Avoid lightning.

- If you hear thunder, move quickly to a safer place.
- Go inside or in a vehicle if possible.
- If that's not possible, avoid hilltops, ridges. and flat, open areas.

Be mindful when encountering wild plants and animals.

- **Cactus:** If you're going to spend time outdoors, picking up a few cactus spines now and again is almost inevitable. Carry tweezers and a multi-tool to flick off cactus segments and remove spines.
- **Rattlesnakes:** Rattlesnakes and other snakes are not inherently aggressive toward people and would rather avoid you. Most snakebites happen when people handle or accidentally touch them. Keep your eyes and ears out for snakes—take out those earbuds and put the phone down! If you see a rattlesnake, stop and stay calm. Don't jump, scream, or run away. Move away slowly until you are out of striking distance. A rattlesnake can strike up to a distance of one-half its body length. If you are bitten, remain calm and restrict movement (less movement means slower blood flow). Elevate the bite and call 911 or get to a doctor as soon as possible. Nonvenomous snakes can also bite if harassed, so leave them alone as well.
- **Bees:** Africanized honeybees ("killer" bees) are found throughout the area. These bees will attack only when they feel their hive is threatened. Stay alert for sounds of bee activity and watch for them entering or exiting a colony. Near a colony, individual bees may "bump" you, without stinging, as a warning. If you are attacked, run away as fast as you can.

If possible, cover your head and face with clothing. Africanized bees will usually cease attacking once you are a quarter-mile to a half-mile (0.4–0.8 km) away from their hive. If you are stung, scrape away embedded stingers with a fingernail or credit card. Call 911 or get to a doctor as soon as possible if you have numerous stings.

- **Javelinas:** Javelinas have been known to attack people and dogs. If you see them, walk in the other direction. If they are coming toward you, make loud noises (hand claps, yells) and throw things in their direction to deter them from following you.
- **Black bears:** When camping in the high country, keep a clean camp. Don't store food, trash, clothes worn during cooking, or toiletries in your tent. Store these in approved bear-resistant containers, in a locked vehicle, or suspended 10 feet (3 m) from the ground or any part of the tree. Cook as far from the tent as possible. When hiking, walk and talk loudly to avoid surprising a bear. If you see a bear, talk calmly to it and do not scream. Stop and slowly wave your arms, raise them above your head, and try to look big. A bear might stand on its hind legs to get a better look or smell, but this is generally a sign of curiosity and not threat. It may bluff by charging or making sounds, but continue to talk to it calmly and in low tones. If it is stationary, you can move away slowly and sideways, keeping an eye on the bear and where you are going. If the bear follows, stop and stand your ground until the bear moves away. On the very rare occasion of a black bear attack, try to escape into a car or building. If you can't escape, fight back, using whatever you have to hit the bear in the face. EPA-approved bear spray is very effective at stopping an attacking bear.
- **Mountain lions:** Encounters are rare, and attacks even rarer. If you see one, don't run. Stop and back away slowly. Make noise, yell, or speak firmly in a loud voice. Make yourself look bigger by waving your arms slowly. Throw objects that you can reach without crouching down. Throw them in the lion's direction, but don't try to hit it. All these activities will likely convince the lion to leave. In the extremely rare case of an attack, fight back. Bear spray is effective with mountain lions as well.

THE MAIN CHARACTERS

PART TWO

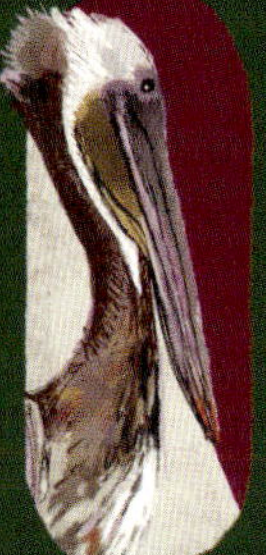

Sonoran Desert Plants and Animals

PRICKLY AND PLENTIFUL: PLANTS

DESERT PLANTS TEND TO look very different from native plants of other regions. They are often swollen, spiny, hairy, or have tiny leaves of many colors. Their unusual appearance is a result of their remarkable adaptations to the aridity and extreme conditions of the desert climate.

Wildflowers

The Sonoran Desert has two rainy seasons—one in the late winter/spring, the other in summer. Typically, spring and fall are considered drought periods. After the winter rains, the desert spring begins in earnest, with sunny days and cool nights. Days warm up in the high country—enough to melt the snow and fill the creeks—and the sound of running water pervades many canyons.

The winter/spring wildflower season peaks in March. The dominant flowers will change from year to year depending on the timing of fall and winter rains as well as especially cold and warm spells. Some of the most ubiquitous species are globe mallow, penstemons, evening primroses, desert marigolds, blue dicks, chia, and bladderpods. In years with the right combination of rain and temperature, you'll encounter beautiful fields of California poppies, lupines, and owl's clover.

Clockwise from upper left: Globe mallow, Parry's penstemon, desert marigold, spring wildflower bloom at Picacho Peak, owl's clover, blue dicks, evening primrose

When good summer rains occur, they trigger another wildflower season, and each species has its own particular timing requirements to produce abundant blooms. Summer poppies, devil's claw, and morning glories as well as flowering woody plants add color to the landscape.

Succulents

CACTI AND SUCCULENTS

▾ Flowering saguaros

All cacti are succulents, but not all succulents are cacti. Agaves and yuccas are succulents; they are frequently mistaken for cacti because they have spines or succulent leaves and stems. Such similarities of outward appearance are often examples of convergent evolution and are not reliable indicators of a family relationship. Convergent evolution is the independent development of similar features in species over different periods or epochs in time as well as from widely separated locations, including different continents. Different non-related species can evolve independent, yet analogous, structures with similar form and function, adapting to shared conditions.

Saguaro, *Carnegiea gigantea*, Spanish: *saguaro*

The iconic saguaro is one of about 50 types of columnar cacti found in deserts and thorn forests from Argentina to Arizona. The saguaro's range is almost completely restricted to Southern Arizona in the United States and western Sonora in Mexico.

It can take about 10 years for a saguaro to grow just a few inches and about 25 years to reach a couple of feet in height. When fully grown, its towering height of 40–60 feet (12–18 m) and tremendous weight of up to 8 tons (7257 kg) are supported by a woody skeleton of about two dozen spongy cylindrical ribs running up the length of the plant and branching out into the arms. Accordion-like pleats enable the plants to expand and contract as they gain and lose moisture during wet and dry seasons. Water comprises most of a saguaro's weight. A fully hydrated large stem can weigh about 80 pounds per foot (120 kg/m).

THE SENTINEL OF THE DESERT

The saguaro is the largest columnar cactus in the United States. Not surprisingly, this magnificent cactus has become a symbol of the American West, appearing everywhere from classic western art to smart phone cases. No calendar about the American Southwest would be complete without saguaro images. Its charismatic appearance and commanding presence across the landscape have made it

▸ Saguaro fruit

◂ Saguaro flowers

one of the defining plants of the Sonoran Desert. It is also a keystone species upon which many other species depend for food, shelter, shade, and more. Without saguaros, this desert community would be completely different.

Most of the plant's white flowers open after nightfall throughout the month of May, closing by late afternoon the following day. Their abundant nectar attracts pollinators—solitary bees, honeybees, nectar-feeding bats, white-winged doves, and other birds. The fleshy red fruits, avidly eaten by a great variety of birds and mammals (including humans), are sometimes mistaken for flowers from a distance.

The fruit of the saguaro has been an important food source for many desert dwellers, including insects, birds, mammals, and humans. The Tohono O'odham consider saguaros (*ha:şañ*, pronounced "hashan") to be their relations and ancestors, and the cactus figures prominently in O'odham ceremonies and desert lore. The O'odham annual calendar begins when the saguaro fruit (*bahidaj* in Tohono O'odham) ripens during the hottest time of the year. The moist red pulp is boiled down into syrup and used to make ceremonial wine for rainmaking ceremonies; the fruit is also consumed fresh and dried.

Agave, *Agave* spp., Spanish: *maguey*

Agaves, or century plants, are not cacti and are among the most useful plants in the Americas. In general, agaves have evergreen succulent leaves arranged in a rosette around a short stem. Though exceptions exist, the leaves are generally tough, ending in a sharp

▲ *Agave americana* in bloom

spine, some bearing sharp lateral thorns along the edges. In most agaves, flowers are produced only once in the plant's lifetime, usually at the 10- to 30-year mark, after which the mother plant dies. The long period leading up to this unique flowering event has led to the misconception that an agave flowers once a century, hence its alternate name, century plant.

Agaves range from southern Utah and Colorado in North America through Mexico, where the most of the 150 species are found, with a few in northern South America and the Caribbean Islands. About 40 species occur in the Sonoran Desert.

THE PLANT OF THE CENTURIES

Of great significance to the Indigenous peoples in the Americas, agaves have been utilized extensively for food, fiber, tools, medicine, fermented beverages, and liquor for thousands of years. Just before flowering, the hearts are cut and roasted, yielding sweet and nutritious food and drink. Some species are better suited for this than others. The Nahuatl word *mescal* means "cooked agave," and the Mescalero Apaches were so named for their use of this plant. Before them, people cultivated agaves as major food crops during the Hohokam period. Nowadays, amid climate change, agaves also

◂ *Agave tequilana* fields

◂ Prickly pear cactus in flower

play an important role in public and private landscaping as well as erosion control. Arid-adapted, agaves are also considered a crop of the future, especially in California and Southern Arizona.

Prickly pear, *Opuntia* spp., Spanish: *nopales*

With its elaborate network of upright stems, the prickly pear sprawls along the ground, though it can grow up to 20 feet (6 m) tall. Its prolific pads (or paddles), sprouting large, bright yellow blooms in late spring and early summer, are speckled with long, dark spines. The flowers turn orange as they age and eventually give rise to deep red, juicy prickly pear fruits (*tunas* in Spanish), known for their anti-oxidant and anti-inflammatory properties and used to make juice, syrup, and jam.

The genus *Opuntia* is identified by the presence of true leaves or leaflets on the young, tender pads and by glochids (hair-thin spines that are hard to see, but can prick just the same). Engelmann's prickly pear are the most common in the desert around Tucson; many other species are found from southern Canada to Tierra del

▸ Prickly pear fruit

Fuego. The common name for prickly pear cacti throughout Mexico is *nopal* (plural: *nopales*). In the Tucson Mountains, they occur in association with cholla cactus, ocotillo, palo verde, and saguaro.

DELICIOUS NOPALES

The pads and fruit are eaten by a wide variety of animals, including rabbits, javelinas, packrats, desert tortoises, numerous birds, and cactus beetles. The pads are actually stems, not leaves. Very small, fleshy leaflets appear on the new tender pads (*pencas* or *nopalitos* in Spanish) but later on in spring, these leaflets soon wither and drop.

The juicy, palatable, though somewhat acidic fruit ripens in tremendous numbers in July and August and can be harvested for a few months. Some of the tender nopalitos are edible, but require thorough cleaning. They contain spines and thousands of microscopic glochids that could make harvesting tunas or nopalitos an unpleasant experience if you don't know what you're doing. Over the decades, the practice of eating nopales has diminished, overtaken by modern diets and prepared, commercial, processed foods. In recent years, however, there's been a revival of eating local and native plant foods, especially cacti such as prickly pear. The large fruits are as tasty as watermelon and, once the spines are removed, the pads can be diced or sliced for cooking or pickling. In urban areas, there are several varieties of *Opuntia ficus-indica*, also known as Indian fig cactus (*nopal de Castilla* in Spanish). These more domesticated varieties grow fast and upright, reaching heights as tall as 15 feet (4.6 m), and some are spineless, though they require some irrigation and extra care to produce a good crop.

Cholla, *Cylindropuntia* spp., Spanish: *cholla*

Besides the majestic saguaro, chollas are probably one of the most widespread and successful cacti in the Sonoran Desert. The reputation of the jumping cholla has concerned many a first-time visitor. Yes, there is one species called just that—they have barbed spines that readily detach onto passersby or other animals at the slightest touch. This is the main method of propagation for this species. Once dropped anywhere near or far, those cholla segments or fruits will take root.

MEETING THE CHOLLAS (CAREFULLY!)

There are at least half a dozen cholla species in the Tucson area, including jumping, teddy bear, pencil, Christmas, buckhorn, and staghorn chollas. In early spring, buds and flowers of these last two species are an abundant food source for bird and insect pollinators as well as humans. Because they contain the least number of spines and glochids, they're easier to harvest and consume. A dietary staple for millennia, cholla buds contain significant protein and are valued for their high calcium and soluble fiber content.

The Tohono O'odham and other desert-dwelling people eat the sizable flower buds of some chollas. First, the spines and glochids are

◂ Teddy bear cholla

◂ Cane cholla with yellow fruit

▲ Ocotillo

➚ Ocotillo flower

removed by rolling the buds on a screen or basket until clean. Then they are pit-roasted or boiled and either eaten immediately or dried or pickled for later consumption. They are definitely not fast food.

Ocotillo, *Fouquieria splendens*, Spanish: *ocotillo*

Another recognizable resident of Southern Arizona, the ocotillo is one of the flashiest, most unique and useful plants, though they can resemble dead sticks much of the year. The branches are used by local Indigenous and ranching communities to construct fences, ramadas, and shelters.

Found throughout the Sonoran Desert and in Texas and Chihuahua, this unusual woody shrub has numerous elongated, flexible, spiny branches bursting forth from a very short trunk and grows 10–20 feet (3–6 m) tall. The red-orange flowers at the tips of the plant's long skinny branches bloom in April regardless of rainfall. Each flame-like cluster resembles a small torch—an *ocotillo* in Spanish, the word derived from the Nahuatl *ocote*, meaning torch.

In the Tucson Mountains, ocotillos grow in association with palo verdes, chollas, and saguaros. They are succulents, not cacti, and are one of the most successful arid-adapted plants in the desert, growing in direct proportion to the amount of moisture available to them. The branches are leafless for most of the year, but after a rain, leaves appear within 48 hours.

THE HONEYSUCKLE OF THE DESERT

Hummingbirds are the ocotillo's main pollinators, feeding on the nectar from the red tubular flowers. This is a crucial energy source for passing hummers as they migrate to northern breeding grounds, often the only option during the region's rainless springs. When you encounter an ocotillo on a hike, you can taste this sweet nectar. Bend a long branch—careful of the thorns!—to pluck the stamens from the flowers and suck them as if they were honeysuckle. The sweetness is subtle, but the experience is as unique as the Sonoran Desert.

Barrel cactus, *Ferocactus wislizeni*, Spanish: *viznaga*

The Southwestern barrel cactus (also called Arizona or candy barrel cactus) is the largest and most common of this cactus type in Southern Arizona. Like other columnar cacti, such as saguaro and organ pipe cactus, this barrel cactus is pleated and can swell or shrink with the availability of moisture during the rainy seasons. The thick barrel-shaped body of this cactus is usually 2–4 feet (0.6–1.2 m) tall, but occasionally can reach 8–10 feet (2.4–3 m) in height. Flowers range in color from yellow to orange and shades of red.

⇞ Barrel cactus

▲ Barrel cactus laden with fruit

IS THERE WATER IN THE BARREL?

According to desert folklore, Native Americans and knowledgeable pioneers could obtain water from a barrel cactus, and those who retain this passed-down skill today still can, but most city dwellers could not if their lives depended on it. Really, the best preemptive measure to survive the desert heat is to bring water with you.

To retrieve water from a barrel cactus, you must first get to the pulp inside the tough, spiny, armored skin. A pocketknife won't cut it. In fact, the whole enterprise is likely to cause more water loss from sweating—though hopefully not bleeding—than could be obtained from the plant. The water within cacti is tightly bound in a gooey mucilage. Most of the year, the texture of this inner tissue is more like that of a damp sponge than that of a watermelon; even so, it's not really possible to squeeze much liquid from it. In addition, some species of cacti have toxic levels of oxalic acid and bitter alkaloids—exposure to these substances causes diarrhea, which only worsens dehydration.

The Seri (Comcáac), Tohono O'odham, and other Indigenous groups of the region rely on the fruit, flowers, and buds of the barrel cactus as an emergency food. The pineapple-shaped fruits can be eaten fresh, though not in large quantities due to the presence of oxalic acid. The seeds, similar to poppy seeds, can be consumed without risk, and the juicy, tart rinds can be sliced and added to salads, pastas, beverages, chutneys, and preserves. Barrels do have a lot to offer, as long as you don't expect water from them.

Soaptree yucca and banana yucca, *Yucca elata*, *Yucca baccata*, Spanish: *palmilla*

Along with cacti and other succulents, yuccas are also familiar silhouettes of North America's western desert landscape. Looking like spiky miniature palms, soaptree and banana yuccas stand out

Clockwise from upper left:
Soaptree yucca

Soaptree yucca bloom

Banana yucca flowers

Banana yuccas

among neighboring plants and are found in grasslands and mountain slopes throughout central and southeastern Arizona and Sonora at elevations ranging from 2000 to 6000 feet (610 to 1829 m). Unlike agaves, yuccas are perennials once they reach maturity, flowering year after year. Their blooms are creamy white, borne in clusters on a long central stalk in May and June. The yucca moth (*Tegeticula yuccasella*) is the plant's chief pollinator.

DESERT BANANA SPLIT

After their showy blooms fade, both soaptree and banana yuccas produce fruit. However, the fruit of the banana yucca gets the award for best-tasting. As the plant's name implies, the fruits resemble a bunch of bananas on the central stalk, but they are shorter and rounder. They also differ from bananas in that they are mostly seeds with very little meat. Because banana yucca populations are relatively small and many animals (insects, mammals, and birds) feed from them, the fruits can be tricky to procure in the wild. In addition, fruit production varies from year to year. In a good year, however, plants produce multiple bunches of healthy fruit.

Both species of yucca also provide basket-weaving material, used in combination with other desert fibers by local Tohono O'odham communities who produce some of the finest weavings in the American Southwest and northern Sonora.

Organ pipe cactus, *Stenocereus thurberi*, Spanish: *pitahaya*

Distinguished from a saguaro by its thinner, multiple unbranched stems that rise from ground level, organ pipe cacti have solid wooden cores. A tropical plant, this unusual shrub-like cactus is more frost-sensitive than the saguaro and, therefore, restricted to the warmest microhabitats—the western part of the US-Mexico borderlands is its northernmost limit. In Mexico, it occurs throughout much of Sonora and the southern half of Baja California.

A PIPE ORGAN LIKE NO OTHER

In Sonora, the organ pipe is the dominant columnar cactus. Known as *pitahaya dulce* (Spanish for "sweet dragon fruit"), this plant is synonymous with summer rains, thunderstorms, and its large, delicious fruit. Some communities engage in commercial harvesting, and fruits are sold in local markets and on the streets of Sonora and Baja California. You can even find organ pipe ice cream and popsicles sold in downtown Hermosillo food stalls, markets, and restaurants.

Nectar-feeding bats are the organ pipe's primary pollinators and among its major seed dispersers. Because the flowers close at

◣ Organ pipe cactus in its eponymous National Monument

▾ Organ pipe cactus at the Arizona-Sonora Desert Museum

▲ Organ pipe cactus flower

daybreak, diurnal animals (active in daylight hours) are not significant pollinators as they are for saguaros. Coastal populations of columnar cacti, including organ pipe, constitute the most important migratory superhighway for bats and bird species on their way from Sonora to Arizona.

Trees and Shrubs

Mesquite, *Prosopis* spp., Spanish: *mesquite, algarroba, chachaca*

The mesquite is one of the Sonoran Desert's most ubiquitous, beautiful, beneficial, and useful trees. One of the three most common native edible leguminous (bean) trees that thrive in this region—along with palo verdes and ironwoods—the trees are heat- and drought-tolerant, ideally adapted to the desert's extreme conditions. This tree is another keystone species and, as a nurse plant, offers protective habitat for a great number of native plants and animals to grow and develop.

MEET THE MARVELOUS MESQUITE

Mesquite trees are also native to the arid and semiarid areas of North and South America. Over time, some species have been introduced to Africa, Asia, and Australia where they are now considered invasive. There are at least 44 mesquite species worldwide, three of which occur in the Sonoran Desert: honey mesquite (*Prosopis glandulosa*), velvet mesquite (*Prosopis velutina*), and screwbean mesquite (*Prosopis pubescens*). All of these species produce varying levels of sweet, edible seedpods. Valued for their sweet taste,

▼ Honey mesquite

◢ Velvet mesquite

nourishment, storability, abundance, and easy harvesting, mesquite pods can be milled into flour and have been a staple food for people living in the Sonoran Desert for millennia.

In addition to providing flour, syrup, and fermented beverages, mesquite trees are the source of firewood, building materials, medicines, paints and dyes, adhesives, tools and utensils, weapons, and other culturally important items. In the past, O'odham people used coils of wheat straw splinted with mesquite bark to make large storage baskets that were used to store seed crops and other dry goods.

In Southern Arizona, the trees grow along desert washes and on plains and, in the past, formed some of the largest mesquite *bosques* (Spanish for forests) along major riverways, such as the Santa Cruz River. However, in some rangelands, mesquite has become an invasive tree/shrub introduced by cattle.

Yellow palo verde, blue palo verde, *Parkinsonia microphylla, Parkinsonia florida*, Spanish: *palo verde*

As spring arrives in the Sonoran Desert, the desert landscape turns yellow as far as the eye can see, and these trees (with some help from the wildflowers) are the main reason. Both species—yellow palo verdes and blue palo verdes—produce exuberant clusters of yellow flowers, creating the most impressive spectacle of golden blooms in North America.

Blue palo verdes grow up to 35 feet (10.7 m) in height and have bluish-green branches, leaves, and trunks. Yellow palo verdes, on the other hand, are more shrub-like with yellowish-green branches, and reach an average height of 15 feet (4.6 m). Both trees occur in the lower Sonoran life zone on rocky slopes (*bajadas* in Spanish), alongside dry desert washes, or in desert mountains. Chlorophyll accounts for their green bark and their ability to photosynthesize.

◭ Palo verde tree

▾ Palo verde flowers

Like many other plant species, palo verdes drop their leaves to conserve water during the dry season. Typically associated with saguaros, ocotillos, chollas, and prickly pear, palo verdes serve as nurse plants for baby saguaros. The primary range of palo verdes and saguaros often overlaps in the Arizona Uplands subdivision of the Sonoran Desert, also known as the saguaro/palo verde forest.

SONORAN DESERT EDAMAME?

After bees, birds, and various insects pollinate the bright yellow flowers, green seed pods develop from mid-May into June. When the pods swell, you can harvest them and snack on the fresh, bright green seeds inside as you would edamame or sprinkle them on salads. They can also be blanched while still in their pods.

Ironwood, *Olneya tesota*, Spanish: *palo fierro*

Of the three edible leguminous trees of the Sonoran Desert, this delicious native bean tree is the least common. Like mesquite and palo verde trees, ironwood is one of the main food-producing legumes of the Sonoran Desert. One of the desert's tallest trees, an ironwood grows up to 35 feet (10.7 m) tall, with gray-green, doubly compound (twice divided) leaves. For a short flowering period during May and June, ironwood boasts gorgeous grayish lavender flowers, blooming in clusters. This tree grows slowly, so a large, mature ironwood could be several centuries old. In association with soil bacteria and mycorrhizal fungi, desert ironwoods fix nitrogen, an essential nutrient often in low supply, in desert soil.

SHARPEN YOUR AXE

As the name suggests, ironwood is so dense and solid it actually sinks rather than floats in water. It is also nearly indestructible, with

▾ Ironwood tree

▴ Ironwood flowers

chemicals in the heartwood that resist decay and decomposition. Dense wood burns hot, so ironwood was heavily harvested for firewood and charcoal production in earlier times.

A few decades ago, a trend of locally produced ironwood carvings by the Seri Indian community in the coastal region of Sonora, Mexico also decreased the tree's population. The exploitation intensified when sales of these originally hand-carved figurines expanded the industry to non-Indigenous neighbors who increased production by using power tools. Nowadays, these commercial threats seem to have decreased somewhat, but new ones have arisen, such as urban and agricultural development as well as the proliferation of invasive species.

In summer, ironwoods offer both flowers and protein-rich seeds, which taste great. Seeds can be collected and eaten when fresh, green, and soft or after drying when hard. They can be added to salads, rice, and savory dishes. For long-term storage, the beans are typically blanched, steamed, boiled, or dried.

Brittlebush, *Encelia farinosa*, Spanish: *incienso, rama blanca*

This attractive flowering plant is widespread and common in most of the Sonoran Desert. Brittlebush is very drought-resistant and often forms uninterrupted stands in extremely arid habitats. The leaves range from bright green and nearly hairless to gray-green or white, often with a dense covering of soft matted hairs. In spring and sometimes summer through winter, small yellow flowers are borne on skinny branched stalks that rise above the leafy stems, so that the whole bush looks like a bouquet of flowers. This species grows 2–5 feet (0.6–1.5 m) tall with a spread of 2–4 feet (0.6–1.2 m).

▾ Brittlebush

O'ODHAM CHEWING GUM

This magnificent composite plant (characterized by flower clusters) has become quite popular in urban xeriscapes (gardens that require little or no irrigation) throughout the arid American Southwest. In Spanish, brittlebush is called *incienso* because its yellow sap, produced during its spring flowering season, was burned as incense in Mexican churches. As the flowering season ends and aridity rises, brittlebush sap hardens to a gum-like consistency. In fact, the Tohono O'odham enjoy it as chewing gum, and a piece of sap can last hours or even days. Just pocket it—it's not sticky—and save it for later.

Triangle-leaf bursage, *Ambrosia deltoidea*, Spanish: *chicurilla, estafiate*

Triangle-leaf bursage is typical of the Arizona Uplands, where it is often the dominant understory plant. It is a densely branched subshrub, about 2 feet (0.6 m) tall with triangular, finely toothed, gray-green leaves that fall away during very dry periods. Though it can be confused with brittlebush when not in flower, bursage is a smaller plant with smaller, duller gray leaves. Its growth and flowering periods occur in late winter to early spring. Because the flowers are green, this plant is easy to miss, but they're more visible when the flowers turn into burs (seed vessels), which ripen in late spring.

▾ Triangle-leaf bursage

BURSAGE BACK FROM THE BRINK

In Southern Arizona, about half of the Lower Sonoran desertscrub habitat is covered by small shrubs, including triangle-leaf bursage. Though small in stature, it plays an important ecological role as a nurse plant, providing protection for baby saguaros, palo verdes, and other young cacti as they sprout and get established and, with other shrub species, it greatly contributes to the overall color and texture of the terrain.

At the Arizona-Sonora Desert Museum, triangle-leaf bursage happens to be the dominant small-shrub species. When it came under threat after some construction projects inside and outside museum grounds, Desert Museum staff stepped in to restore the natural areas disturbed by human intrusion by replanting this bursage. The goal was to integrate, repair, and make the restoration as undetectable as possible for human visitors and most especially for the resident wildlife. It seems to have worked.

Whitethorn acacia, *Vachellia constricta*, Spanish: *vinorama*

A large deciduous shrub, whitethorn acacia has leaves that resemble those of the mesquite, but the leaflets are smaller. The white thorns are about an inch (2.5 cm) long, but mature shrubs are often thornless. Usually growing to 6 feet (1.8 m) and occasionally as tall as 12 feet (3.7 m), this plant is common in arroyos and washes in Southern Arizona and south through to central Mexico.

FRAGRANT YELLOW PUFFY BALLS

The flowers of the whitethorn acacia, blooming in spring and again in summer, are small, striking yellow balls, 0.5 inches (1.3 cm) in diameter with a strong scent, but no nectar and sparse pollen. Though pollinators do not visit in large numbers, whitethorn acacias are good seed crops. In Sonora, Mexico, the Seri people use the leaves and seeds in a medicinal tea for stomach problems. Their thorny branches are also ideal for building fences.

Desert broom, *Baccharis sarothroides*, Spanish: *romerillo*

Desert broom is a pioneer plant, efficient at establishing itself in newly disturbed soil. Therefore, it's often abundant in washes, roadsides, and abandoned plowed fields. Like many pioneer plants, it is rather short-lived, lasting perhaps a couple of decades. Due to its aggressively invasive nature, desert broom is not always a favorite among gardeners, but it can be useful. The flowers attract hundreds of butterflies, bees, wasps, and beetles. Because it flowers in autumn, it helps extend the season of a butterfly garden. These plants are dioecious (male and female reproductive organs occur in separate plants) and the more plentiful female seeds are a particular woe for allergy sufferers as they take to the air in cloudy puffs that look like snow.

From top to bottom: Whitethorn acacia flowers

The white thorns of whitethorn acacia are a formidable defense.

Desert broom

GRAB A BROOM

As the vernacular name suggests, this plant's thin terminal twigs can be bundled together at the end of a pole to make a broom. Traditionally, they were the broom of choice not only for household chores but also for harvesting native foods (prickly pear and cholla buds) and threshing grains (wheat and barley).

BONELESS AND BOUNTIFUL: INVERTEBRATES

FOR EVERY SPECIES OF VERTEBRATE on this planet, there are nearly 10 that lack a backbone. This holds true regionally, too. Thousands of arthropods (invertebrates with jointed appendages) inhabit this region, ranging from minuscule (and harmless) pseudoscorpions to large spiders, centipedes, butterflies, and beetles. With such a large number of organisms, this will serve as a primer for some of the common arthropods as well as some of the bizarre ones.

If "bugs" aren't your thing, don't worry—you're not alone. Many people view them as things rather than animals. And often, as things to be feared, avoided, and eliminated due to a perception that these organisms lack redeeming qualities in a world dominated by humans. But if you can open your eyes, ears, and minds to "things" that differ from us, you will see how few of them can—let alone want to—really hurt us, and you will learn about some highly unusual methods of survival. In the process, a new world may open before you, providing untold hours of discovery and entertainment while you come to appreciate the beauty, diversity, and value of these sometimes creepy, often crawly, animals to humankind.

In desert areas, many of the species listed here can be found in spring through autumn, though for several, surface activity is tied to and dependent upon the summer monsoon.

Beetles

With about 350,000 named species of beetles (a number that increases as new discoveries are made), it is estimated that beetles account for 25 percent of Earth's living organisms. High beetle diversity is also a feature of the Sonoran Desert, which provides habitat for an incredible array of species ranging from miniature to massive, from drab and subtle to bright and showy. As a group, their high numbers, diverse body forms, broad food palates, and wide range of habitats are reasons why they're among nature's most important recycling agents. They are the ones that "bring back the dead," by cycling the nutrients needed to create new life. Here's a sample of some of the more common species.

June bugs/beetles, *Phyllophaga* spp., Spanish: *mayate de mayo*

This member of the scarab beetle family shows up in great numbers in Southern Arizona during the warm summer months. It is attracted to light and is known for what humans may think of as a rather clumsy flight pattern, often bouncing off (or landing on) screens, pools, and your clothes. Though the beetle's behaviors may be slightly annoying (again, to humans), what might not be apparent is the critical role this beetle plays in nutrient cycling. The adult beetle is food for other animals, as is its larva (grub).

Pinacate (or stink) beetles, *Eleodes* spp., Spanish: *pinacate*

Known for lowering its head to the ground and pointing the tip of its abdomen upwards when approached, this common 1-inch-long (2.5-cm-long) black beetle isn't bowing—it's giving you fair warning that if you don't leave it alone, it will release an extremely intense and smelly chemical intended to convince you (the potential predator) that it's anything but a tasty meal. This defense strategy works well, except with animals like skunks, who roll the beetles on the ground, or grasshopper mice who "plug" them into the ground. This beetle cannot fly because its outer wings (called *elytra*) are fused to create a form of armored protection and to reduce water loss.

Clockwise from upper left: June bug, pinacate (or stink) beetle, ironclad beetle, green fig beetle, cluster of green fig beetles, shining leaf chafer

Ironclad beetle, *Asbolus verrucosus*, Spanish: *escarabajos acorazados*

Sturdily built 0.75 inches (1.9 cm) long, this slow-moving black beetle is commonly encountered at lower elevations. It can be differentiated from the stink beetle by its wider and flatter body, and its thick outer wings (elytra) generally have a dimpled appearance.

Green fig beetle, *Cotinis mutabilis*, Spanish: *mayate verde*

Another scarab, this sizable beetle is known for its vibrant green coloration and slow, deliberate, relatively loud flight. Particularly attracted to ripening fruits and nectar-rich flowers, it is an important pollinator. It can also be found around the wounds of mesquite and desert broom, where it feeds on the tasty sap.

Clockwise from upper left: pleasing fungus beetle, pleasing fungus beetles enjoying some fungus, palo verde root borer, tiger beetle, lady beetle, convergent lady beetles congregate in the warmer months at higher elevations.

Shining leaf chafer, *Anomala binotata*, Spanish: *escarabajo brillante de las hojas*

Another showy form, this species' metallic sheen adds a touch of brilliance to the region's beetle diversity. Activity correlates with the monsoon season, and it is more common at higher elevations.

Pleasing fungus beetle, *Gibbifer californicus*, Spanish: *escarabajos de hongos*

Another higher-elevation species, this beetle, as its name suggests, prefers to eat various fungi. Look for these colorful, harmless animals on the forest floor, near or under rotting logs, tree branches, and trunks. Females lay their eggs on fungus and, upon hatching, the grayish grubs, which sport dark hairy projections from the top and sides of their bodies, eat the fungus. Some of the fungi they eat could be harmful to the host plant, so these beetles share a mutually beneficial (or symbiotic) relationship with the trees.

Palo verde root borer, *Derobrachus hovorei*, Spanish: *torito de palo verde*

At 2 inches (5 cm) or more in length, this sizable beetle is hard to confuse with any other in the region. The male possesses impressive, oversized mandibles, but don't let its size or formidable jaws concern you—though it can bite if you stick your finger in front of it, it's not aggressive and rarely does so.

The beetle's above-ground life is short—about a month in summer—as opposed to its years spent underground prior to metamorphosis as a grub. There it can grow several inches long, munching on its favorite food—the woody roots of various desert trees.

Tiger beetles, family Cicindelidae, Spanish: *escarabajos tigre*

Many beetles are herbivores. Tiger beetles differ in that they are predators of smaller insects. While most beetles move slowly, tiger beetles use exceptional speed and agility to chase and capture their prey.

Lady beetles, family Coccinellidae, Spanish: *mariquitas*

Though they're often called bugs, they're actually small, brightly colored beetles that play a vital role in natural pest control by eating aphids and other garden pests—one lady beetle can eat 5000 aphids during its lifetime! Species often have a specific number of distinct spots on their wings that is reflected in their common names (such as "twice-stabbed lady beetle").

Lady beetles show up where/whenever aphids are common and are often associated with succulent new plant growth in spring. In fall you're most likely to see them on pines and other evergreens.

Grasshoppers

Several species of grasshoppers are found in this region, many of which employ crypsis (camouflage) to avoid detection, while others use vibrant contrasting colors (aposematism) to warn predators that they are toxic and unpalatable, or to distract predators with flashes of color to avoid capture.

▲ Horse lubber grasshopper

◄ The gray bird grasshopper gets its name from its imposing size and choppy flight.

Horse lubber, *Taeniopoda eques,* Spanish: *saltamonte perezoso norteamericano*

When hiking in the Sonoran Desert, especially in grasslands during late summer through early fall, you're likely to see a large, heavy-bodied grasshopper—up to 2.5 inches (6.4 cm) long—flashing bright pinkish-red hind wings in flight. Unpalatable due to stored toxins from food plants, the horse lubber warns off predators with its bright contrasting wing color and greenish-yellow lines on its black body.

Pallid-winged grasshopper, *Trimerotropis pallidipennis,* Spanish: *chapulín de alas pálidas*

Plentiful and common in the desert, this grasshopper possesses bright orange, red, or yellow hind wings set against its drab brown body and forewings that startle predators upon flight and help it disappear as it lands by blending in with the ground and vegetation.

Gray bird grasshopper, *Schistocerca nitens,* Spanish: *langosta gris norteña*

This large (up to 3 inches/7.6 cm long) common grasshopper frequents gardens and home vegetation. When it's time to lay eggs, the female deposits them underground in loose soil, where they stay through winter, yielding a tiny bright green nymph in early spring. Though the nymph is vibrantly colored, the adult is mottled gray or tan. Its neutral color and relative inactivity through most of the day as it lingers on a single plant allow it to hide in plain sight.

The Real Bugs and Their Relatives

We often refer to the invertebrates running and flying around us as "bugs," but this group is the only one that are *true* bugs. True bugs are those with a unique pair of wings that are leathery at one end and membranous toward the tips—hence their order classification name, Hemiptera, which means half-wing. They also sport needle-like mouthparts that arise from the front part of the head and which they use to pierce and suck fluids out of their food. Most feed on plant sap while some are predatory, and still others, like the kissing bug, are parasitic, feeding on the blood of other animals.

Giant mesquite bug, *Thasus neocalifornicus*, Spanish: *xamues*

As you'd expect from its name, this bug is found feeding on the fresh green stems and pods of mesquite trees during early summer. Adults are brownish-black with orange bands on their legs and along their wing veins. Nymphs show up in spring and are bright red and white. Though harmless, they release a stinky secretion if handled. Eggs look like rows of tiny brown pillows glued along tree stems. Adults lay eggs at the end of summer, then die.

Clockwise from left: Giant mesquite bug adults

Giant mesquite bug nymphs (immature form)

Giant mesquite bug adults

Cicadas and Cochineals

Close relatives to the true bugs are the fascinating cicadas and cochineals. They also have piercing/sucking mouthparts, but located further back on the underside of the head. Another difference is that their wings are uniform in structure. The cicada is a common, easily identified insect while the cochineal scale insect doesn't even look like a bug.

Cicadas, family Cicadidae, Spanish: *chicharras, cigarras*

Most of us are familiar with the large, loud cicada and the males' mating "songs," intense buzzing sounds emanating from trees and other plants and intended to attract females as well as establish territory. Several species occur here, perhaps the most common of which is the Apache cicada. Adults emerge before the monsoon, feed on plant sap, mate, and deposit their eggs under the surface of plant stems. When the eggs hatch, the larvae drop to the ground and burrow into the soil, where they feed on plant roots. Nymphs live and feed underground for three or more years before emerging as adults.

Clockwise from upper left: Cicada

Dried cochineal bugs, and yarns dyed with the pigment released when they are crushed

The white scale on the pads and fruit is the wax produced by cochineal insects. The bugs live under the wax.

Cochineals, *Dactylopius* spp., Spanish: *cochinillas*

Cochineals are scale insects that feed on cacti, where evidence of their presence—white, fuzzy splotches made from a wax secreted from the abdominal glands of females and nymphs—dot the plant's surface and conceal the insects inside. Females are dark red, lack wings and legs, and attach to the plant, looking like tiny grapes. Males look more insect-like, resembling tiny pink and white gnats, and are most visible when they emerge to mate during late summer.

Cochineals have impacted our lives, too. Inside their bodies, cochineals contain carminic acid, which produces an intense red dye harvested by Indigenous peoples of the Southwest United States, Mexico, and Central and South America. Though synthetic dyes replaced it in the mid-1800s, it is making a comeback due to synthetic dye toxicity as well as the desire for the subtle hues this natural dye offers.

Pollinators I: Butterflies and Moths

Butterflies are one of the most easily recognized and popular groups of insects. About 250 species occur in Southern Arizona, representing several families, among them swallowtails, gossamer wings, brush-footeds, metalmarks, snouts, skippers, whites, and sulphurs.

Butterflies and their heavier, furrier, and more nocturnal cousins, moths, are critical pollinators. While a lot of people like butterflies, fewer appreciate moths (which can destroy your favorite sweater and outnumber butterflies, species-wise, about 15 to 1) or caterpillars (which chomp through your favorite plants). But without caterpillars there would be no butterflies—or moths—so consider adopting a "live and let live" philosophy and marveling at the circle of life.

August and September are the best times for butterfly sightings in Southern Arizona. Moths are very active then, too, but also peak in April through May. You can see them in flight, on plants, and "puddling" (congregating near damp, muddy areas or puddles) to extract nutrients (salts and minerals) critical to their diets and reproductive success.

Above, left to right:
Giant swallowtail

Two-tailed swallowtail

Pipevine swallowtail

Pipevine swallowtail caterpillar

Swallowtails, *Papilio* spp., Spanish: *mariposas cometa*

At up to 5 inches (12.7 cm) across, swallowtails are some of the largest and most beautiful butterflies in the world. They're a stunning and fascinating addition to any garden, desert, or riparian scene. They seemingly float unaided as they traverse the skies. All the while, they're searching for suitable habitat and pollinating plants. Many lepidopterans (moths and butterflies) rely on a few obligate host plants, particular plants on which the animal's survival depends at some point in its life cycle. For example, many of the larger yellow and black butterflies need to feed on the tender new leaves of citrus plants during their caterpillar stage. Southern Arizona is home to various swallowtail species, like the giant swallowtail, anise swallowtail, and the state butterfly, the two-tailed swallowtail.

Giant swallowtail, *Papilio cresphontes*, Spanish: *mariposa cometa gigante*

With a 4-inch (10 cm) wingspread, this is one of the region's largest butterflies. Brown and yellow, this species is more common in urban areas. Its larvae, which feed mostly on citrus leaves, look like bird droppings. If disturbed, the larvae release an unpleasant-smelling substance from an organ just behind the head. Both their appearance and smell are defenses against predation.

Two-tailed swallowtail, *Papilio multicaudata*, Spanish: *mariposa cometa Xochiquetzal*

With a wingspan of up to 5.5 inches (14 cm), this is the largest swallowtail in western North America; the females are larger than the males and more brightly colored. You're most likely to find them

near streams, canyons, and lower-elevation cities, such as Tucson. Like katydids and stick insects, they feed on Arizona rosewood (a great nontoxic alternative to oleander) as well as Arizona sycamore, chokecherry, and ash.

Pipevine swallowtail, *Battus philenor*, Spanish: *mariposa cola de golondrina azul*

While not as bright or quite as large as other swallowtails of the region, this species is a more subtly beautiful insect, easily identified by its iridescent blue wings with brilliant orange spots. Its caterpillars are showy, too, announcing their toxicity (garnered from pipevines, their host plants) with reddish-orange spikes along the topside of the body.

Monarch, *Danaus plexippus*, Spanish: *mariposa monarca*

Monarchs are famous for their annual migration, covering thousands of miles—Canada to Mexico and back!—and taking three or more generations to complete. Migration routes aren't taught; rather, they are inherited. Monarchs come through the Sonoran Desert and Tucson en route to their main overwintering sites in Mexico or California. Those headed to high-elevation oyamel fir forests in Mexico communally roost in groups estimated to be in the millions. A careful eye might spot a butterfly with a small white ID tag on its left hind wing, and any observer can report a sighting to the Southwest Monarch Study at swmonarchs.org.

▸ Check out the hind wing of a butterfly to discern if it's male or female. The males have an extra black dot that is a pheromone factory, helping communicate the individual's availability to mates.

Climate and land-use change appear to have had devastating impact on monarch migrations by reducing hospitable habitat throughout their range. The best way to help? Participate and encourage conservation efforts such as protecting wild spaces, planting milkweeds, and eliminating pesticide use.

Monarchs feed on milkweeds, known for producing a milky latex. These plants are required eating for caterpillar survival and therefore integral to the species' life cycle. Although milkweeds are distasteful to the majority of animals, monarchs can utilize many, if not all, of the 108 species found in North America. As caterpillars, monarchs ingest the toxins from milkweeds to their favor. The caterpillars and adults are then distasteful to predators, and their bright black, white, and orange coloration advertises the "yuck" factor to curious birds.

▸ You can tell the difference between monarchs and queens by looking at the white spots. These spots on a monarch will all be within the black borders; on a queen, white spots are in the orange sections as well.

Clockwise from upper left:
Queen butterfly caterpillar. Queen and monarch caterpillars look similar to each other.

Gulf fritillary caterpillar

Gulf fritillary butterfly

Gulf fritillary with wings closed

Rabbles of monarchs can be seen in Southern Arizona during September and October migrating south and March and April migrating north. You'll find these flyers anywhere there's milkweed. Don't forget to look for caterpillars and chrysalises in and around gardens. Pro tip: If there are three pairs of tubercles (projections) on the caterpillar, it's a queen; monarchs have two pairs.

Queen, *Danaus gilippus*, Spanish: *mariposa reina*

Similar in appearance and closely related to the monarch, the queen butterfly also feeds on milkweeds and is much more common in the region.

Gulf fritillary, *Agraulis vanillae*, Spanish: *mariposa pasionaria motas blancas*

The Gulf fritillary is a large orange and black butterfly (a deeper orange than that of the queen and monarch) adorned with silver spots on the undersides of its wings. Its caterpillars feed exclusively on passion vines. Planting these vines around the house will greatly increase local abundance.

Clockwise from upper left:
Great blue (or purple) hairstreak butterfly

Tobacco hornworm, *Manduca sexta* caterpillar

White-lined sphinx moth

White-lined sphinx moth caterpillar

Great blue/purple hairstreak, *Atlides halesus*, Spanish: *mariposa sedosa gigante azul*

The great blue (or purple) hairstreak is one of the largest and most spectacular of the gossamer-winged species. Solitary and uncommon in our region, its caterpillar feeds on desert mistletoes. Look for them around desert broom or seepwillow when they are in bloom.

Carolina sphinx moth/tobacco hornworm, *Manduca sexta*, Spanish: *polilla del cuerno del tabaco*

Often considered a crop and garden pest, due to its voracious caterpillar (or hornworm, so named for the protruding "horn" on its head), few people recognize the importance of this moth as a pollinator to the very same plants. And with the region's favorable climate, moth pollination is incredibly important in the desert. This amazing caterpillar avoids nicotine-rich veins in tobacco leaves while feeding, though tolerant of the toxin, and the plant retains enough nicotine to protect itself from other herbivores.

White-lined sphinx/hawk moth, *Hyles lineata*, Spanish: *polilla esfinge de rayas blancas*

One of the most abundant hawk moths in North America, this common moth feeds on and pollinates a variety of plants. It's sometimes mistaken for a hummingbird due to its large size and habit of hovering near and feeding from flowers by sipping nectar through a long proboscis. As with the Carolina sphinx moth, caterpillars are known as hornworms and, in large numbers, can damage crops and gardens.

Pollinators II: Bees, Wasps

Another critical and well-documented part of the Southwestern pollination story belongs to bees and wasps. When people consider bees, they often think of the honeybee. Though common and important in Sonoran Desert ecosystems, this bee is an introduced species that originally came from Italy to North America via English colonizers as early as 1622. Later, Africanized (hybrid) forms migrated from Brazil. Much more defensive than their European relatives, these honeybees can be aggressive when their hive is approached, so steer clear of hives and, if a group pursues you, quickly distance yourself from them.

Clockwise from upper left:
Mason bee

Mason bee nest

Cactus bee

▲ Male carpenter bees

▼ Female carpenter bee

More relevant to the desert than this naturalized (non-native, but successfully established) species are the native forms, most of which are solitary and often nest in the ground or the hollow tunnels left behind by wood-boring beetles. The Sonoran Desert hosts one of the most biodiverse assemblages of bees, ants, and wasps in the world. A thousand or more species call this region home, making it among the top hot spots in the world. Just a few are listed below.

Mason and leafcutter bees, family Megachilidae, Spanish: *abejas cortadoras de hojas y abejas albañil*

Many desert bees, including mason and leafcutter bees, don't make their own nesting holes. Instead, females use abandoned tunnels of wood-boring beetles in dead limbs or standing dead trees. Once a tunnel is located, the bees lay an egg then import pieces of leaves, resins, pebbles, and mud balls to line and cap a small cell.

Cactus bee, *Diadasia* spp., Spanish: *abejas de los cactos*

This species pollinates prickly pear, cholla, and saguaro cacti. Though they create individual nests in the ground, hundreds of thousands of bees may aggregate when spring blooms appear.

Carpenter bees, genus *Xylocopa*, Spanish: *abejorro carpintero*

You'll see and hear these large bees—the original woodworkers—as they clumsily fly around, sometimes bouncing off objects, gravitating to palo verde tree flowers in late spring to early summer. Black-colored females lay their eggs in holes they excavate themselves and leave pollen and nectar for the larvae to eat once they hatch. The males are gold-colored and lack stingers.

Paper wasps, genus *Polistes*, Spanish: *avispa*

A quizzical paper wasp

Velvet ant

Common, conspicuous, and generally about an inch (2.5 cm) long, these social wasps build honeycomb-shaped nests anchored to vegetation, such as the undersides of palm fronds. Though unaggressive, they can be intrusive and are not opposed to doing the same with the eaves in your backyard or the underside of outdoor furniture; if you see them building nests in these locations, remove them before their numbers grow. When away from the nest, seeking food or moisture from flowers or your favorite sugary drink, they only sting if bothered. Several species occur in the region.

Velvet ants, genus *Dasymutilla*, Spanish: *hormiga de terciopelo*

Though called an ant, this species is actually a type of solitary wasp. The wingless females are often seen on sandy or bare soil surfaces during warmer seasons as they search for other ground-nesting bees and wasps, the targets for the velvet ants' extremely potent and paralytic venom. Afterward, they lay an egg on the bee, which then hatches and feeds on the immobilized bee, eventually killing it. More than three dozen species live in the region and range from 0.25–1 inch (0.6–2.5 cm) long. Covered in setae (stiff, hair-like structures) that may be red, orange, yellow, or silvery white in color, these animals look like fuzzy cotton balls. They can emit a squeaky sound that is used to warn potential predators of their *incredibly* painful sting. Males are much smaller and can fly.

Tarantula hawks, genus *Pepsis*, Spanish: *avispa*

The *Pepsis* wasp (also called the tarantula hawk) shares a remarkable predator-prey relationship with tarantulas in the Sonoran Desert.

▲ *Pepsis* wasps

Blue-black in color, except for highly contrasting rusty-orange or iridescent purple wings, this extremely large wasp—up to 1.75 inches (4.45 cm)—looks for tarantulas in spiders' burrows or out in the open and will attempt to sting them, delivering a powerful paralytic venom. Once the prey is immobilized, the wasp drags the tarantula underground, where the wasp lays an egg on the spider and seals up the burrow. After the egg hatches, the wasp larva feeds on the live, paralyzed spider, eventually pupating and metamorphosing into an adult wasp. Note: These wasps are unlikely to sting humans, but on the rare occasion that this occurs, the sting can be extremely painful.

Ants

Family Formicidae, Spanish: *hormiga*

Ants are equally common and important to the local ecology, though perhaps a little underappreciated and labeled pests because of their tendency to bite or sting in defense or find their way into our homes and foods. While native bees are generally solitary, ants live in cooperative colonies with populations that may number into the thousands. As any horned lizard would tell you if it could, ants are important to many animals as food.

Some of the more interesting forms are the harvesters (*Pogonomyrmex* and *Messor* spp.) and the leafcutters (*Atta* and *Acromyrmex* spp.). Harvester ants gather the seeds of grasses and several annuals as food for their larvae; leafcutters, the farmers of the ant world, grow a "crop" of edible fungus that grows on the cut and masticated leaves they place in their underground tunnels.

Seed harvesters are good-sized and often clear good-sized patches of ground around the openings to their nests. They are most active spring through autumn. Similarly, leafcutters are active in the warmer parts of the year. When you encounter what look like miniature versions of cinder cone volcanoes, you've probably found the nest of the smaller form of leafcutter ant.

Clockwise from upper left: Harvester ant

Leafcutter ant

Leafcutter ants bringing leaves back to their nest

Millipede

Giant desert centipede

Many-legged arthropods

Millipedes: Industrious Gardeners (class Diplopoda, Spanish: *milpiés*)

Millipedes are dirt diggers, eaters, and movers. As detritivores, they eat dead plants and animals and create fertile soil when they defecate. They are also called "rain worms" because they tend to emerge from underground during the monsoon season.

Giant desert centipede, *Scolopendra heros*, Spanish: *ciempiés*

Despite the name, which implies they have 100 legs, centipedes often have fewer than 50. Relatively fast-moving predators, they're equipped with an impressive and painful bite, used to immobilize prey. Some grow to over 8 inches (20.3 cm) in length.

Arachnids: Spiders and Scorpions

Tarantulas: Gentle Giants (family Theraphosidae, Spanish: *tarántula*)

As spiders go, tarantulas are among the largest. While the size can at first be intimidating, they are relatively calm and gentle. They aren't fast runners or jumpers, and their slow, deliberate movements only add to their charm. When a tarantula is forced to defend itself, it uses its back legs to flick irritating hairs off its abdomen in the direction of the aggressor. These urticating (stinging) hairs cause itchiness, and a young predator—or curious human—will learn to be more careful when approaching these super spiders in the future.

Giant crab spider, *Olios giganteus*, Spanish: *cazadora del desierto*

Known for its amazing ability to climb smooth vertical surfaces, this large spider earns its name by locomoting like a crab—extending its legs at right angles to its body and rapidly scuttling sideways. Such abilities, combined with a flattened body, allow the giant crab to enter narrow spaces. It's found in dead saguaros, under rocks, or in human dwellings, where it often rests high on walls or ceilings. Its climbing ability, movement pattern, and light-colored body distinguish it from the wolf spider.

Below, left to right:
Tarantula

The shorter appendages in front of the face are not legs, but pedipalps that help the tarantula feel its environment.

Giant crab spider hunting crane flies

Wolf spider, *Hogna carolinensis*, Spanish: *araña lobo*

A common, large, fuzzy-looking spider, the wolf spider is generally afoot at night in the warmer months of the year, staying close to or on the ground. An adult spider carries its babies on its back after

Clockwise from left: The Carolina wolf spider (also known as giant wolf spider) is the largest of the wolf spiders in North America.

Black widow spider with egg case

Black widow spiders make messy webs.

they hatch. Wolf spider burrows usually have a turret (slightly raised ridge) around the opening. At night, their eyes reflect light in a hue of blue-green, resembling broken shards of glass.

ARACHNIDS OF MEDICAL CONCERN (BLACK WIDOW, BROWN SPIDERS, SCORPIONS)

With the high number of spiders in the desert and the fact that almost all but one group of spiders are venomous, it may seem surprising that the venoms of almost all of them are *not* of medical concern to humans. This means that most spiders can live harmoniously with us, especially if they are outdoors. As an added benefit, they help control other pest populations, chemical-free.

To avoid encounters with spiders of medical concern, seal cracks that could allow them into your home and remove webs around outdoor furnishings. Avoid bites and stings by not putting your hands or feet anywhere you haven't visually inspected first.

Black widow spider, *Latrodectus hesperus*, Spanish: *viuda negra*

The venom of black widows is neurotoxic, which means that it results in systemic reactions in humans. Symptoms, including pain, tingling, and numbness near the sting site, can last around 24 hours. The affected region of the body tends to correlate with the location of a bite (upper versus lower body).

Brown spider, genus *Loxosceles*, Spanish: *uvari*

Arizona brown spider venom is entirely different from that of widow spiders and results in completely different symptoms and outcomes. The initial bite is painless, but pain and blistering in the area can follow, sometimes with more severe symptoms. Some bites result in tissue death (necrosis) that can take weeks or months to heal.

Antivenoms have been produced for both of these spider groups. Though very few people die from their bites, if you are bitten, immediately consult with a poison center. If that isn't possible, then contact your doctor or local ER or urgent care center.

Scorpions, order Scorpiones, Spanish: *alacran*

The desert is home to scores of scorpion species. We'll describe three common forms here. The desert hairy scorpion (*Hadrurus arizonensis*) is the largest in the region and noted for the hair-like projections on its body. It's generally found at lower elevations, in flatter, open desert areas. Though impressive in size, its venom and that of the stripe-tailed scorpion (*Vaejovis* spp.) are not very strong. The latter scorpion is named for the dark lines on its tail and is the most widely distributed form in the region.

The most infamous species in the region, the bark scorpion (*Centruroides exilicauda*), is small and seems innocuous, but what it lacks in size it makes up for in its venom strength, which is highly neurotoxic. Slender with a tendency to climb vertical surfaces, this species finds its way into our homes much more often than others, leading to more stings to humans and, due to venom toxicity, stings of consequence. Stings are not to be taken lightly, especially to very young children and older or ailing adults. That said, most stings can

▾ Brown spider

◢ Scorpion mothers carry their babies on their backs for one to three weeks.

▲ Scorpion under ultraviolet light

be managed at home by calling your local poison center, and severe stings can be counteracted by an effective antivenom that's available through local hospitals.

You can usually differentiate scorpions with highly toxic venoms from those with less potent ones by the shape and size of their pincers (pedipalps). Those with weak venoms have more robust, bulbous pincers while those with strong venoms have slender, more delicate ones.

Scorpions fluoresce under ultraviolet light. The special proteins that help them light up under blacklight are found in chitin (in their exoskeletons). Recently molted scorpions, who've recently shed their exoskeletons, don't fluoresce, and very young scorpions must wait 10–20 days to develop exoskeletons and glow up.

Monsoon Magic

In the Sonoran Desert, invertebrate activities undergo a dramatic and awe-inspiring transformation during the monsoon season. With higher humidity, somewhat lower temperatures, and temporary rainpools created by short-lived heavy rainfall, life explodes in and on this landscape. Insects, like cicadas, emerge from their long underground slumber, filling the air with deafening, mate-attracting choruses, and many other animals also seek mates during this season. This is the only time of year when millipedes, vital nutrient recyclers, are active, and winged ants and termites engage in mating flights.

From top to bottom:
Flame skimmer dragonfly

Praying mantis

Walking stick

This sudden burst of plant and invertebrate life creates a ripple effect throughout the ecosystem. Many herbivores capitalize on fresh shoots, seeds, and flowers. Predators—not only spiders and scorpions, but also lizards, birds, small mammals, and snakes—take advantage of the increased number of small animals available to eat.

Aquatic Environments

Naturally occurring surface water is rare in the desert, but wherever you encounter it, life abounds. In fast-moving streams, caddisflies protect themselves with cases they make from sand and plant material while stoneflies use flattened bodies and gills to navigate high water flows. In slow-moving systems, fishing spiders, whirligig and diving beetles, water striders, backswimmers, water boatmen, and giant water bugs take up residence. Some, like dragonflies, are only aquatic for the first (larval) part of their lives.

Backyard Biodiversity

When we think of the wild, we often focus on what's out *there*, but so much can be found in your backyard. The more space and plants you have, the more likely you are to have nature all around you. And if you avoid using pesticides and keep cats indoors, you're much more likely to see and hear wildlife, including lizards, birds, small mammals and, in particular, invertebrates. Butterflies, moths, grasshoppers, crickets, katydids, walking sticks, mantids, ants, bees, wasps, flies, and others will take up residence. Of course, some may be less desirable than others, but learning about them allows you to enjoy more of them and figure out how to prevent the unwanted ones from living inside your home, often the result of human actions that attract them.

YES, THERE ARE FISH IN THE DESERT

IT MAY SEEM STRANGE to pair the words "fish" and "desert" but, yes, you will find fish in the Sonoran Desert. Though aquatic environments are scarce, at one time the region had plenty of rivers and streams, hosting dozens of freshwater species—more than 30 species in Arizona alone. For a number of reasons, this vibrant interconnected network of surface waterways has nearly disappeared, leading a majority of native fishes to become scarce and at risk of extinction.

Desert fish are typically small to medium in size and well-adapted to aquatic environments with widely fluctuating conditions. (Note: Most lakes in the desert have been artificially created. Likewise, most of the fish found in them have been introduced and compete with or prey upon native species.) Some desert denizens, such as pupfish, can withstand high levels of salinity (even greater than seawater) and temperatures up to, or above, 100°F (38°C). Despite these remarkable adaptations, many of these desert fish are now among the rarest, though less specialized ones, like many small minnows, are still found in a number of streams.

Several hikes in this book offer opportunities to see desert fish. The easiest places to find them are clear streams and smooth, flat backwaters. During daylight hours, polarized sunglasses (which reduce surface reflections) can help you peer into the watery

Above, left to right:
Gila chub

Gila topminnow

Longfin dace

Desert sucker

Yaqui chub

Beautiful shiner

shadows, around rocks or banks that provide visual cover for fish. In these areas, it can be easier to make out their tiny young, called fry, often less than an inch long (2.5 cm). Don't worry about figuring out *which* fish species you've found—native fish are hard to identify as adults and even fish biologists have difficulty categorizing the young darting around in the water. Just revel in the pleasure of stumbling upon fish in the desert.

Gila chub, *Gila intermedia*, Spanish: *charalito del Gila*

This minnow can grow to 9 inches (22.9 cm) long and feeds mostly on diatoms and other algae at night, but also eats ants and caterpillars that fall into the water.

Locales: Restricted to the Gila River basin; look for them in Sabino Canyon

Gila topminnow, *Poeciliopsis occidentalis*, Spanish: *charalito*

Unlike most fish species, topminnow have internal fertilization and are live-bearing (giving birth to living young rather than laying eggs). Males are smaller than females as adults and develop dark brown to black coloration. Despite its small size of 1–2 inches (2.5–5 cm), this species is one of the easier ones to spot because it lingers close to the water's surface (looking for food) and moves more slowly, rarely swimming far, even when spooked.

Locales: Ciénega Creek

Longfin dace, *Agosia chrysogaster*, Spanish: *pupo panza verde*

This extremely adaptable minnow is the most geographically and topographically widespread of all native Sonoran Desert fish species. Small (up to 4 inches or 10 cm in length) and omnivorous, it is a stream

dweller that uses its fin rays for positioning and speed when it swims. Breeding males develop tubercles (tiny raised bumps) on the upper part of their heads and bodies to facilitate reproduction.

Locales: Ciénega Creek, Sonoita Creek

Sonora sucker, *Catostomus insignis*, Spanish: *matelote de Sonora*

Desert sucker, *Pantosteus clarkii*, Spanish: *matelote del desierto*

These two fish look nearly identical, differentiated by the shape of their lips, especially the lower one. Though they can grow to a foot (30 cm) or more in length, they're usually about half that size. During the spring breeding season, male desert suckers develop striped patterns.

Locales: Relatively common in Arizona, particularly in the middle and southern parts of the state

Loach minnow, *Tiaroga cobitis*, Spanish: *charalito adornado*

Yaqui chub, *Gila purpurea*, Spanish: *charalito yaqui*

Mexican stoneroller, *Campostoma ornatum*, Spanish: *rodapiedras mexicano*

Beautiful shiner, *Cyprinella formosa*, Spanish: *carpita yaqui*

Though these species may be more common in northern Mexico, all four are extremely rare, with few locales left in Arizona. Mountain wildfires have put them at extreme risk of extirpation (local extinction) due to post-fire habitat loss and water contamination.

Locales: Chiricahua Mountains

AND THERE ARE FROGS AND SALAMANDERS, TOO!

LIKE FISH, YOU MIGHT NOT EXPECT to find amphibians in the Sonoran Desert. After all, they easily dehydrate in dry heat and need freestanding water for reproduction. Indeed, intense desert conditions can be particularly taxing for aquatic and semiaquatic wildlife, but over millennia, these environmental challenges have produced a number of well-adapted desert specialists that are right at home in Southern Arizona and northern Sonora.

In physiology, morphology, and behavior, many of the two dozen or so amphibian species native to the region are fine-tuned to their environments. Some common behavioral adaptations are avoiding dry, hot, or cold conditions (limiting most species to nocturnal activity) and synchronizing reproduction with rainy summer nights. Physiologically, most Sonoran Desert amphibians have thick, protective dorsal (upper) skins which are spotted or blotched and heavily pigmented in hues of olive, green, tan, and brown while their ventral (under) sides are creamy white. Though many frogs, particularly toads and spadefoots, don't appear to drink water, their thin, highly vascularized undersides allow them to readily absorb water instead merely by sitting in it.

Beyond these generalized adaptations, amphibians have developed some incredibly specialized ways of living large in the desert—read on and be amazed! However, before we get into the specifics, let's take a moment to review a set of often misunderstood terms.

Frog or Toad?

For our purposes, a frog is four-legged amphibian that (almost always) lacks a tail as an adult (though the larvae—called tadpoles or pollywogs—do have tails).

A toad (sometimes called a "true toad," depending on the context) is a specific type of frog that has a large paratoid as well as other skin glands that produce and store potent toxins designed to defend against predators.

Yet another kind of frog, a spadefoot has a hardened (keratinized) projection on the undersides of the rear feet for digging into softer soil to burrow deep underground for protection from the elements and predators. Spadefoots lack paratoid glands and have smoother skin (rather than the lumpy, glandular skin of true toads), though they still produce some skin toxins. Another difference is that they possess vertical, elliptical pupils (like cats); true toads have horizontal pupils.

Except for true toads, all other types of frogs are classified as frogs. When they reach adulthood, almost all have mating calls that help them find one another during the breeding season. Learning these frog calls will allow you to identify species in the middle of the night without even seeing them. It's a fun way to impress friends and a useful skill when looking for other nocturnal animals that may share temporary rainpools with frogs.

▾ The Sonoran Desert toad is a true toad.

◢ Canyon tree frogs are classified as frogs.

Couch's spadefoot at night. Notice the elongated "spade" on the hind foot.

Couch's spadefoot by day

Common Sonoran Desert Amphibians

SPADEFOOTS

Couch's spadefoot, *Scaphiopus couchii*, Spanish: *sapo cavador*

At 3.5 inches (9 cm) long, Couch's spadefoot is small in size but big on reputation, setting a high bar for desert adaptation. Like all spadefoots, it uses "spades" to dig deep underground with a twisting motion to find a depth of suitable temperature and humidity where its respiration and metabolism can slow down. It may remain underground and dormant for ten or more months per year, an adaptation that allows it to survive in the driest parts of the Sonoran Desert, even in areas with minimal or no rainfall.

As the summer rainy season approaches, spadefoots move around and move up to the ground surface, waiting for signals (thunder and raindrops) of the first summer downpours. Then they emerge and locate to temporary rainpools. Males will do their best to attract females with a call that sounds like a herd of tiny sheep, a *waaah-waaah* sound. When a pair breeds, their eggs hatch within 24 hours and rapidly metamorphose, transforming from egg to tadpole to froglet in as few as nine days. This same process takes bullfrogs up to a year or more.

Locales: Southern Arizona, portions of Baja California, and most of Sonora

Mexican spadefoot, *Spea multiplicata*, Spanish: *sapo de espuelas*

Similar in size, shape, and behavior to Couch's spadefoot, the Mexican spadefoot also shares habitat with its more well-known cousin. However, the two species differ in coloring and calls—Mexican spadefoot is greenish-gray or tan with minimal orange spotting (compared to the greenish-yellow or olive and dark spots of Couch's spadefoot) and emits a call that sounds like a gentle snore. If you ever handle one, you may notice a faint odor reminiscent of roasted peanuts.

Locales: Eastern and central Arizona and the extreme northern part of Sonora

TOADS

Sonoran Desert toad, *Incilius alvarius*, Spanish: *sapo del desierto de Sonora*

Growing up to 7.5 inches (19 cm) long, this is the largest toad native to North America. Aside from several raised skin glands, including the paratoids, its olive green dorsal skin is smoother and more uniform in color than is typical for toads, with just a few white bumps at the angle of the jaw. (Note: As a juvenile, it may have a profusion of orange-to-red spots on its back.)

This toad's defensive toxins, which include cardiotoxins and a unique hallucinogen, are so potent that predators may suffer significantly or even die when attempting to eat this well-protected amphibian. The hallucinogen is among the strongest produced by any animal, and the toad itself or toxin-laced tea/tobacco have been used for medicinal purposes historically and today.

Locales: Sonoran Desert region

▸ Sonoran desert toad

Great Plains toad, *Anaxyrus cognatus*, Spanish: *sapo de espuelas*

At up to 5 inches (12.7 cm) long, this toad is considerably smaller than the Sonoran Desert toad. However, what it lacks in size, it more than makes up for in voice, with one of the loudest, more incessant rapid-fire calls of all desert amphibians. Tan and brown, with paired blotches down its back. Deafening choruses of male mating calls can last up to a minute at a time. Females lay strings of eggs that can number into the thousands.

Locales: Widespread throughout the Southwest and Great Plains of the United States as well as portions of northern Mexico, except at higher elevations and in extremely dry areas

Red-spotted toad, *Anaxyrus punctatus*, Spanish: *sapo de puntos rojos*

The red-spotted toad is one of the smaller (3 inches/7.6 cm in length) but most widely distributed desert species. More active in dry seasons than other toads, it has the remarkable ability of surviving dry spells even after losing up to 40 percent of its body weight (mostly in water). It is the only toad with round, rather than oblong, paratoid glands and has a pleasant mating call—a whistling trill that sounds much like a loud cricket and lasts up to 10 seconds. This species is the only amphibian in the Sonoran Desert that lays its eggs singly rather than in long strings.

Locales: The Sonoran Desert region at lower elevations, including Isla Tiburon in the Gulf of California

◂ Red-spotted toad

Less Common Forms of Desert Amphibians

TREE FROGS

Canyon tree frog, *Hyla arenicolor*, Spanish: *ranita de las rocas*

Tree frogs have enlarged toe-pads with a specialized surface allowing them to climb and hang from vertical structures, including rocks, leaves, trees, walls, and windows. This 2-inch-long (5-cm-long) gray, tan, and brown frog prefers streamside boulders and uses extreme camouflage to become virtually indistinguishable from the rocks. At times, it avoids predation by resting on rocks that are too hot for garter snakes (a common predator in riparian areas) while secreting stored body water, which evaporates and prevents overheating. It has a loud, rather short, rattling trill.

Locales: Widely distributed *outside* of true desert areas. In the Sonoran Desert, it's found in and near streams within desert grassland, oak and pine-oak woodlands, and thornscrub and tropical deciduous forests. These tree frogs hide in shadows and crevices, resembling shiny spots on a rock's surface. When one leaps from its hiding place, it looks as if a small chunk of the rock just popped off.

▾ Canyon tree frog

TRUE FROGS

▾ Lowland leopard frog

▴ Bullfrog

Lowland leopard frog, *Lithobates yavapaiensis*, Spanish: *rana leopardo de Yavapai*

Chiricahua leopard frog, *Lithobates chiricahuensis*, Spanish: *rana leopardo Chiricahua*

Tarahumara frog, American bullfrog, *Lithobates tarahumarae, Lithobates catesbeaina*, Spanish: *rana Tarahumara, rana catesbeiana*

The "true" frogs use their long, powerful rear legs and webbed toes to leap and swim in permanent bodies of water. Several species occur in the Sonoran Desert, the most common of which are the two leopard frogs listed above. They are recognizable by their heavily blotched skins and protruding dorsolateral folds (ridges that run from each eye down their backs).

Introduced to Arizona wetlands throughout the twentieth century, the extremely large and highly invasive American bullfrog outcompetes the native leopard frogs and, for that reason, is encountered more often. This frog takes competition to a new level, eating native amphibians, reptiles, and mammals. You can identify it by its large size, relatively uniform green color, and lack of dorsolateral folds. Though a long-standard effort to reintroduce the Tarahumara frog into southern Arizona is ongoing, you are very unlikely to see one unless you travel south of the Mexican border.

Locales: Southern Arizona, in or near permanent water, usually slower-moving streams, but also natural ponds and lakes as well as cattle tanks (especially true for bullfrogs)

▸ Tiger salamander in hand for scale

SALAMANDERS

While many frogs successfully call the Sonoran Desert home, the demands of desert living appear to be a bit too challenging for salamanders—only one species (the tiger salamander) occurs in Arizona, and two others (Tarahumara and Bell's salamanders) barely enter the most southern part of the Sonoran Desert. Here, we'll focus on the most common one.

Tiger salamander, *Ambystoma tigrinum*, Spanish: *ajolote tigre norte* (3 subspecies: Arizona, barred, Sonoran)

Nose to tip of tail, the tiger salamander grows up to a foot long (30 cm) and has a rounded snout and small eyeballs. As aquatic larvae, their color is light to slate gray, with filamentous gills, outlined in red, emanating from the back of the head. Terrestrial adults vary in color from yellow to olive to black, with numerous spots, blotches, or bars of contrasting colors. (Light salamanders have dark blotches whereas dark salamanders have light blotches.) Lizards are the only animal in our region that superficially resemble salamanders, but lizards have dry scaly skins; tiger salamanders have smooth, moist skin and costal grooves (or furrows) along both sides of their bodies.

As an adult, the tiger salamander spends most of its time in underground burrows (often borrowed from rodents, but sometimes self-made in soft, moist soil). Generally, it surfaces only during the breeding season, migrating to ciénagas (swamps or marshes),

◂ Tiger salamander

ponds, and cattle tanks to reproduce. It can also breed in larval form, in which case it can spend its entire life as an aquatic animal.

The most common type in southern Arizona is the barred tiger salamander, an invasive species that can interbreed with native salamanders, such as the Sonoran tiger salamander, designated as endangered due to competition, genetic swamping (wherein local species are replaced by hybrid species), and introduction of disease (such as iridovirus, carried by insects). In the northern part of the state, the Arizona tiger salamander is more common, a native species subject to some genetic pollution from genetically similar species introduced through bait fishing from the neighboring states of Colorado and Utah.

Locales: Widely distributed throughout the region but rarely seen, especially in desert areas. More commonly seen at higher elevations, particularly in grasslands and mountain foothills. Adult salamanders can be found on roads during summer rainstorms and larvae in small permanent water bodies.

A REPTILIAN PARADISE

REPTILES ARE MADE FOR DESERTS, and the Sonoran Desert is rife with reptiles. Like other deserts, it offers plenty of open sunny areas that provide the heat and the UV rays most lizards and turtles need for overall metabolism, vitamin D_3 synthesis, and calcium assimilation (for strong, healthy bones). Equally important is the availability of sheltered or shaded areas, allowing these ectotherms (a more precise label than "cold-blooded animals") to choose places to rest that suit their thermal needs. Unlike other deserts, the Sonoran Desert's bi-seasonal rainfall figures prominently in the diversity of reptile species and their activity patterns.

When to Look

If you want to see (or avoid) reptiles, season matters, but ground and air temperature are better predictors of activity. Peak lizard activity takes place between March and early May, particularly in the morning to early afternoon, though some (especially youngsters) are active throughout the year. Similarly, snakes can be found any time of year, but many species are most active at night during the summer monsoon due to the combination of higher humidity and warm temperatures. Most reptiles don't seem to care for the rain itself—they leave that for the frogs!

Note: If the weather calls for short sleeves and a skirt, shorts, or kilt, then snakes are around—day or night, January or June. Keep this in mind, particularly if you wish to avoid rattlesnakes.

Reptile Round-up: The Usual Suspects

TURTLES

Though the Sonoran Desert is home to scores of reptiles, only a small portion are turtles; many of these (particularly the freshwater, semiaquatic ones) are non-native and threaten the existence of indigenous species. The red-eared slider and painted turtle, for example, have become Sonoran Desert dwellers because people released them as unwanted pets. These species have thrived and reproduced, all the while eating large numbers of native invertebrates and small vertebrates.

If you see an aquatic turtle that is largen than a human palm or hand, chances are that it's one of these introduced species. As you search, keep in mind that non-native aquatic turtles often rest on branches or rocks, either in or adjacent to bodies of water, while mud turtles tend to hide in deeper pools of streams and are often covered with filamentous algae.

What's the difference between a turtle and a tortoise? Like the frog-versus-toad question addressed in the section "Frog or Toad?" (page 168), one category—turtles—encompasses the other. All tortoises are turtles, but there are many types of turtles that are not tortoises. Put another way, it's fine to call a tortoise a turtle, but not necessarily the other way round.

TORTOISE ADOPTION

Though many people keep desert tortoises as pets, it is now illegal to collect tortoises from the wild. Even so, because so many have bred in captivity and are long-lived, there are hundreds, if not thousands, that reside in local backyards. This has led to adoption programs, like the one administered through the Arizona-Sonora Desert Museum, which place unwanted or surplus captive tortoises with private individuals designated as custodians, not owners—the State of Arizona retains legal jurisdiction over all wildlife.

Clockwise from upper left:
Sonoran Desert tortoise

Sonoran Desert tortoise

Close-up of a Sonora mud turtle

Sonora mud turtle

Sonoran Desert tortoise, *Gopherus morafkai*, Spanish: *tortuga del desierto de Sonora*

Among native terrestrial turtles, this is the largest and most commonly encountered species, usually found in rocky foothill areas. These tortoises resemble small boulders, up to a foot (30 cm) long or more, and move ever so slowly on south-to-east facing slopes. Tortoises are a reptilian version of cows when grazing, searching and feeding on more than 100 types of plants, sometimes eating them when they are crispy and dead (likely for mineral content).

With their affinity for wedging into rocky crevices and burrowing under or around boulders and the bases of desert shrubs, their boulder-like appearance is an ideal adaptation, providing protection from extreme temperatures, low humidity and, importantly, predators. There's a cost to carrying one's "house" around—speed.

Keep in mind that the Sonoran Desert tortoise inhabits the same areas as Gila monsters and various rattlesnake species—keep an eye out to avoid these reptiles in your tortoise search.

Sonora mud turtle, *Kinosternon sonoriense*, Spanish: *tortuga pecho quebrado de Sonora*

A stream dweller, this and other mud turtle species are usually found on the bottoms of creeks, ponds, and intermittent streams that wend their way through low-altitude mountain areas and desert habitat.

Small in size (3–4 inches/7.5–10 cm) and secretive by nature, they use camouflage to avoid detection—their shells naturally blend into their surroundings and, even more effective, they're heavily coated by algae. In addition, if captured, mud turtles release foul-smelling fluids from musk glands that likely save many from an untimely end.

LIZARDS

Dozens of lizard species are native to the Sonoran Desert, two dozen in the greater Tucson area alone. These lizards range from 2 inches (5 cm) to nearly 2 feet (60 cm) in length, with most of them 4–8 inches (10–20 cm) long. (Because many lizards lose portions of their tails in their lifetimes, the lengths listed here are snout-to-vent measurements—from the tip of the nose to the cloaca, the opening at the base of the tail.)

Lizards are the most easily spotted group of reptiles, though identifying each species takes patience, persistence, and a lot of practice. Use geographic location to narrow down the list of possibilities, then body shape and size, followed by color and pattern. If you stick with it, before long you'll be able to identify the most common forms rather quickly.

Each species has specific tendencies and often microhabitat associations. In general, look for protrusions from rocks that don't seem to fit the lines of the rock as well as tree bark that seems to curve up and away from trunks and branches. You may be rewarded with a lizard sighting.

SELF-DEFENSE: LIZARD-STYLE

Gila monster, *Heloderma suspectum*, Spanish: *monstruo de Gila*

The Gila monster is one of the few venomous lizards in the world with a bite that can result in severe medical problems in humans, such as burning pain, swelling, vomiting, dizziness, and increased heart rate (and, in a handful of cases, death). As such, its notoriety has given rise to an over-amplified fear of the species as well as misinformation and myths—for example, its jaws *don't* lock when biting, its tongue *doesn't* sting, and its breath *isn't* toxic.

The Gila monster can indeed look intimidating—at up to 22 inches (56 cm) long, it's the largest lizard in the United States.

Clockwise from upper left:
The black and orange color of Gila monsters warns other animals of danger.

Gila monster with an artistic sunset setting

Gila monster portrait

And it does bite—in self-defense only, dispensing small amounts of venom via grooved teeth (rather than through hollow fangs as snakes do). That venom is toxic to predators (intrusive hikers included), but its study has also benefited humanity, inspiring the development of drugs that combat type 2 diabetes.

Black with contrasting pink or peach markings, the Gila monster's skin serves as both camouflage (when it's hiding amidst rocks or vegetation) and warning (for potential predators). Its diet includes small birds (mostly eaten as eggs) and newborn mammals, as well as lizards, frogs, and insects. Spending three quarters or more of its life underground, it emerges for short periods in spring and during the monsoon season to eat massive meals (up to one-third of its body weight), mate, and lay 2 to 12 eggs, which hatch many months later.

GECKOS: TALKING LIZARDS

Western banded gecko, *Coleonyx variegatus*, Spanish: *geco de bandas occidental*

House gecko, *Hemidactylus turcicus*, Spanish: *geco*

Though other lizards may hiss, geckos are the only lizards that vocalize, producing various clicks, chirps, and squeaks used to establish dominance and to attract mates. Though several types of geckos occur in the Sonoran Desert, there are only two that occupy the Tucson area. Both the banded gecko (named for the pattern

‣ Western banded gecko

on its body and tail) and the house gecko (a non-native species) are smooth-skinned and nocturnal, feed on small invertebrates, and easily drop their tails when threatened by potential predators. Each has additional defense/escape mechanisms as well: the house gecko's adhesive toe-pads allow it to skitter up smooth, vertical surfaces, and the banded gecko can scare off predators by mimicking a scorpion and curling its tail. Both species readily drop part of the tail if handled.

SPINY LIZARDS: PUGNACIOUSNESS WITH PURPOSE

Desert spiny lizard, *Sceloporus magister*, Spanish: *lagartija-escamosa de desierto*

Clark's spiny lizard, *Sceloporus clarkii*, Spanish: *lagartija espinosa del noroeste*

Spiny lizards are named for the thick and sharply pointed scales along their backs, a deterrent to predators and a water-conservation adaptation. Here we focus on the two large forms prevalent in the Tucson area, though several smaller species occur in the nearby mountains. Both are stout and robust in form, omnivorous in eating patterns, and similar in size (up to 5.5 inches/14 cm), but small details differentiate the two. Check out the features called out in the photographs. Their subtle differences in habitat use may also help with identification. The desert spiny tends to inhabit fairly flat terrain while the Clark's spiny favors trees and rocky hillsides. Because these lizards are relatively bold around humans, you may spot one (usually a male) performing push-ups—quick up-and-down motions of the head and forebody—to communicate territoriality and dominance to other lizards or species.

Clockwise from upper left:

Desert spiny male

Desert spiny female

Male spiny lizards have blue patches on the throat and sides, but Clark's usually have dark brown crossbands on the forearms.

Zebra-tailed lizard

Clark's spiny lizard

LITTLE DOG OF THE DESERT

Zebra-tailed lizard, *Callisaurus draconoides*, Spanish: *cachora arenera*

One of the smaller (2.5–4 inches/6.5–10 cm) and more pervasive species of the region, especially in open, sandy areas, the zebra-tailed lizard is known for wagging its banded black-and-white tail back and forth right before and after it runs away from potential predators. Hence, its nickname—*perrito* (Spanish for "little dog").

Typically, you'll notice this lizard when it suddenly dashes away as you approach. Look for them in and near desert arroyos (dry riverbeds) or in areas with scant vegetation.

HORNED LIZARDS/HORNY TOADS

Clockwise from upper left: Regal horned lizard

Regal horned lizards are hard to spot against most local rocks.

Close-up of "horns" on greater short-horned lizard

Greater short-horned lizard

Regal horned lizard, *Phrynosoma solare*, Spanish: *camaleón real*

Greater short-horned lizard, *Phrynosoma hernandesi*, Spanish: *camaleón cuernitos de Hernández*

The family name of these lizards, Phrynosoma, translates to "toad body," a reference to their flat, wide body form. Perhaps it's this unusual and endearing morphology that accounts for the great fondness people feel for these particular reptiles.

There are at least eight species in the Sonoran Desert, roughly six of which are in Southern Arizona. The most common species around Tucson are the two highlighted here. The regal horned lizard thrives at lower elevations (feeding on harvester ants and tolerating

their stings) while the greater short-horned lizard is found at higher, cooler elevations (likely a reason for giving birth to their young rather than laying eggs). For protection, many horned lizards collect blood in their ocular sinuses and squirt it from their eyes to deter potential predators, particularly canines (coyotes, wolves, foxes, and dogs).

OVERLY CAFFEINATED LIZARD?

Whiptail lizard, *Aspidoscelis* spp., Spanish: *lagartijas corredoras*

There are over a dozen whiptail species in the Sonoran Desert, many of which strongly resemble one another—slender heads, bodies, and tails; 2.75–5.25 inches (7–13.3 cm) in length; small scales; often with stripes down the back—especially when young. Unless you're a seasoned "herper" (avid fan of reptiles and amphibians) or study up on minute differences in scales and patterns (detectable only if you are actually holding a lizard), you'll have to be satisfied recognizing them as a category rather than a particular species. "There goes another whiptail!" might be all you're able to say.

Despite their many micro-differences, whiptails as a group share a particular way of moving that distinguishes them from other lizards of the region. Their herky-jerky, stop-and-start movements, accompanied by faint foraging sounds, mark them as whiptails.

Many whiptail species, such as the Sonoran spotted whiptail, are all female and reproduce asexually (parthenogenesis), producing unfertilized eggs that are clones of the parent. Despite the lack of males, pseudocopulation (females mounting other females) is common and serves a critical role in reproduction by elevating relevant hormones in the mounted females.

▾ Whiptail lizard

CAMOUFLAGE, SILENT COMMUNICATION, AND NICHE PARTITIONING

Ornate tree lizard, *Urosaurus ornatus*, Spanish: *roñito ornado*

Side-blotched lizard, *Uta stansburiana*, Spanish: *lagartijas de manchas lateral*

These lizards have considerable overlap in their range and distribution but occupy different microhabitats. The smaller tree lizard (up to 2.3 inches/5.8 cm) prefers trees and larger rocks, while the side-blotched (up to 6 inches/15.2 cm) stays closer to the ground. This is an example of niche partitioning, allowing competing species with similar habits to occupy the same general areas.

Both species are well-camouflaged, making them a challenge for us to see, but they exhibit colorful adaptations to show off and communicate with one another. Sexually mature males have dark bluish patches on their bellies and stretch their throat skin (called the *dewlap*) downward, flashing colors to attract females and send territorial signals to rival males. The throat can be blue, blue-green, green, yellow, or orange; side-blotched lizards cycle through different colors over the years depending on which is most successful at breeding.

▾ Ornate tree lizard

◣ Side-blotched lizard

Snakes

Dozens of snake species inhabit the Sonoran Desert—nearly 60 in Arizona alone. This section covers a small sampling of some of the most common forms. For more information on the full range of snakes in a particular area, consult a field guide for the location you are in.

In our experience, people often aren't that curious about specific snake species; instead, they want to know if a snake can hurt them. Differentiating between harmless snakes and venomous ones isn't too hard, since there are only two types that you need to be wary of in this region—coral snakes and rattlesnakes.

Outside of the southern part of Sonora, Mexico, there is only one tiny coral snake found in the Sonoran Desert region, and encounters with this species have never resulted in a human fatality. For this reason, avoiding venomous snakes is fairly straightforward—basically, look out for rattlesnakes. Fortunately, they're easy to identify by their rattles.

Live-born rattlesnake young begin life with the first segment of a rattle, which resembles a stumpy, gnarled fingernail and, like fingernails, is composed of keratin. As rattlesnakes grow, so do their rattles—a new segment is added each time they shed their skin, making that signature sound when they bump against each other. Its rattle is the species' most defining visual characteristic, even if you don't hear the buzzing sound associated with it, and the rattle, or the stumpy appearance it gives the tail, is readily visible from a safe distance of 5 feet (1.5 m). (Note: Rattlesnakes without rattles are *extremely* rare.)

As you're walking through the desert, pay attention to sounds that emulate the buzzing of a rattle—a sprinkler or running faucet, for example. If you hear a noise that sounds like a deflating balloon, it could be a rattlesnake (or gopher snake) breathing rapidly to warn you of its presence. In each of these instances, use caution, stop moving, and look around. And look around again. Snakes can be really hard to detect amidst the low-lying vegetation and rocks of the desert. If you do spot a rattlesnake, quietly veer around it, giving it a wide berth, and move on—generally, a snake is not even remotely interested in biting unless threatened and, by walking away, you essentially remove any threat.

Rattlesnakes, *Crotalus* spp., Spanish: *vibora de cascabel*

More than two dozen rattlesnake species can be found in the Sonoran Desert. Some are widespread generalists, like the western diamondback rattlesnake, which eats a variety of prey and can exceed 4 feet (1.2 m) in length, though the record is over 6 feet (1.8 m) long,

Clockwise from upper left:
Western diamondback rattlesnake

Mohave rattlesnake

Tiger rattlesnake

Sidewinder rattlesnake

a highly rare occurrence. Other species in this family are the black-tailed rattlesnake and the Mohave rattlesnake, a bit shorter in length and more specialized in habitat preference—rocky slopes for the former, semi-desert grassland and creosote flats for the latter.

Maxing out at 3 feet (0.9 m) long, the tiger rattlesnake occupies a much more limited range, preferring rocky hillsides. It's the only rattlesnake with a banded pattern rather than one composed of blotches, diamonds, or rhomboids. The sidewinder is similar in length but more slender, with a strong affinity for open sandy terrain. It's the only snake in North America with scales that look like thorny triangular points arching above the eyes, and its common name derives from its peculiar side-to-side locomotion, a way to overcome the lack of friction for moving through loose sand. Other snakes, too, may adopt these movements when confronted with loose or slippery surfaces.

Three other rattlesnakes—the banded rock, ridge-nosed, and twin-spotted—dwell specifically in the Sky Islands of the Sonoran Desert and, due to their restricted habitat, are protected by state

and/or federal laws. Banded rock rattlesnakes grow to almost 3 feet (0.9 m) long and have a strong affinity for large rock outcrops, while the 2-foot-long (0.6-m-long) ridge-nosed tends toward the lower reaches of these same hillsides, their reddish-brown, tan, and cream patterns blending well with leaf litter on the ground. Barely reaching 2 feet (0.6 m) long, the twin-spotted rattlesnake prefers rock-fragment slopes called taluses. All three have a varied diet consisting of rodents, birds, lizards, and even invertebrates, such as scorpions and centipedes.

Clockwise from upper left: Black-tailed rattlesnake

Black tail of black-tailed rattlesnake

Ridge-nosed rattlesnake

Twin-spotted rattlesnake

Banded-rock rattlesnake

THE ART OF DECEPTION

Gopher snake, *Pituophis catenifer*, Spanish: *cincuate casero*

Growing up to 8 feet (2.4 m) long and native to a variety of habitats, the gopher snake is one of the largest and most wide-ranging snakes in the Sonoran Desert. It is also nonvenomous and relatively harmless to humans, though a bite can be painful. To avoid predation, this species has developed a suite of physical characteristics and behaviors to look, act, and sound like a rattlesnake. It is similarly patterned, large, and heavy-bodied; vibrates its tail and flares its

head when threatened; and emits a rattle-like sound (from a special membrane in its windpipe) to keep predators at bay. You'll know it's a gopher snake because it lacks a rattle. Still, steer clear, respect the snake's turf, and admire from afar—no need to provoke even a nontoxic bite.

Long-nosed snake, *Rhinocheilus lecontei*, Spanish: *culebra nariz-larga*

Peaking at a slender 3 feet (0.9 m) in length, this nonvenomous species is one of many snakes that resemble a coral snake, encircled by red, black, and cream/white bands of color. As with the gopher snake, mimicry—when a harmless/palatable species imitates a harmful/unpalatable one—discourages predators and affords the long-nosed snake some protection.

OTHER NONVENOMOUS SNAKES

Kingsnakes, *Lampropeltis* spp., Spanish: *culebras reales, falsas coralillos*

Kingsnakes are midsized generalists, 3.5–5 feet (1–1.5 m) in length. High-elevation forms sport bright red, white, and black patterns (like the long-nosed) making them popular in the pet trade. Desert forms are typically decked out in black and white bands, speckles, or a combination of both, though near the international border some are solid black.

Though kingsnakes are generalized predators of birds, rodents, and other reptiles, they are constrictors with a specialized talent, namely, to capture, kill, and eat rattlesnakes. Though they possess a high tolerance, if not immunity, to rattlesnake venom, kingsnakes nevertheless avoid the fangs of their prey, incapacitating them by grasping and squeezing around the head/neck region.

Whipsnakes, *Coluber* spp., Spanish: *chirrionero*

Named for their thin bodies (4 feet/1.2 m) and quick movements, whipsnakes are another type of snake frequently seen in the Sonoran Desert. Depending on where you travel, you may encounter three species, recognizable by their coloring. The largest and most widely distributed is the coachwhip, in shades of speckled brown, black, red, or even pink. The slightly smaller Sonoran whipsnake

Opposite, clockwise from upper left: Gopher snake pattern is similar to the diamondback rattlesnake.

Gopher snakes have black and white tail bands like many rattlesnakes.

Common kingsnake close-up

Coachwhip (dark variety)

Coachwhip pink variety)

Long-nosed snake

Opposite, center: Arizona mountain kingsnake

is olive with a light stripe running down each side of the body. The striped whipsnake is similar to the Sonoran, but with two stripes instead of one. All three forms differ from many other snake species in being most active during the day. They are also known to periscope, raising the forebody above grasses and other vegetation to scan the horizon for prey (small mammals, birds, and lizards).

Opposite, top to bottom:
Night snake coiled

Night snake on the move

Lyre snake

Patch-nosed snakes, *Salvadora* spp., Spanish: *culebra nariz de parche*

Another medium-sized, day-active snake, 1.25–3.25 feet (0.4–1 m) in length, is the patch-nosed. These snakes possess an unusual patch-like scale at the tips of their noses and are considered a harbinger of summer because they are among the first species to become active as temperatures rise.

REAR-FANGED SNAKES

Desert night snake, *Hypsiglena chlorophaea*, Spanish: *nocturna verde-oscuro*

Sonoran lyre snake, *Trimorphodon lambda*, Spanish: *ilamacoa de Sonora*

Beyond rattlesnakes and coral snakes, a third group, known as rear-fanged snakes, are also venomous. Two of the most common, the small night snake (1–2 feet/0.3–0.6 m) feeds on lizards and the somewhat larger lyre snake (2–3 feet/0.6–0.9 m) eats many things, including bats. Though these animals are venomous, their venom type and its delivery system are designed to subdue small animals and pose no danger to humans.

To identify the pale gray, light brown, or beige night snake, note the pair of large dark brown or black blotches on its neck immediately behind the head and the dark gray, brown, or black blotches on its back and sides; its underside is white. The smooth-scaled lyre snake is light brown to light gray with dark brown saddles on its back; the underside is white or yellow with scattered brown spots.

BIRDS: THE MAGIC OF MIGRATION

RENOWNED AS A BIRDER'S PARADISE, the Sonoran Desert boasts an immense diversity of wildlife that isn't limited to birds. The Sky Islands surrounding Tucson in the northern Sonoran Desert (and Southern Arizona) are a source of elevational diversity, while pockets of wetlands, grasslands, oak forests, and pine stands offer other inviting ecosystems. Along with built attractions such as parks, golf courses, and artificial lakes, these varied habitats attract more than 500 recorded bird species in Pima County alone. Among them are familiar and frequently sighted resident birds, such as Cooper's hawks, Gambel's quails, Anna's hummingbirds, verdins, and Gila woodpeckers and, throughout the year, migrating species pass through, too, dappling yards and ponds with flecks of bright color and adding new calls and trills to the ever-changing avian symphony.

In spring, the orioles, grosbeaks, warblers, and flycatchers return to Southern Arizona as do turkey vultures and black vultures. The longer days of summer bring lesser nighthawks—it's a treat to step outside at dusk and watch the doves and sparrows fly home as the bats and nighthawks dance together against a fiery sunset. In fall, the white-winged doves and vultures leave while the northern migrants start coming back, an influx of bright hummingbirds, warblers, and robins. Winter welcomes returning phainopeplas (also called goth cardinals) with their quiet *wurp* call and intimate ties to mistletoe (the birds feed on the berries and then spread the seeds). Yellow-rumped warblers (or "butterbutts" to birders) dominate mesquite groves and wetlands, and some fascinating waterfowl show up, too. Truly any time of year is the right time to step outside, look up, and listen to birds.

Resources: Merlin and eBird are extremely helpful apps for identifying birds by picture or sound recording and for logging personal sightings. If you explore eBird and search for any of these field trips, it will list the most recent species sighted, and you can dig deeper into historical records.

Owls: Brilliant or Birdbrained?

Great horned owl, *Bubo virginianus*, Spanish: *tecolote cornudo, buho*

Barn owl, *Tyto alba*, Spanish: *lechuza, mono*

Western screech owl, *Megascops kennicottii*, Spanish: *tecolotito chillón*

Thanks to fairy tales, poetry, and marketing schemes, we consider owls to be wise, an assumption firmly ensconced in our collective knowledge and celebrated across cultures worldwide. But is it true? Owls do have wide, intense, perhaps knowing stares, but their big eyes, related muscles, and scleral rings (bones surrounding the eyes) leave less headroom for gray matter. Their enlarged eyes (1.4 to 2.2 times larger than birds of the same weight) are useful for detecting fierce predators—bobcats, coyotes, snakes, ringtails, even other owls— but they are not thought to be among the most intelligent birds.

Largely nocturnal creatures, owls rely on their famed silent flight for hunting food, the result of a fascinating feather adaptation. Tiny eyelash-like combs on the outer edges of their wings break up noisy, turbulent air, allowing them to fly slowly, stealthily, and quietly as they sweep down on their prey.

Thirteen owl species have been recorded in Southern Arizona, ranging in size from the elf owl, with a height of about 5 inches (13 cm), to the great horned owl, up to 3 feet (90 cm) tall. They cover categories such as diurnal (daytime) owls, burrowing owls in the

▸ Burrowing owl

Above, left to right:
White-winged dove

White-winged doves help pollinate saguaro flowers, then enjoy the fruits of their labor.

Juvenile mourning dove

Mourning dove with two young

Common ground dove

Doves

White-winged dove, *Zenaida asiatica*, Spanish: *paloma pitahayera*

Mourning dove, *Zenaida macroura*, Spanish: *paloma huilota*

Inca dove, *Columbina inca*, Spanish: *tortolita de cola larga*

Common ground dove, *Columbina passerine*, Spanish: *tortolita pico rojo*

Eurasian collared dove, *Streptopelia decaocto*, Spanish: *paloma turca*

The doves of the Sonoran Desert bring melody and harmony to our regional symphony overhead. In her "Edge of Seventeen" lyrics, Phoenix native Stevie Nicks, perhaps captivated by the white-winged doves of her youth, references this particular dove who sounds like she's singing "Ooh, ooh, ooh." Doves can be found in very large flocks during migration or, at other times of year, in pairs or singly, and they are granivorous (feeding on seeds, grains, and fruits).

The return of white-winged doves to Southern Arizona during migration is a signal that summer has arrived. This species pollinates the iconic saguaro and disperses its seeds. Saguaro flowers bloom during the night and close by the following midday; bats take the pollination night shift while white-winged doves cover the daytime hours. Known for their vivid blue eye rings and distinctive,

white-trimmed feathers, they are easy to recognize. When they depart at summer's end, cooler weather is on its way.

Mourning doves, on the other hand, are ubiquitous throughout the year, regardless of season, time of day, or temperature. Sometimes considered less than conscientious parents for their slapdash nest-building technique—"two sticks and call it quits"—this species, in fact, raises several broods a year. On the lookout for food, these birds often drain bird feeders before the less common and "more interesting" birds, like quail, cardinals, and grosbeaks can get there, making it difficult for some naturalists to explain their positive role in the ecosystem. But they are an integral part of the desert's web of life as prey for other yard birds, such as Cooper's hawks, corvids, and Gila woodpeckers, and mourning dove eggs are welcome snacks for snakes, roadrunners, and even feral cats.

A few other notable dove species are Inca (or Mexican), common ground, and Eurasian collared doves. At 6.5–9.1 inches (16.5–23 cm), the Inca dove, characterized by fish-scale-patterned feathers, is by far the smallest and can be abundant in urban areas, where it feeds on grasses. The common ground dove (5.9–7.1 inches/15–18 cm), usually found alone in dense thickets or on trails, has a pink beak, very short tail, and gorgeous scaling on its neck and breast. Finally, the Eurasian collared dove is larger (12–14 inches/30–33 cm), with a sleek, elegant body shape and a black ring on the back of its neck.

▲ Roadrunner close-up showing its patch of bare blue, white, and orange skin behind the eyes. The orange becomes a deeper red during mating season.

Ground Birds

Though famed for flying, many Sonoran Desert bird species spend more time on the ground than in the sky due to niche factors, adaptations, and body size. Keep this in mind when bird-watching and remember to glance down from your binoculars occasionally to spot them.

Greater roadrunner, *Geococcyx californianus*, Spanish: *correcaminos, churea, paisano*

A member of the cuckoo family and fairly synonymous with the Sonoran Desert, the greater roadrunner (20–24 inches/56–62 cm) is zygodactyl (having two toes in front and two in back), leaving X-shaped tracks in its wake. Roadrunners are ubiquitous throughout Tucson, especially in flat open desert areas and near washes. They feed on insects and occasionally baby quail, but mostly on lizards and small snakes. Known for their speed, this species can run up to 20 mph (32 kph). However, unlike their cartoon namesake, they make a short, barking/yipping sound rather than *meep-meep*. They also make rapid clacking calls to communicate.

◤ Greater roadrunner

▲ Gambel's quail

Nests can be found in cholla, mesquite, and palo verdes. Both parents incubate the eggs, usually two to six in number, which hatch within three weeks, and teach their young to hunt for another couple weeks before sending them out on their own. Interestingly, roadrunners use their dark skin to absorb heat in winter seasons and develop bright red and blue splotches of skin behind their eyes during breeding season (March to October).

Gambel's quail, *Callipepla gambelii*, Spanish: *codorníz de Gambel*

Often heard before seen, Gambel's quail (about 10 inches/25 cm) can be found in any low desert area. Their easily recognized call is the sound of the American Southwest, a repetitive, pitch-varying four-note call. Males, identified by their black masks and chests (females are uniformly gray), caw loudly from perches and all covey members respond with a *chip-chip-chip* sound to relay information about surroundings, potential threats, or locations. If startled or in danger, quail actually fly short distances (quite noisily) to get out of harm's way, but are otherwise found on the ground, the adults foraging for seeds and the young feeding on small insects. With their signature topknots and lineup of tiny chicks ambling behind them, Gambel's quail are beloved among naturalists, birders, and artists and can be found in paintings, metalwork, and yard art.

Southern Arizona also hosts several other quail species—scaled, Montezuma, and bobwhite. The Buenos Aires National Wildlife Refuge has undertaken a multiyear reintroduction project for the

▸ Wild turkey profile

▸ Wild turkey back

endangered masked bobwhite, and eastern bobwhites are also commonly purchased and released by people to train hunting dogs throughout the Sonoita and Las Cienegas areas.

Wild turkey, *Meleagris gallopavo*, subspecies *intermedia* (Rio Grande), *merriami* (Merriam's), *mexicana* (Gould's), Spanish: *guajolote, chihui*

There are three types of wild turkeys in Arizona—Merriam's, Gould's, and Rio Grande—all found at higher elevations. Among the largest birds in the Sonoran Desert, turkeys are easy to spot, and their "gobble-gobble" calls are very recognizable. If you encounter a turkey or an entire gaggle in the forest, note the way the dappled light reflects off their velvety iridescent feathers; in full sunlight, the shimmering black and metallic greens are even more vivid. When mating, the large toms mingle with the hens, but otherwise keep to themselves while the hens and poults (turkey young) travel, feed, and sleep together until the brood grows into adulthood after about a year.

Woodpeckers

Gila woodpecker, *Melanerpes uropygialis*, Spanish: *carpintero del desierto*

Ladder-backed woodpecker, *Dryobates scalaris*, Spanish: *carpintero mexicano*

Arizona woodpecker, *Dryobates arizonae*, Spanish: *carpintero de Arizona*

Acorn woodpecker, *Melanerpes formicivorus*, Spanish: *carpintero harlequín*

Northern flicker, *Colaptes auratus*, Spanish: *carpintero de pechera común*

Gilded flicker, *Colaptes chrysoides*, Spanish: *carpintero de pechera amarillo*

Woodpeckers are headstrong—literally and figuratively. Their perseverance matches their rhythmic pounding as they hammer away on trees and saguaros, inspecting and consuming each insect, morsel, and stashed acorn. Their zygodactyl toes (like those of the roadrunner) provide a stabilizing grip on branches, and their surprisingly long tongues reach deep recesses to find food. Their tongues also serve double duty by cushioning their brains as the woodpeckers hammer away. Northern flickers hold the record for longest tongue—it sticks out 2 inches (5 cm) past the tip of the bill when extended.

◣ Gila woodpeckers excavate nests in saguaros. When they are done with them, other birds will use them.

▾ Ladder-backed woodpecker

Clockwise from left: Evidence of woodpeckers

Arizona woodpecker eating from a suet feeder

Acorn woodpecker

Gilded flicker

Northern flicker

In Southern Arizona, Gila woodpeckers are extremely common, hollowing out and nesting in saguaro cavities for protection against the elements. When Gilas peck into the soft flesh of a saguaro, the cactus forms a scab along the recessed interior, resulting in a "saguaro boot" (named for its shape). Over time, these boots are used over and over by multiple species, such as owls, kestrels, flycatchers, purple martins, and more.

Sharing the habitat with Gilas are ladder-backed woodpeckers. Slightly smaller, but just as noisy, ladder-backs are active and fun to watch. Like Gilas, males have red crowns. They forage on tree trunks rather than the ground for bugs and occasional fruit. In urban areas, they often feed at hummingbird and suet feeders.

You can also look for the Arizona woodpecker and the acorn woodpecker. Arizona woodpeckers have brown backs (in contrast to the black-and-white coloring of most regional woodpeckers), speckled chests, and, in males, a flash of red on their heads. They favor higher elevations of 5000 to 6000 feet (1524 to 1829 m) above sea level where oaks, pines, junipers, sycamores, and cottonwoods dominate the landscape. They feed on insect larvae like wood-boring beetles in addition to berries and acorns.

You'll recognize acorn woodpeckers by their striking white eyes juxtaposed against black face feathers, giving them a surprised look.

Noisy and gregarious, they maintain a complicated social structure—suffice to say, when you see one, you'll see many. Acorn woodpeckers are associated with oaks (they're named for the trees' nuts), and they stash their finds tightly into holes they carve in the upper reaches of the trees. These birds fiercely defend their granaries, and you'll detect evidence of their work in any pine-oak habitat.

Flickers are similar to Gilas in size, habitat, and behavior. You'll see and hear northern flickers and gilded flickers in and around Tucson, particularly in the cactus forest of both districts of Saguaro National Park. Unlike other woodpeckers, northern flickers hunt for bugs on the ground. As for gilded flickers, you'll recognize them by their brown heads, as opposed to northerns, which appear golden (or gilded) in the right light. Different types of flickers can be hard to tell apart—if you can get a picture or record its call, identification apps can help you identify the species.

Sure, We Have Shorebirds (and Other Surprises)

Not many experienced birders expect to have to differentiate spotted versus solitary sandpipers in the middle of the desert, but the Sonoran Desert is unique and always defies assumptions. Anywhere there are wetlands and water, shorebirds, wading birds, and ducks will show up—they welcome the plentiful pit stops on their migration routes.

Herons and egrets are reliably spotted at Sweetwater Wetlands, Canoa Ranch, and golf courses. So much so, that one can catch them flying over Tucson houses—not bad for a desert yard bird! These waders share several traits, for example, long skinny legs with agile feet that help them keep balance and stability in streams, lakes, and currents. Their necks are long, sometimes comically so, compared to their bodies, but those seemingly ungainly necks are powerful, providing the strength to adjust their posture ever so slightly to gain advantage while searching for prey. Keep an eye out for the majestic great egret, the beautiful and more common great blue heron, the green heron, and the shy, bulky, black-crowned night heron.

In wetlands, along the water's edge, look for more shorebirds foraging. They're probing in the soft mud and finding tiny invertebrates. Sandpipers, avocets, snipes, and stilts have all been seen in Arizona and Mexico, but the killdeer can be seen in flooded

agricultural fields, too. They are active singly, or sometimes in groups, and totally entertaining to watch. Killdeer add another auditory layer with their plaintive *kill-deer* call.

As for ducks, the list is long, weird, and inconsistent. Your best bet for identifying them is to rely on field guides, signage, and the ever-present bird expert in the vicinity. Take some photos and try to learn them later. You'll most likely see mallards (the classic catalogue duck), northern pintails, gadwalls, American wigeons, pie-billed grebes, northern shovelers, and of course, American coots. You can't *not* see a coot—they won't let you, as they dominate the water. But coots are cute (check out their wildly colored lobey feet!), so no one's complaining. Rarities are less predictable, but it's always a treat to see teals, buffelheads, and mergansers show up.

Opposite, clockwise from upper left: Black-crowned night heron

Egret (white) and cormorant (dark)

Great blue heron

Green heron

Sandpiper

Killdeer

Vulture Culture

Turkey vulture, *Cathartes aura*, Spanish: *aura común*

Black vulture, *Coragyps atratus*, Spanish: *zopilote*

Crested caracara, *Caracara plancus*, Spanish: *quebranta huesos, caracara*

Vultures are the sanitation engineers of the ecosystem—as scavengers, they help clean up roadkill and carrion by feeding on sick, dying, and dead animals. You'll often spot them along roadsides for that very reason and, equipped with stomach fluids more powerful than battery acid to digest efficiently, they're up to the task. However, while their gastric chemistry can zap diseases like botulism and salmonella, these birds are not completely invincible and can fall victim to accumulated lead toxicity from hunters' bullets found in their food.

Another adaptation is regurgitating their last meal to shed weight for quick flight when escaping a fast car or a hungry predator. They're also capable of urohidrosis, eliminating urine and feces on their legs to cool off—as the droppings (excreted together) evaporate, the wet skin cools. This process has a disinfectant function, too, killing bacteria and parasites that could be harmful.

In Tohono O'odham culture, the vulture appears in their origin story. In the very beginning, I'itoi (Elder Brother), Ban (Coyote), and Nuwï (Vulture) were the first beings created by Jewed Makai (Earth Medicine Man) to help complete the Earth. Today, O'odham claim membership in one of two clans: the Nuwï clan or Ban clan.

Black vultures and turkey vultures can be seen in Southern Arizona, especially during migrations. In spring, they travel from Central America and South America, dispersing throughout North America, then returning south in fall. Both birds are largely black and can be identified by a couple of differing physical features—the slightly larger turkey vulture has a red head and pale feathers on the undersides of its wings, while the black vulture has a black head and white patches on the inner edges of its wings. When flying, the black vulture glides, wings spread wide and flat; the turkey vulture slowly flaps its wings, raising them above its body in a V-shape, often teetering from side to side. These species can often be found together in communal roosts.

Part of the falcon family, the caracara is also a scavenger, but it also hunts small birds, mammals, and fish. They range from South America north through Central America and have become more common in Southern Arizona, where their population has grown due to their considerable ecological flexibility and adaptability to human presence. Look for them feeding on carrion in grasslands or ranchlands and chasing vultures away from roadkill. Caracaras have a flat-footed gait that aids in chasing prey, an unusual hunting strategy among birds. Their name comes from a South American Indigenous word that emulates the rattling quality of their calls.

Opposite, clockwise from upper left:
Black vulture

Black vultures (like all vultures) stick their faces into some pretty messy places, and their bare facial skin is easier to keep clean than feathers.

Turkey vultures on cleanup duty

Turkey vulture in flight

Caracaras

Caracara

▸ Male rufous hummingbird

Opposite, clockwise from upper left: Anna's hummingbird visiting penstemon flowers

Male Anna's, perched

Black-chinned hummingbird

Male broad-billed hummingbird

Broad-billed sipping nectar from a fairy duster

Male Costa's hummingbird

Female rufous hummingbird

Hummingbird nests are glued together with spiderweb strands.

Hummingbirds

Anna's hummingbird, *Calypte anna*, Spanish: *colibrí cabeza roja*

Black-chinned hummingbird, *Archilochus alexandri*, Spanish: *colibrí barba negra*

Broad-billed hummingbird, *Cynanthus latirostris*, Spanish: *colibrí pico ancho*

Broad-tailed hummingbird, *Selasphorus platycercus*, Spanish: *zumbador cola ancha*

Costa's hummingbird, *Calypte costae*, Spanish: *colibrí cabeza violeta*

Rufous hummingbird, *Selasphorus rufus*, Spanish: *zumbador rufo*

Describing hummingbirds, tiny though they are, requires a series of superlatives. This family includes the world's smallest birds, with the most brilliant iridescent colors, the fastest wingbeats, and the most amazing ability to fly up, down, sideways, and backwards. Among the Sonoran Desert's avid pollinators, they spend their days hovering at flowers to sip nectar, feeding almost constantly—every 15 to 20 minutes from 1000 to 2000 flowers each day—to sustain their racing metabolisms.

There are more than 300 species of hummingbirds, all native to the Americas. The majority are found in the tropics, where flowers abound year-round. Only a handful of species reach the United States, and Southern Arizona is home to more than a dozen, which vary from 2.5–5 inches (6.4–12.7 cm) in length and from 0.07–0.35 ounces (2–10 g) in weight—four average-sized hummingbirds weigh about as much as a US penny!

You'll encounter the greatest variety of hummers in late summer, when several species are heading south. All have long, pointed

HUMMINGBIRD FUN FACTS

- **Hummingbird hearts are larger in proportion to body size than those of any other warm-blooded animal.**
- **Hummingbirds have the most rapid heart rate for a bird—up to 500 beats per minute at rest and 1260 beats per minute when active.**
- **Their flight muscles account for 25 to 30 percent of body weight, compared to 15 to 25 percent in other flying birds.**
- **Hummers have the most rapid rate of wingbeats among birds—up to 80 beats per second.**
- **Their unique flight mechanisms allow them to hover for long periods of time, move in any direction (even backwards), and dive at over 60 miles per hour during courtship displays.**
- **Hummingbird body temperatures are quite high, varying from 105–109°F (40.5–42.5°C).**
- **Hummingbirds may consume up to 70 percent of their body weight in solid food per day (8 to 12 calories) and 4 to 8 times their body weight in water.**

beaks, ideal for extracting nectar from flowers; saber-like wings for hovering as they feed and pollinate; and in most instances, shimmering bronze or green backs. To impress the females, the males are brightly colored with ornate patterns, vibrant head patches, and equally vivid throat feathers, called a gorget (pronounced GOR-jit).

After mating, the male is done with family duties. The female builds the nest, incubates the tiny eggs (about 0.5 inches/1.3 cm long), and feeds the young. Considering the amount of energy that a hummingbird needs just to feed itself, it's remarkable that one female can raise her brood all alone.

Talon-ted Hunters of the Sky

Cooper's hawk, *Astur cooperii*, Spanish: *gavilán pollero, gavilán palomero*

Red-tailed hawk, *Buteo jamaicensis*, Spanish: *gavilán cola roja*

American kestrel, *Falco sparverius*, Spanish: *falcón cernícalo*

Harris's hawk, *Parabuteo unicinctus*, Spanish: *aguililla cinchada, gavilán de Harris*

Hawks, eagles, falcons, birds of prey—many names for many birds! Due to their keen eyesight, sheer strength, and magnetic appeal, these birds are celebrities all over the world. Think of all the mascots, emblems, national flags, and shields that all sport hunting birds. There are about 45 species in the Sonoran Desert region and between the largest (ferruginous hawk) and the smallest (American kestrel), chances are high you'll see hawks on many of the outings in this book.

▾ Red-tailed hawk

Clockwise from upper left:
Cooper's hawk, back

Cooper's hawk, front

Harris's hawks

Harris's hawks and other raptors often perch on utility poles. Contact your electrical utility if you see active or injured birds around electrical equipment. Utility technicians can modify equipment to protect birds.

Harris's hawk

Red-tailed hawks are widespread, numerous, and common year-round. On a recent 55-mile drive through Southern Arizona, one of our authors counted 25 red-tails on telephone poles. When not perched, red-tails circle overhead, taking updrafts and always hunting. They have incredible variation in color—either light or very dark or anywhere in between, but you can count on seeing a noticeable red-tail, especially as it hits the light.

Cooper's hawks are common backyard birds and can be seen in open areas and within the city. They don't mind making their presence known, almost constantly *cak-cak-cak*-ing, whether perched or flying. While walking in a neighborhood, take note when a burst of doves and pigeons scatter and fly, then wait a second to check if a Cooper's hawk is on the hunt. Their short wings and long tails allow for adept hunting, changing directions easily, and flying through thick tree stands. Fun fact: if you see one up-close (or with binoculars), check out the color of their eyes. The youngest fledglings have blue-gray eyes that become bright yellow when the hawks are juveniles and finally deepen to dark orange or even stunning claret red in older hawks.

Birds of prey are generally solitary, but there are exceptions. Harris's hawks, sharply patterned raptors of warm climates, live in

Want to see aerial acrobatics in an up-close environment? Check out the Raptor Free Flight show at the Arizona-Sonora Desert Museum during winter months.

▲ American kestrels

small family groups. Three or more adults often care for the young in a single nest, and two or three may hunt cooperatively as a pack, actively flushing prey animals out into the open. A classic desert sight involves three or four Harris's hawks perched on adjacent arms of the same giant saguaro. This sophisticated behavior is rare among raptors, and possibly even rare among Harris's hawks. Some research suggests this behavior is especially common in the Sonoran Desert. If you are lucky enough to see one bird, keep an eye out for the rest of its social group.

Our most familiar falcon, the American kestrel, is also our smallest, about the size of a mourning dove. Kestrels nest in large tree cavities or holes in saguaro cacti. Although they can shore up bursts of speed when they are pursuing rodents, small birds, and lizards, they mostly feed on large insects; their most impressive flying trick is hovering in one spot, on rapidly beating wings, as they scan the ground for prey. Look for kestrels on power poles and telephone lines—they sit solo, not in flocks like doves. The American kestrel has false eyespots on the back of its head and vertical black stripes on its face. Also noteworthy: it is sexually dimorphic (males and females look different).

▲ Chihuahuan ravens

Curious Corvids: A Caw-caw-caw Cacophony

Common raven, *Corvus corax*, Spanish: *cuervo común*

Chihuahuan raven, *Corvus cryptoleucus*, Spanish: *cuervo de Chihuahua*

American crow, *Corvus brachyrhynchos*, Spanish: *cuervo americano*

Among the most intelligent of animals, particularly among birds, corvids (ravens, crows, jays, and magpies) have incredible adaptability, memory, and resourcefulness.

Because corvids are found just about everywhere, you're likely to run into at least one type of corvid whenever you're outside. Of course, identification between ravens and crows is easiest when they're compared side by side, but rarely has nature been so obliging. Here are some generalized hints: ravens are larger than crows with larger, thicker bills; ravens have very long, swept-back wings while in flight, a longer tail, and slow steady wingbeats; and, unlike crows, ravens are an NFL mascot.

Ranging from sea level to mountaintops, ravens can be predators or scavengers; are comfortable in the wildest of places or in urban cities; and though hawk-sized, are classified as songbirds. Their vocalizations are just as varied—and also entertaining. With more than 30 documented types, raven calls encompass everything from empathic barks to deep *quork-quork* sounds, from gurgling croaks to alarm calls. Just as impressive are their aerial antics—these birds are strong fliers and can even do acrobatic displays in flight.

Because ravens are opportunistic scavengers, plants, animals, carrion, discarded human food, eggs, berries, nuts, and mice are all on the menu at any time. Much like coyotes, they take advantage of available resources and even cache food if necessary.

The Chihuahuan raven, found in southeast Arizona, northern Mexico, and parts of the lower United States, is slightly smaller than the common raven, but all the same superlatives apply: agile, adaptable, entertaining, intelligent. They tend to occupy areas where other ravens and crows are less prevalent, such as desertscrub and grasslands. Like other corvids, pair-bonding is an important part of their life cycle. The birds court through head bobbing, mutual preening, bill contact, and aerial displays. They mate for life, and nesting occurs on high perches like cliffs, telephone poles, and treetops. Pairs can reuse and build on their nests for multiple seasons.

The American crow is not as geographically widespread as the common raven, found only within the United States, part of Canada, and just barely into northern Mexico. Crows emit a robust *caw-caw-caw* and can be found in large flocks. They're seemingly happy in nearly any habitat, from mountains to beaches, around human habitation or not. Agricultural fields, soccer pitches, garbage dumps, and campgrounds are all potential homes for a murder of crows.

As for other corvids you'll encounter in the desert, look out for jays and magpies, especially at higher elevations. They add beautiful, raucous calls to the soundscape, accompanied by bright pops of color on Sky Island hikes.

Common Raven	American Crow
Weigh 2–3 pounds	Weigh 1 pound or less
Wingspan 4–5 feet	Wingspan 2–3 feet
Long, wedge-shaped tails	Short, rounded tails
Long, thick beaks	Short, thin beaks
Soar in flight	Flap wings in flight
NFL Mascot	Not an NFL mascot

Common ravens

American crows

▸ Cactus wren with red-stained beak from prickly pear fruit

▸ Cactus wren on cleanup duty, removing a fecal (poop) sac from a juvenile in the nest

Wonderful Wrens

Cactus wren, *Campylorhynchus brunneicapillus*, Spanish: *matraca del desierto*

Canyon wren, *Catherpes mexicanus*, Spanish: *saltapared*

Rock wren, *Salpinctes obsoletus*, Spanish: *saltapared*

Active and inquisitive little brown birds, wrens spend their days snooping about, peering into shadows, prying with their thin bills, and seeking the insects on which they feed. Often hard to see, they are easy to hear as male wrens are nonstop singers. They are also industrious nest-builders—in some wren species, the male may build several dummy nests before the female chooses one, adds a soft lining to it, and lays her eggs there. The dummy nests serve to dissuade and confuse predators.

Wrens are pretty ubiquitous inhabitants within areas of the Sonoran Desert, and in rocky, canyon, and cactus flats (where many of our adventures unfold), wrens will be your constant companions. In more barren rocky zones, the canyon wren and rock wren manage to thrive in places where there is not enough plant life to create habitat for most birds. They play hide-and-seek among the boulders, bouncing from one rock to the next, probing into deep crevices for spiders and insects lurking there. Canyon wrens produce a rippling, descending cascade of loud clear whistles, fitting music for the most majestic canyons of the West.

While most wrens are small, plain, secretive, musical, and solitary, the best-known wren in the Sonoran Desert breaks all those rules. Cactus wrens, strikingly spotted and striped, found in pairs or family groups, clamber and scramble about in the open. They cry out in rough scratchy voices from high perches and boldly peer in house and office windows. Their brash behavior has earned them the admiration of their human neighbors—the cactus wren is designated as Arizona's official state bird.

Warbler Whimsy

Warblers are visual and auditory staccatos to any desert experience. As they fluctuate in species dominance, these small birds mark the change of the seasons throughout the year. You know winter is coming when the yellow-rumped warblers (or "butterbutts" to birders) arrive.

Of all the warblers, the only species truly adapted to the desert is Lucy's warbler (*Leiothlypis luciae,* Spanish: *chipe rabadilla castaña*). This small gray-and-white bird arrives from Mexico in spring, settles into mesquite *bosques* (groves) and sings its sweet, simple song all summer long.

Below, left to right:
Yellow warbler

Yellow-rumped warbler

Lucy's warbler

Warblers forage in the treetops of cottonwoods, mesquites, acacias, and anywhere small tasty insects are found. Some bird-watchers might experience "warbler neck" after spending long hours looking up, but warblers also forage along the ground and bathe in streams. Due to their small size and quick movements, warblers are not the most cooperative photo subjects. To locate them, stay perfectly still for a few minutes and take note of the tiny hops, drops, and flights between twigs. Then you can train your binoculars to get the details.

Almost all warblers are migratory and more than 50 species occur in North America. So many come through the Sonoran Desert, we won't list all the species names. They include yellow warblers, orange-crowned warblers, black and white warblers—they're definitely colorful! On fall and spring hikes in wetlands, warbler influx is a fun event, revealing new birds to watch.

The Aptly Named Flycatchers

Phainopepla, *Phainopepla nitens*, Spanish: *capulinero negro*

Vermilion flycatcher, *Pyrocephalus obscurus*, Spanish: *mosquero cardenalito*

Ash-throated/brown-crested flycatchers, *Myiarchus cinerascens*, *Myiarchus tyrannulus*, Spanish: *mosquero copetón*

Flycatchers in North America feed mainly on insects and forage by watching from an exposed perch and then sallying forth to pick flying insects out of the air. The dipping, diving, and returning to perch is indicative of this group, often leaving one unable to identify particular species with a "welp, I know it's a flycatcher" shrug.

Although most flycatchers are dull-colored, a striking exception is the vermilion flycatcher, common along streams, wetlands, parks, and golf courses in the desert. In brilliant contrast to the drabness of its relatives, the male glows red and black, and in his courtship display, puffs himself up like a ball and flutters about the sky while singing madly. Look for this species on the outer branches or tops of trees.

Ash-throated flycatchers frequent desertscrub, pinyon-juniper, oak groves, creek bottoms, and dry open woodland. Brown-crested flycatchers are found in association with saguaros, but also frequent

Good thing flycatcher species can tell themselves apart, because it's quite a challenge for humans. Some species are so similar, it's their call that sets them apart. For example, the brown-crested and ash-throated flycatchers are almost identical except for size, but their songs and calls are different. Free apps like Merlin can narrow down or identify birds based on their calls, photos, or other information.

Clockwise from upper left:
Ash-throated flycatcher

Vermilion flycatcher

Phainopeplas commonly perch at the tops of trees, making them more visible.

river groves and other areas where trees are large enough to provide sites for cavity nesting. Both feed by flying out from a perch to hover and eat insects from foliage or in midair.

The goth cardinal, or phainopepla, often takes people by surprise. It's not a black cardinal but a flycatcher associated with desert mistletoe. Few other birds in North America have such an intimate relationship with a single plant species. Mistletoe is a parasitic plant that grows on the branches of trees, and it is planted there through the actions of birds. When birds eat its berries, the seeds often pass unharmed through their digestive systems; if bird droppings happen to land on a suitable branch, the seeds may stick long enough to germinate. The phainopepla, by specializing on the berries of desert mistletoe, is unwittingly planting its own future food supply.

In addition to eating mistletoe berries, phainopeplas eat a variety of other small fruits, and they fly out to catch insects in midair. At times they congregate by the hundreds when food is abundant, such as when elderberries are ripening along rivers at the edge of the desert. When food is scarce, they virtually disappear. Their numbers vary tremendously from season to season. As long as the mistletoe is in fruit, however, there will be at least a few phainopeplas around. A classic winter sight in the desert is a lone phainopepla perched atop a mesquite, red eyes blazing, its spiky crest raised, ready to chase away any other birds that might approach the clumps of mistletoe in the branches below it.

Cardinals and Cousins

Northern cardinal, *Cardinalis cardinalis*, Spanish: *cardenal norteño*

Pyrrhuloxia, *Cardinalis sinuatus*, Spanish: *cardenal pardo*

The northern cardinal is among the most popular garden birds in eastern North America, chosen as the official state bird of seven states and mascot of a few professional sports teams. Travelers are often surprised to discover that, in the very different surroundings of the Sonoran Desert, the same cardinal is abundant along with several other related birds.

All the members of this group have thick bills, good for crushing hard seeds, which make up a high percentage of their diet during some seasons. Many people set out black sunflower seeds to attract these striking birds. In all cardinal species, the males have bright colors and complex whistled songs. When not singing, they often hide their colors amidst dense foliage.

Very closely related to the cardinal is the pyrrhuloxia. The male pyrrhuloxia is mostly gray, with red accents and highlights, but otherwise remarkably similar to the cardinal. And some of their whistled songs are essentially identical. The two species live side by side in dense brush along desert washes, but the pyrrhuloxia also ranges out into more open and arid places. To tell the difference, look at their bills. Cardinals have a red pointy bill with relatively little inside curve while pyrrhuloxias have a parrot-like yellow bill with a more pronounced curve.

At the other end of the color spectrum from these red birds are the varied bunting (mostly dark purple), the blue grosbeak, and the black-headed grosbeak, which is mostly a summer denizen of oak woods, but migrants show up all over the desert in spring and fall.

▲ Male northern cardinal

▲ Male pyrrhuloxia

Ornate Orioles

Opposite, clockwise from top:
Hooded oriole

Hooded oriole

Bullock's oriole

Scott's oriole

Hooded oriole, *Icterus cucullatus*, Spanish: *bolsero enmascarado, calandria*

Bullock's oriole, *Icterus bullockii*, Spanish: *bolsero de Bullock, calandria*

The blackbird family is hard to characterize because it includes such diverse types: orioles, meadowlarks, grackles, cowbirds, and others. Most have at least some black in the plumage, and their other colors run to warmer tones, such as yellow, brown, and orange. All the species have sharply pointed bills. Most are omnivorous. None is adapted to extreme desert conditions, but several species can be found in the Sonoran Desert. While these birds are brightly colored with conspicuous black patterns, they can disappear surprisingly well in tree canopies. The foliage of cottonwoods, ash, and palms can hide an oriole, but their nonstop chatter, a mix of sharp tweets and musical songs, gives them away.

Orioles in general are treetop birds, moving methodically through the foliage in search of insects, often stopping at flowers to add some nectar to their diet. In the lowlands of the American Southwest, hooded orioles and Bullock's orioles occur mainly as summer residents, seen everywhere from riparian areas, city parks, and the Sky Islands to backyards and the grounds of the Desert Museum. A popular and easy bird to identify, the hooded oriole has a special liking for palm trees. Their intricately sewn hanging nests are often found on the undersides of palm fronds. In nature, orioles feed on insects, caterpillars, fruit, and nectar-filled flowers, and humans can attract them to yards with orange slices, grape jelly, and nectar feeders.

MARVELOUS MAMMALS

Desert Dogs

THREE SPECIES OF CANID (mammals in the dog family) inhabit the Sonoran Desert: coyotes, gray foxes, and kit foxes. The highly endangered Mexican gray wolf used to range throughout the region as well, from central Mexico through the southwest United States. In the late 1800s, increasing livestock herds and declining numbers of deer and elk led wolves to prey on cattle, prompting intensive efforts to eradicate wolves. By the mid-1900s they were effectively extirpated from the United States, and the Mexican population was severely reduced. Captive breeding of wolves for reintroduction in the United States began in 1979, and the first 11 wolves were released in 1998. Currently, Mexican gray wolves are closely monitored and managed in both wild and captive populations in southeastern Arizona, southwestern New Mexico, and northern Mexico, and the population is growing slowly and steadily.

Above, left to right: Coyote colors match their desert surroundings

Howling coyote

Coyote

Coyote, *Canis latrans*, Spanish: *coyote*

An icon of the American West, the coyote figures prominently as a trickster, wise-one, or divine being in many Plains and western Native American stories as well as the wily, yet hapless, victim of many a roadrunner prank in Warner Bros. cartoons. Due to their amazing adaptability and the removal of their predators from many areas, coyotes now range from Central America all the way to Alaska and from coast to coast. Wherever you are in North America, whether Saguaro National Park or New York City's Central Park (and certainly on any of the adventures covered in this guide), you can spot a coyote and hear the eerie canine chorus of the "song dogs," especially at dawn and dusk.

COYOTE CHARACTERISTICS

Slim and wiry, coyotes have long legs; small feet; a long, bushy, black-tipped tail; big ears; a pointy face; and the stature of a medium-sized domestic dog. Coyotes are intelligent, curious, and playful, with excellent hearing, sharp vision, and an extremely sensitive sense of smell. These keen senses help them both locate their next meal and avoid becoming a meal. Coyotes are omnivorous, which means they will eat just about anything, including rodents, rabbits, fruit, lizards, snakes, flowers, beans, and insects, depending on what's in season.

COYOTE COMMUNICATION

Coyotes are social animals that live in small family groups. They mark their group's territory using scent—urinating on bushes, leaving scat, and scraping the ground with their paws, which have scent glands. Their yips, barks, growls, and howls communicate a range of messages, from "good morning" to "let's hunt" to "I'm here/where are you?" and others that humans can only guess at. The chorus of howls can be prolonged, leading people to overestimate the number of coyotes in a pack based on sound alone.

CHUPACABRA OR COYOTE?

The chupacabra is a mythic creature thought to attack cattle and other animals to feast on their blood. Said to have red eyes and reptilian skin, chupacabras were first reported in Puerto Rico in the 1990s, but the stories and sightings have spread throughout Latin America. Several chupacabra observations have been confirmed to be mange-afflicted coyotes; the highly contagious, mite-caused disease results in severe itching and hair loss in mammals. The altered appearance of the coyotes may have sparked the imaginations of human observers, but the impact of mange is all too real for the animals—excessive scratching can lead to secondary infections, a common cause of disease-related death for coyotes and foxes. Because it's spread only by direct contact, transmission to people and pets is unlikely.

FOXES

Gray fox, *Urocyon cinereoargenteus*, Spanish: *zorro gris*

Kit fox, *Vulpes macrotis*, Spanish: *zorrita del desierto, el zorro kit*

Foxes are the smallest of the desert canines. Gray foxes are a bit less than half the size of a coyote (13–44 inches/79–112 cm long, including its tail), and kit foxes are even smaller than that, about the size of a house cat. The gray fox has a coat that is, not surprisingly, gray with

Clockwise from upper left:
Juvenile gray fox

Gray fox parent with pup

Gray fox

Kit fox

brown patches while the kit fox, though similarly colored, is distinguished by its relatively large ears and pointy muzzle.

The gray fox is the only desert dog that can climb trees and does so to hunt, forage, escape, or sleep. They have even been seen napping in the arms of a saguaro. Gray foxes prefer rocky slopes and canyons while kit foxes live in the drier, open flats and dig underground dens. Both fox parents participate in pup-rearing, bringing food, and protecting the pups.

Kit foxes are pickier eaters than coyotes and gray foxes, subsisting mostly on kangaroo rats, but they sometimes supplement their diet with other small animals. As for water, kit foxes can survive without drinking free water for days, absorbing it from their food instead. Sadly, kit fox populations are in decline due to habitat loss and poisoning (often from rodent poisons).

Rabbits and Hares

Desert cottontail, *Sylvilagus audubonii*, Spanish: *conejo del desierto*

Antelope jackrabbit, *Lepus alleni*, Spanish: *liebre antílope*

Black-tailed jackrabbit, *Lepus californicus*, Spanish: *liebre cola negra*

Whether you are strolling through a Tucson neighborhood or hiking on a trail, the desert cottontail is a common sight. They're found throughout the Sonoran Desert and prefer thick brushy habitat where they can hide from their many predators, such as snakes, owls, and larger mammals. You'll have to be much luckier to spot the jackrabbit, a rarer sight, but you may see one in more open, less vegetated areas, where they are more likely to be.

RABBIT OR HARE?

Although we call them all rabbits, the desert cottontail, antelope jackrabbit, and black-tailed jackrabbit are different species, and the jackrabbits are scientifically classified as hares. The easiest way to tell them apart is by size—desert cottontails are small, generally 1 to 2 pounds (0.45 to 0.9 kg) while jackrabbits can be up to 10 pounds (4.5 kg) and an astonishing 2 feet (0.6 m) tall.

Cottontail rabbit (left) and Jackrabbit (right): Note the size of the Jackrabbit's ears compared to the cottontail's.

Hares are known for their speed. Black-tailed and antelope jackrabbits can run up to 44 miles per hour in short bursts.

MY, WHAT LARGE EARS YOU HAVE!

Both desert cottontails and jackrabbits have large ears. Jackrabbit ears are especially impressive, but even desert cottontail ears are larger compared with those of cottontails in more temperate climates. These large ears help them to not only hear predators but also to release heat and cool down.

BREEDING LIKE RABBITS

For many other desert animals, rabbits are prey, and their prodigious ability to breed helps ensure the survival of the species. Cottontails breed throughout spring and summer and usually give birth to at least two litters per year. The mother rabbit digs a shallow nest in the ground, lines it with grasses and fur, and then covers the babies with more grass and fur to hide them from predators. The young are ready to leave the nest within about two weeks. Due to their many predators, desert cottontails only live up to about two years in the wild.

Rodents

With more than 2000 species, rodents comprise the largest and most diverse group of mammals—mice, rats, squirrels, chipmunks, beavers, porcupines, marmots, and many others. All rodents have continually growing front teeth, or incisors (two upper and two lower), with thick enamel on the outer surfaces that helps maintain sharpness as their gnawing and chewing wears away the inner edge more quickly. Most rodents are herbivores (species that eat only plants), but some eat insects as well. Rodents are important seed dispersers, spreading plants to new locations. In the Sonoran Desert, the rodents you are most likely to see are packrats, Harris's antelope squirrels, round-tailed ground squirrels, and rock squirrels.

▾ The packrat's large eyes and rounded ears are endearing. The damage they cause to cars and homes is not!

◂ Packrat

Packrat (white-throated woodrat), *Neotoma albigula*, Spanish: *rata-cambalachera garganta blanca*

Packrats are medium-sized rodents, growing up to about 8 inches (20.3 cm) in body length, with another 5–7 inches (12.7–17.8 cm) of furry tail. Like many desert rodents, they get most of the water they need from the plants they eat. In the Sonoran Desert, their diet consists of a lot of prickly pear cacti along with seeds, fruits, and leaves of other plants. Packrats construct large homes of sticks, grasses, and other plant parts, defended with spiny cholla cactus segments and cemented together with urine. Scientists have used these multi-material dwellings to reconstruct the climate history of this region.

GROUND SQUIRRELS

Harris's antelope squirrel, *Ammospermophilus harrisii*, Spanish: *ardilla antilope de Sonora*

Round-tailed ground squirrel, *Xerospermophilus tereticaudus*, Spanish: *ardillón cola redonda*

Rock squirrel, *Otospermophilus variegatus*, Spanish: *ardillón de rocas*

Harris's antelope squirrels are commonly mistaken for chipmunks, but chipmunks live in cooler, higher elevations while the Harris's antelope squirrel inhabits rocky deserts. They mostly eat the fruits, seeds and beans of cactus and desert shrubs and have developed behavioral adaptations for coping with desert heat—finding shady spots or holding their bushy tails over their backs like umbrellas to create their own shade. You may also see them engaged in "heat dumping"—splaying out on their bellies to release heat into the ground.

▲ Harris's antelope ground squirrel

▼ The Harris's antelope ground squirrel is identified by its distinctive stripes and bushy tail, often held high.

RODENTS AND HUMANS

People have been waging campaigns to control rodents since the earliest civilizations and have good reasons to exclude wild rodents from their living areas—these prolific animals often eat food stores, chew wires, and pose the threat of spreading disease to humans. However, rodent poisons should only be used as a last resort. As the base of the food web for many larger animals, poisoned rodents can end up inadvertently killing a bobcat, coyote, or owl.

▲ Round-tailed ground squirrels are lighter in color than the Harris's antelope ground squirrel.

Rock squirrels and other rodents will flatten their bodies against a cool surface to cool down in a process called "heat dumping."

Round-tailed ground squirrels look a lot like prairie dogs but are much smaller. They live in underground colonies on lower mountain slopes and open flat areas. Their burrows are about 3 feet (1 m) deep with many openings to allow for airflow and multiple entry/escape routes. They stay close to their burrows, eating nearby seeds, cacti, and other vegetation.

Rock squirrels are the largest of the local ground squirrels, with bodies up to 10–12 inches (25.4–30.5 cm) long. They can be solitary or colonial and prefer rocky arid canyons and boulder piles, although they have adapted to urban living, too. They live in underground burrow systems, concealing the entrances under rocks. They climb nearly as well as tree squirrels.

Javelina/collared peccary, *Tayassu tajacu*, Spanish: *jabalí, pecarí de collar*

Javelinas are named for their long sharp canine teeth, which resemble javelins. They look something like feral hogs (wild boars) with pig-like snouts, but they are not pigs, hogs, or boars. Peccaries and pigs share a common ancestor, but their lineages diverged 37 million years ago—peccaries populated the Americas while pigs spread throughout Europe, Africa, and Asia. Unlike pigs, peccaries have inconspicuous tails and scent glands on their rumps that produce a musky, oily liquid that helps them identify each other and mark their territory. Javelinas, also called collared peccaries, are the smallest of the peccary species, about the height and length of a medium-sized dog. Long stiff hairs encircle their necks and shoulders, creating a collar that is most visible when they have their full winter coats.

DINING

Javelinas are common throughout the Sonoran Desert, in both urban and wild areas, where you're most likely to see them at daybreak or twilight. Chewed prickly pear pads and uprooted plants are often signs that they've been around and, if they've rummaged through recently, you may detect their skunk-like scent. In addition to prickly pear, they eat roots, seeds, mesquite beans, green vegetation, cactus fruits, and agave leaves. Their excellent sense of smell compensates for their poor vision and, in urban areas, they often find and feed on the trash strewn about from toppled bins.

Below, left to right: Javelinas

Note the javelina's collar made from stiff fur.

Javelinas do not have curly pig tails.

▸ Baby javelinas are known as "reds" due to their reddish fur.

LIFESTYLE

Javelinas live in herds of about 8 to 12 animals and defend territories as large as 700–800 acres (about the size of Central Park). They are social animals and generally stay with the same group throughout their lives, moving, eating, playing, and bedding down together. Each herd has its own distinctive scent, shared by rubbing against each other, affectionately called a "javelina handshake." They can breed year-round and usually have two babies with each pregnancy. Although mountain lions are the only significant predator of adult javelinas, coyotes, bobcats, and other animals prey upon reds (baby javelinas). In the wild, a javelina's lifespan is about 10 years.

Wildcats

Bobcat, *Lynx rufus,* Spanish: *gato montés*

Mountain lion, *Puma concolor*, Spanish: *puma, león de montaña*

Powerful, elusive, and lithe predators, five wildcat species make their homes in the Sonoran Desert. From largest to smallest, they are jaguars, mountain lions, bobcats, ocelots, and the rarely seen jaguarundis. Of these, only bobcats and mountain lions are common in Southern Arizona, though because they are more numerous

and widely distributed, you are more likely to see a bobcat than a mountain lion.

Mostly nocturnal and, like most felines, masters of concealment, bobcats have nevertheless adapted to living among humans, and Tucson residents spot them on occasion. Bobcats appear in many Tucson home security videos, and some are even regular backyard visitors, especially if there is access to a fountain or pool.

Bobcats live throughout the United States and range from southern Canada to central Mexico. As carnivores, they ambush rabbits, birds, snakes, and rodents, their favored foods. Though they prefer the solitary life, males and females gather to mate in spring. Kittens stay with their mothers until the following fall and then set out on their own to hunt and establish home ranges of a few square miles.

Mountain lions, also known as cougars or pumas, are apex predators (animals at the top of the food web) and, as such, help maintain a healthy web of life by keeping populations of other animals in check. Adult lions are normally solitary, except when they meet with females to breed for a few days, which can occur at any time of the year. Kittens (2 to 3 per litter) stay with their mothers for up to a year and a half, and then siblings may stay together for a while as they perfect their hunting skills.

Clockwise from left: Bobcat and her kitten caught on a wildlife camera in Tucson

Bobcats are 15–22 pounds (7–10 kg); 24–36 inches (60–90 cm) long, nose to rump; have broad cheek ruffs; and a short tail (2–8 inches/5–20 cm), black tip, and white underside.

Bobcat

▲ Mountain lions are 75–145 pounds (34–66 kg), measure about 6 feet (1.8 m) long from nose to rump, and have a 3-foot (0.9-m) black-tipped tail.

◀ Mountain lion at the Arizona-Sonora Desert Museum

You are more likely to spot signs of a mountain lion than a lion itself. Their tracks are quite large (3–5 inches/8–13 cm wide) with no claw indentations, and their scat is cylindrical and segmented. A mountain lion kill will be partially eaten with scrape marks in the surrounding dirt from the lion covering what's left behind.

Mountain lion sightings are very rare, so if you see a wildcat in Southern Arizona, it is almost certainly a bobcat. Still, knowing that mountain lions are also in our region makes a walk in the wilderness a more exciting adventure.

▲ Male jaguar in the mountains of Southern Arizona as seen on a wildlife research camera

◀ Ocelot at the Arizona-Sonora Desert Museum

JAGUAR, OCELOT, AND JAGUARUNDI

Southern Arizona is the far northern limit of the range of these marvelous cats. Jaguars and ocelots are both listed as endangered in the United States and are the subjects of ongoing study and conservation in both Arizona and Sonora. In recent years, it's a rare and celebrated occasion in Arizona when one or the other makes an appearance in an image or video captured by a wildlife research camera. People have reported seeing jaguarundi, a smaller weasel-like cat, around Tucson, but their presence has never been confirmed with a photo or any other evidence.

Black bear, *Ursus americanus*, Spanish: *oso negro*

Despite their name, black bears can be black, brown, cinnamon, or dark blond. They are found only in North America and are the smallest and most numerous of the continent's three bear species. As omnivores, their diet includes mostly acorns, berries, cactus fruit, insects, small rodents, and carrion. In the Sonoran Desert region, they generally live on forested Sky Islands but will occasionally roam through lower elevations in search of food or new habitat. Black bears are also good climbers, scaling trees and rock formations to find food, escape predators, or sleep.

Mostly crepuscular (active at dawn and dusk), black bears are solitary animals with territories that range from 15–100 square miles (39–259 sq km). In winter, their body temperatures drop about 10 degrees, and their breathing and heart rates also decrease. However, they are not true hibernators, alternating between sleep and a groggy wakefulness. True hibernators burn their protein reserves while dormant, while black bears use their fat reserves for energy. Urea from their urine is recycled back into muscle production. Remarkably, female bears give birth during the winter while semi-hibernating, usually bearing two or three cubs that nurse and snuggle with mom until the warmth of spring. In the wild, black bears live 20 to 30 years.

↖ Black bear

▾ Breakfast with the black bear at the Arizona-Sonora Desert Museum. Black bears are about 3–3.5 feet (1–1.1 m) tall when on all fours and 5 to 6 feet (1.5–1.8 m) long.

BEARS AND PEOPLE

Due to suburban expansion and increasing recreation in bear territory, encounters with bears have become more common. Conflicts can be minimized by securing food and trash, whether at campsites or in neighborhoods at the wildland-urban interface. Bird feeders, including hummingbird feeders, pet food, fruit trees, and vegetable gardens have also been known to attract hungry bears. See the section "Exploring the Desert Safely" (page 113) for more information about what to do if you see a bear.

Deer

Mule deer, *Odocoileus hemionus*, Spanish: *venado bura*

Coues whitetail deer, *Odocoileus virginianus couesi*, Spanish: *venado cola blanca de Sonora*

▾ Mule deer on the roadside. How many do you see?

Two species of deer are found in the Sonoran Desert—mule deer and Coues whitetail deer (a smaller subspecies of white-tailed deer). Mule deer are more common in the lower elevation desert and scrublands while whitetails are more common at higher elevations, although there is a good deal of overlap in their ranges. Mule deer are named for their large mule-like ears. Coues deer also have larger ears than other white-tailed deer, leading to some difficulty in telling the two species apart. These large ears help them to shed excess heat and listen for mountain lions and humans, their main predators.

Deer can live in most habitats in the region, except in the driest, most open, and most urbanized areas where there isn't enough food or cover. During the warmer months they browse shrubs and graze grasses in the evening and early morning hours, or sometimes on moonlit nights. They will also migrate to higher elevations in summer and return to lower elevations in winter. They are herbivores, eating a wide variety of vegetation, and ruminants (like

TIPS FOR TELLING THEM APART:

COUES:

- Tail flap with white underside
- Antler points all split from one main branch
- Smaller than mule deer

MULE:

- White rump
- White rope-like tail with black tip
- Antlers split into two main branches
- Larger ears

cows and sheep) that chew their cud, regurgitating food to chew it again. Male deer grow antlers in summer and fall, then shed them each spring.

Unfortunately, the best way to tell the two species apart is when they are running away from you—their tails tell the tale. Mule deer have fluffy white rumps and a short, rope-like white tail with a black tip. It's difficult to see the white on a whitetail deer's tail until they lift it up, an action called flagging; when the tail is down, it blends with the body. There are also some differences in their faces. If the fur is darker above the eyes than on the snout, it's likely a mule deer. On a whitetail, the fur color around the eyes and the bridge of the nose will be more uniform.

The furry coating on antlers is called velvet. It is full of nerves and blood vessels that allow antlers to regrow quickly each year.

Above, left to right:
Mule deer fawn

Coues whitetail deer

Coues whitetail deer

▲ Raccoons have a rounded body, bandit-like face mask, and ringed tail.

Raccoons, Coatis, and Ringtails

Raccoons, coatimundis, and ringtails are all members of a family called procyonids. They are native to the Americas and are some of the most distinctive, though least known, animals of the Sonoran Desert.

Raccoon, *Procyon lotor*, Spanish: *mapache, batepi, lavador*

For residents of the United States, raccoons are the most familiar of the three species because they're common in various parts of the country and often live near human communities. They have also been introduced in Europe. Many people are surprised to learn that raccoons do quite well in the desert as long as there is water nearby. In fact, swimming pools and fountains in urban areas have opened up new habitat for desert raccoons. In the wild, they prefer riparian habitats and brushy or wooded areas.

Raccoons are nocturnal, hunting during the relative cool of night and sleeping during the day. Ordinarily solitary in the wild, racoons congregate when enticed by human food sources, often in picnic areas or at campgrounds. They mate between January and June, and their litters (of 1 to 7 cubs) are mostly born in spring. Raccoons are well-adapted to urban and suburban habitats where their dexterous paws can open trash bins and doors, giving them ready access to our ample food waste. In urban areas, they den in chimneys, attics, and crawl spaces under homes.

Coati or coatimundi, *Nasua narica*, Spanish: *coati, chulo*

Coatis (also known as coatimundis) are native to South America, Central America, Mexico, and the southwestern United States. In Arizona, you can find them in woodlands and riparian habitats.

SOCIAL CLIMBERS

Coatis are very social animals, living in bands of 20 or even 30 individuals. The bands are made up of females and their young, with adult males joining only during mating season. They are also very chatty, communicating with clicks, grunts, whistles, and barks as they forage. Excellent climbers, they use their long tails to help balance on branches. Like racoons and ringtails, they can rotate their ankles more than 180 degrees and descend trees headfirst.

Most active in the morning and late afternoon, they spend the nights in trees or caves and eat an omnivorous diet of bugs, fruits, nuts, small rodents, eggs, snakes, lizards, and carrion.

TAILS UP!

While foraging and walking on the ground, coatis will often hold their tails straight up. This may be to help them keep track of each other in tall brush or grass. From a distance, a band of coatis with tails up looks like a herd of tiny brontosauruses walking backwards!

Coatis have longer bodies than raccoons, along with longer noses and tails.

Coatis are more common in riparian habitats.

Ringtail, *Bassariscus astutus*, Spanish: *cacomixtle*

The ringtail is Arizona's state mammal, though most Arizonans have never seen one in the wild. Their diminutive faces, large black eyes, big pink ears, and long fluffy black-and-white ringed tails are endearing to us, but not to the many smaller animals that are food for this efficient predator. They are omnivores (species that eat both plants and animals), but prefer meat (especially rodents) when they can get it.

▲ Ringtails are between squirrel- and cat-sized. Their large eyes help them see at night.

◀ The ringtail's fluffy banded tail is longer than its body.

ROCK ON!

Ringtails live in rocky habitats, most often in riparian canyons. They are exceptional climbers and can nimbly negotiate ledges, squeeze through small crevices, and leap from wall to wall through narrow gaps. They den in rock niches, mine shafts, abandoned burrows, and tree hollows. Strictly nocturnal, ringtails rely on their large eyes to gather enough light for maneuvering and hunting at night. Ringtails are solitary animals, pairing up for only a few days each year to mate.

WHAT'S IN A NAME?

Early miners domesticated ringtails to help keep rodents and insects in check. Hence, one of their monikers—miner's cat. They are also commonly referred to as ringtail cats or civet cats, though they are not cats. In Mexico, the ringtail is called *cacomixtle*, a Nahuatl (Aztec) word that means "half cat" or "half mountain lion." Its Latin name, *Bassariscus astutus*, means "clever little fox"—but it's not a fox either.

Skunks and Badgers

Skunks and badgers are both relatively common in the Sonoran Desert. Badgers are much stockier than skunks, with smaller, shorter tails. Both animals are nocturnal and have a similar waddling, shuffling gait. This is because they walk with their hind feet flat on the ground, rather than on their toes, like dogs and cats.

SKUNKS

Spotted skunk, *Spilogale gracilis*, Spanish: *zorrillo pinto*

Striped skunk, *Mephitis mephitis*, Spanish: *zorrillo listado*

Hooded skunk, *Mephitis macroura*, Spanish: *zorrillo mofeta*

Hog-nosed skunk, *Conepatus mesoleucus*, Spanish: *zorrillo de nariz porcina*

Southern Arizona is endowed with four species of skunk: spotted, striped, hooded, and hog-nosed. Spotted skunks are the smallest of the bunch with white patches that resemble irregular spots. Striped skunk patterns vary, but they usually have a black back and white stripes down the sides. Hooded skunks look a lot like striped skunks, but have a ruff of fur around the neck and a very long fluffy white plume for a tail. Least common, hog-nosed skunks are all white on top and black underneath with a bare patch of skin on the nose.

Although feared for their malodorous spray, skunks are relatively calm and forbearing, seemingly confident in the effectiveness of their well-known defense mechanism should they need it. Skunks give ample warning before a spray, stamping their feet and, in the

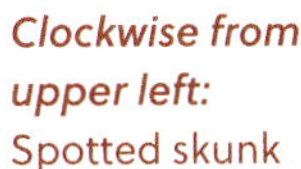

Clockwise from upper left:
Spotted skunk

Hooded skunk

Striped skunk

Hog-nosed skunk

case of the spotted skunk, even doing a handstand before spraying. Skunks generally have enough fluid for 5 or 6 sprays, which they can shoot up to 12 feet (3.7 m).

Skunks live in many habitats, from riparian canyons to woodlands to desertscrub to suburbia. They prefer areas with thick brush or other vegetation where they can seek cover. The spotted skunk tends to inhabit rocky canyons while the hog-nosed is usually found at higher elevations. None of the skunks are common in the lowest, driest parts of the desert. Skunks often share dens with other animals, such as packrats, and also make use of hollow logs, brush piles, mine shafts, and crawl spaces under buildings. They are omnivorous and have adapted to both urban and suburban areas, happily feeding on human trash.

Badger, *Taxidea taxus*, Spanish: *tejón*

The badger is known for its tenacity and testy temperament. When confronted, they may charge, hiss, snarl, or growl. Badgers have even attacked vehicles that veer too close to their dens. Strictly carnivorous, they feed on insects, ground birds, mice, prairie dogs, and groundhogs. Their long, formidable front claws are well-suited to furrowing out small animals from underground burrows and, not surprisingly, they live in open sandy flats where the soil is easy to dig, such as farmland, grassland, and even golf courses. Badgers have transparent extra eyelids they close while digging to keep dirt out

▸ Badgers have a white stripe running from their nose down their back and have a shaggy coat with long guard hairs. They weigh about 20 pounds (9 kg).

of their eyes. Like skunks, they can secrete a musky scent from their anal glands, but unlike skunks, they cannot spray it.

Badgers are nocturnal, solitary, and roam widely within their home ranges. Badgers might den in different spots each day, depending on where they find themselves at nightfall. When tracking prey, a badger plows a shallow burrow about 1 foot (30 cm) in diameter in which it can tunnel after rodents with impressive speed. Competing coyotes sometimes intercept fleeing rodents, though coyotes and badgers generally tolerate each other and even engage in play.

BATS

California leaf-nosed bat, *Macrotus californicus*, Spanish: *murciélago orejón*

Lesser long-nosed bat, *Leptonycteris yerbabuenae*, Spanish: *murciélago hocicudo*

Mexican long-tongued bat, *Choeronycteris mexicana*, Spanish: *murciélago trompudo*

Mexican (Brazilian) free-tailed bat, *Tadarida brasiliensis*, Spanish: *murciélago cola suelta*

There are more than 1400 different bat species in the world—almost one quarter of all mammal species! Bats have adapted to live in a wide variety of habitats and can be found on all continents except Antarctica. Approximately 70 species of bats live in the Sonoran Desert region. Bats are an important part of our ecosystem, helping keep populations of night-flying insects, like mosquitos, in control. They also help disperse seeds and pollinate many plants, including valuable cash crops, such as bananas, cashews, cacao, and agave. They are fascinating animals that are often misunderstood. Bats can navigate in pitch-darkness using sophisticated sonar transmitters and receivers. Contrary to popular opinion, they are not blind, they do not get tangled in your hair, and only one species in the Sonoran Desert region feeds on the blood of mammals. The range of this bat—the common vampire bat (*Desmodus rotundus*)—approaches the southern end of the Sonoran Desert, south of Guaymas, Sonora.

American leaf-nosed bats are the most ecologically diverse family of bats in the world. A few important species in the Sonoran Desert are the California leaf-nosed bat, lesser long-nosed bat, and the

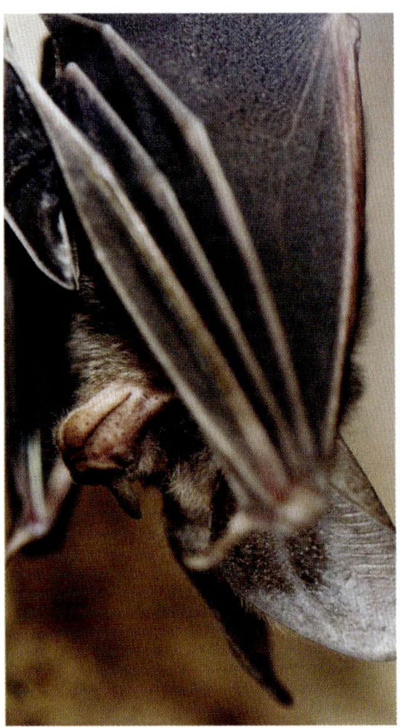

▲ Lesser long-nosed bat sipping on agave nectar

◀ California leaf-nosed bat

Despite the critical roles of bats in keeping ecosystems healthy, they are among the most threatened land mammals in North America due to habitat degradation or destruction, accelerated climate change, and the spread of a deadly disease, white nose syndrome. Thankfully, this fungal disease has not yet been detected in the Sonoran Desert. The use of wind turbines as part of sustainable energy strategies is also a growing threat to bats, although research is underway to find operating parameters that reduce bat deaths.

Mexican long-tongued bat. They all have a triangular fleshy patch of skin protruding above the nose. The California leaf-nosed bat is an insect eater, while the other two are nectar and pollen feeders. Unlike the nectar feeders, California leaf-nosed bats do not migrate. They are well-adapted to aridity and have never been observed drinking in the wild. With their huge ears, they can detect and pinpoint the location of sounds as faint as a cricket's footsteps. Lesser long-nosed bats and Mexican long-tongued bats both migrate. In late spring they follow the blooming of bat-friendly flowers as warm

temperatures spread northward. Lesser long-nosed bats are partial to the flowers of columnar cacti (column-shaped, like saguaros). In the Tucson area, they have also discovered the sugar-rush provided by hummingbird feeders.

Another common species in the Tucson area is the Mexican (Brazilian) free-tailed bat. Thousands of these bats roost under bridges in Tucson and its environs from April to September, returning to Mexico for the winter months.

▲ Mexican free-tailed bats provide a show for city residents when they emerge from their roosts under bridges each summer evening.

Bighorn sheep, *Ovis canadensis*, Spanish: *borrego cimarrón*

Bighorn sheep are superbly adapted to desert living and inhabit some of the driest mountain ranges in the Sonoran Desert. During winter, when vegetation contains more moisture and is coated by dew on cold mornings, the sheep may go for months without drinking any free water. In summer months, they get water from cactus fruits. Enlarged stomach compartments allow them to drink up to 20 percent of their body weight in just a few minutes and store it for

‣ Only the male bighorns have large, curled horns. Bighorn hooves are sharp-edged with spongy centers, allowing the sheep to grip steep slopes.

‣ Bighorn sheep (male with two females)

‣ Bighorn lamb born at the Arizona-Sonora Desert Museum

What's the difference between horns and antlers? Animals do not shed horns, which continue to grow throughout their lives; antlers, on the other hand, are shed and regrow each year.

several days. Their body temperatures of 101–102°F (38–39°C) are ideal for the hot summers, and they can survive body temperatures up to 107°F (42°C).

Bighorns live in and around the most rugged terrain and retreat to these spots to avoid predators. Their hooves are adapted to cling to steep, rocky slopes, allowing them to ascend and descend nearly vertical surfaces. Social animals, bighorns feed with their herds in the morning and evening, bedding down during the heat of the day to rest together in the shade and chew their cud. Bighorn sheep eat many different grasses, shrubs, cactus fruits, and agave.

Bighorn lambs are born in early spring and imprint on the place where they're born. When they are ready to give birth, females return to this place whenever possible. Both males and females have horns, but ewes' horns are narrow and grow about 12 inches (30.5 cm) long whereas the male's horns are broad and massive, eventually curling into nearly a full spiral and weighing as much as 40 pounds (18 kg). When rams butt heads to establish dominance, the cracking sound of their horns colliding can be heard a mile (1.6 km) away.

READY, SET, ACTION

PART THREE

Exploring the Sonoran Desert

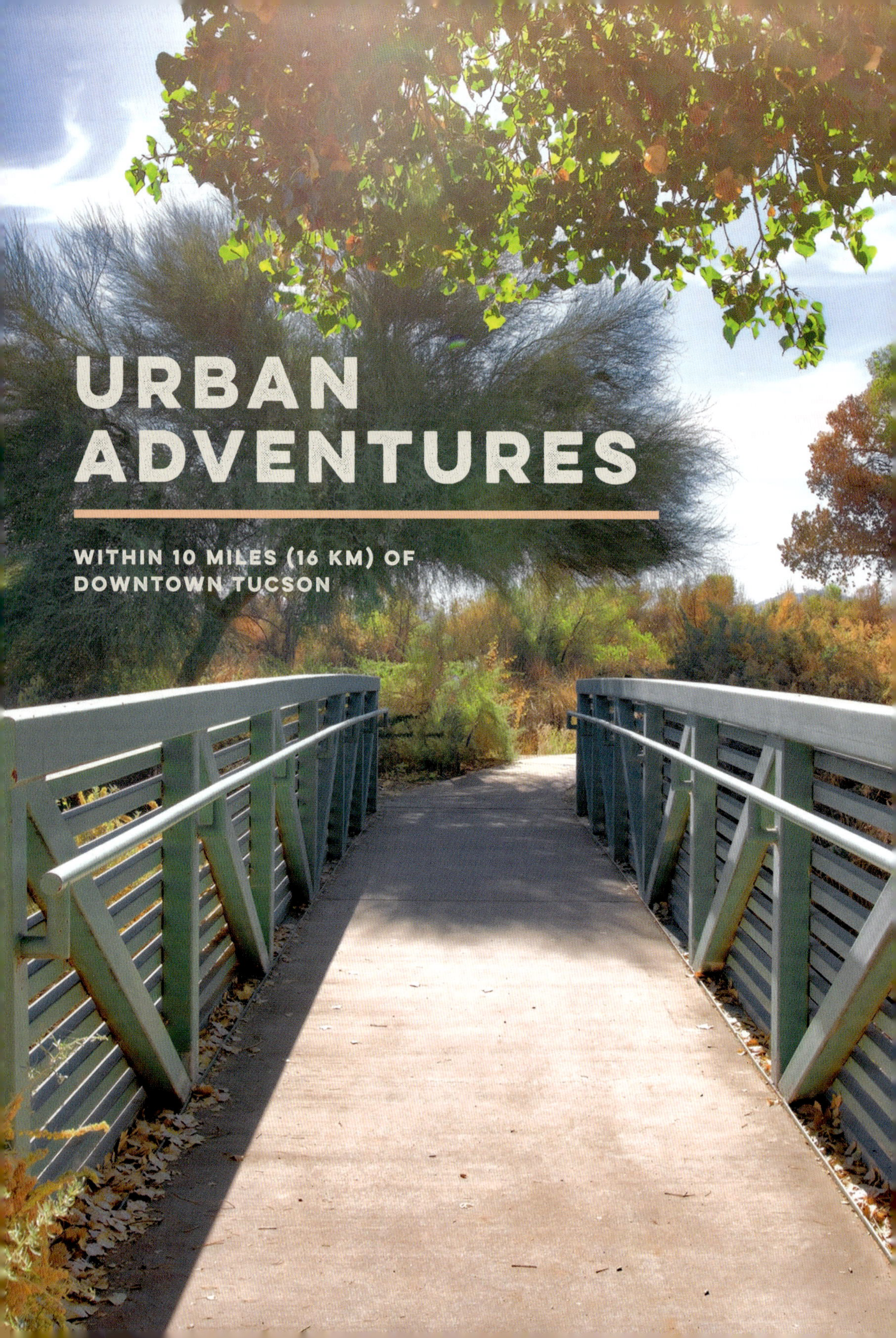
URBAN
ADVENTURES
WITHIN 10 MILES (16 KM) OF
DOWNTOWN TUCSON

ARROYO CHICO GREENWAY

HAVE YOU EVER HEARD of "green infrastructure," but wondered what it really means? Green infrastructure refers to practices and design features that infuse nature into a city by promoting water conservation, enhancing biodiversity, and serving the wider community. The Arroyo Chico Greenway is an example of this approach.

Walking, biking, or running this route is a great way to experience a modern urban greenway that fulfills multiple purposes: flood control, ecological restoration, recreation, public art, and neighborhood health and well-being. This adventure starts in the heart of downtown Tucson, at 4th Avenue and 9th Street, crosses the iconic Rattlesnake and Basket Bridges, and enters the historic Barrio San Antonio neighborhood. Then it loops around floodwater detention basins between Park and Cherry Avenues—yes, it does flood in the desert—and returns through the Lost Barrio shopping district.

Some southwest vocabulary for this trip:

- **Arroyo:** a steep-sided gully formed by swift flowing water
- **Arroyo Chico:** small gully
- **Riparian:** Relating to wetlands, generally along the banks of a stream or river

Fundamentals: Urban hike; begins in downtown Tucson area; fall/winter/spring

THE PATH AT IRON HORSE PARK

This urban hike is a paved loop that begins on Aviation Path at the corner of 4th Avenue and 9th Street, behind the Coronado Hotel Apartments. Head east through Iron Horse Park toward the Rattlesnake Bridge. Lined with drought-tolerant vegetation, the path takes you away from the bustle of 4th Avenue and passes an inconspicuous fenced-in retention basin, thick with desert riparian habitat and ideal for urban wildlife viewing. Halfway to the bridge, among a stand of mesquite trees, you'll find the first public art feature of the route, a towering metal structure with a poem by Genevieve Taggard entitled "Train: Abstraction," a reference to the historic train depot within sight of the park. The Iron Horse, or railway, played a significant role in the history of this area. (You'll hear the trains intermittently throughout the entire route.)

RATTLESNAKE BRIDGE TO SAN ANTONIO PARK

You can cross Broadway in the "belly" of the 280-foot (85-m) Rattlesnake Bridge, a steel rendering of the western diamondback designed by Simon Donovan. A work of art in itself, this unique Tucson icon affords broad vistas of downtown and the Tucson

◂ Arroyo Chico bike and pedestrian path

Mountains to the west and the entryway to the historic Sunshine Mile district to the east with the Rincon Mountains in the distance. The path between the Rattlesnake and Basket Bridges runs adjacent to Aviation Highway, west of Park Avenue.

The 240-foot (73-m) Basket Bridge passes over Euclid and Park Avenues. Its double-bowstring steel structure features decorative metal panels, inspired by Tohono O'odham woven basketry and embellished with horned lizards and geometric designs. Bear grass, a common material used in Tohono O'odham basketmaking, is abundant in the landscaping here.

As you exit the Aviation Path to the left, just beyond the Basket Bridge, walk east on 14th Street toward San Antonio Park, located at the southwest corner 14th Street and Santa Rita Avenue. This stretch of 14th Street features several sunken water-harvesting basins that take advantage of stormwater runoff to divert water to native vegetation. This small neighborhood park is known as "El Parque

▸ Mouth end of Rattlesnake bridge

▸ Tail end of Rattlesnake bridge

◂ Arroyo Chico Greenway is popular with dog-walkers.

de la Gente" (the People's Park) in honor of the Mexican American families who established the neighborhood. It has picnic tables, benches, grills, a playground, and drinking fountains and is beautifully landscaped with native vegetation.

WILDLIFE HABITAT AND PUBLIC ART

The next 2-mile (3.2-km) stretch of the walk circles the floodwater retention basins between Park and Cherry Avenues. From the northeast corner of 14th Street and Santa Rita Avenue, head east, then follow the path south around the basins.

The path ends at the Cherry Fields crossing. Continue along Cherry Avenue and turn left down the alley between Manlove and 13th Streets. This alley features an impromptu outdoor art gallery, founded and maintained by neighbors. When you reach the point where the alley meets Vine Avenue, turn first right (north) and then left (west) onto 13th Street. Follow the sidewalk to rejoin the Arroyo Chico path and stay on the path as it loops north around the basins.

The three basins have been revegetated with native riparian and upland plants. There are also two grassy areas with public art by four different artists:

- Eight cast-concrete mosaic tufts depicting native wildlife by Mary Lucking, offering seating along the path
- A playful metal sculpture on the west side of the Highland turf area
- A metal, glass, and tile sculpture by Joshua Sarantitis and Alex Garza on the turf area at 12th Street and Santa Rita Avenue
- Portraits of neighborhood residents by Chris Rush, inlaid along the 15th Street wall just east of the basin closest to Cherry Avenue

The complex also boasts a historic bridge spanning the arroyo on Highland Avenue and a BMX bicycle park in the northeast basin.

Created by the Pima County Regional Flood Control District and the City of Tucson, in cooperation with the US Army Corps of Engineers, the park serves as a 100-year flood control system as well as an environmental restoration and recreation project, addressing preservation and restoration of about 20 acres of riparian habitat.

RETURN TO STARTING POINT VIA LOST BARRIO SHOPPING DISTRICT

Exit the path at 13th Street and Fremont Avenue. There is a drinking fountain close to the path near the Fremont maintenance building. Head west on 13th Street, then turn right and head north on Park Avenue to traverse the Lost Barrio shopping district with stores selling Southwestern and Mexican home goods, furniture, antiques, and other wares. Turn left at Broadway and head west to Euclid Avenue. Cross Broadway and Euclid Avenue at the traffic signal and rejoin the Aviation bike/pedestrian path. Walk west on the path to return to your starting point at 4th Avenue and 9th Street.

ALTERNATIVE 2-MILE (3.2-KM) LOOP ROUTE

Start at Santa Rita Avenue and 12th Street—or at the cul-de-sac at the south end of Cherry Avenue, immediately west of Cherry Fields—and follow the path around the detention basins.

MORE DETAILS

Hike: 4 miles (6.4 km) with 2-mile (3.2-km) option; mostly flat; easy.

Amenities: Metered and free street parking; drinking fountain, benches, picnic tables, grills, playground, leashed dogs permitted, family-friendly, fully accessible; no bathrooms.

Special Features: Urban walking, running, or biking tour of public art, green infrastructure, two bridges, local neighborhoods, and interesting shops.

Pro Tips: You can also get to 4th Avenue by bike or scooter via the 4th Avenue bike path or by streetcar. From there, it's a short walk to the trail start.

MISSION GARDEN

GET A TASTE OF TUCSON'S deep cultural and ethnobotanical origins right near the heart of downtown. Mission Garden, located on the site of Tucson's birthplace, encapsulates more than 4000 years of agricultural heritage and continuous cultivation of the land. It's this rich history of farming and traditional foods that prompted UNESCO in 2015 to designate Tucson as a City of Gastronomy "for its culture and development of Sonoran Mexican cuisine."

Fundamentals: Garden walk; 1.5 miles (2.4 km) southwest of downtown Tucson; year-round

▲ The garden hosts many cultural festivals.

◄ Mission Garden, with "A" mountain in the background

TUCSON'S HISTORY AND AGRICULTURAL HERITAGE

Mission Garden is a representative microcosm of the diverse ethnic groups who have inhabited and farmed this region, from the early hunters-gatherers to immigrants from around the world to modern farmers. An outdoor living museum, the garden offers multicultural, hands-on educational programming for all ages. The various gardens and heritage crops grown here are presented as a historical timeline, where the plots are exhibits of both agricultural and cultural significance, showcasing the climate and soil adaptability of local species as well as their central place in the lives of peoples who have lived in the region for millennia.

The garden's location is known to the Tohono O'odham as *S-cuk Son* (pronounced Chuk-Shon), meaning "at the base of the black hill," a reference to Sentinel Peak or "A" Mountain. In recent years, archaeological studies at the site and along the Santa Cruz River revealed that humans have continuously lived on and worked these lands for more than 4000 years. Locals and visitors alike can experience the deep cultural, agricultural, and biodiverse history of Tucson at Mission Garden.

RICH CULTURAL AND BIOLOGICAL DIVERSITY

Starting with the ethnohistory of earliest inhabitants to the subsequent immigrants who now call this place home, connections between people and plants have been crucial to community development and survival. Over time, these human populations have included the first Indigenous farmers, Spanish colonizers, Mexicans, Africans, Chinese, European Americans, and, more recently, several waves of refugees from around the world. Each culture has brought unique perspectives and practices to farming, food production, and water use and conservation. The result is a biologically rich oasis within the Sonoran Desert, where human occupation has helped shape the diversity of animal and plant species.

During your visit, note various places to take shelter from the desert sun and the acequia (irrigation canal) that traverses the garden; both features cater to the needs of visiting humans and resident species. Other highlights include a medicinal garden, agave-roasting pit, granary, millstone, chicken coop, and a replica

◂ San Ysidro Festival at Mission Garden

◂ The garden has a few shady ramadas.

of an early pit house (a shelter from extreme weather). Take some time to explore the Bookworm Path, with 20 activity hubs ideal for families and youngsters, all presented in a range of languages, including English, Spanish, Chinese, and braille.

TASTING HISTORY: GROWING AND PRESERVING LOCAL HERITAGE CROPS

Two years after its first trees were planted back in 2012, Mission Garden harvested its first successful crops at the foot of Sentinel Peak. First came the grapes, then the pomegranates, quinces, and figs. Over the years, the diversity and quantity of traditional and native crops have increased dramatically, honoring the connection to the ancestral farmers who originally domesticated and grew these fruits, vegetables, herbs, and grains.

Today, at any time of the year, there's always something fresh to sample from the garden's wild bean trees, cacti, herbs, and crop wild relatives as well as heirloom varieties that crossed oceans more than 400 years ago. One of the garden's aims is to ensure that visitors get to experience the region's history by tasting at least one of the

▾ There are several pathways through the garden.

seasonal crops. Mission Garden's historic location and its ongoing preservation, representation, and interpretation of Tucson's great agricultural and cultural diversity all contributed to the city's designation as the first UNESCO City of Gastronomy in the United States.

GARDENS AS WILDLIFE HABITAT

With its abundant vegetation (consisting of a dense tree canopy, wide array of flowering plants, and more), rich floodplain soil, and organic farming practices, Mission Garden offers a healthy habitat for a wide diversity of insects, birds, reptiles, and mammals. You might cross paths with animals mid- or post-meal:

- A greater roadrunner clutching a lizard in its beak
- A pair of towhees or a curve-billed thrasher turning the soil under a quince tree
- Ground squirrels scuttling into their burrows, half-eaten barrel cactus fruits strewn about
- Hawks stalking doves and cottontails
- A covey of quails hopping up and running along the adobe wall that surrounds the garden

You can also observe the prey-and-predator game of the insect world. When aphids appear on tender plant tips, ladybugs (lady beetles) will not be far behind, showing up to feed on the abundance. Butterflies, bees, wasps, and beetles arrive to pollinate the young

Greater roadrunner with a lizard snack

flowering crops while fig beetles and leaf-footed bugs proliferate and nibble on ripened fruits. After dark, when gardeners and visitors are gone, the night shift begins; bats, moths, owls, bobcats, and raccoons come out for nocturnal nourishment, leaving only footprints and other subtle signs that they, too, are part of the garden ecosystem even if they don't observe visiting hours.

MORE DETAILS

Directions: Drive west on West Congress Street to South Grande Avenue and turn left. It's just a short distance to Mission Garden.

Amenities: Parking; restrooms; water available; shaded areas; leashed dogs permitted; family-friendly.

Accessibility: Two accessible parking spaces; wheelchair-accessible restrooms at the north end of the garden; compacted pathways with level ADA-compatible surfaces (occasional dips); service animals welcome.

Pro Tips: Call or check the garden's website for upcoming events and tours that cover topics such as archaeology, bird-watching, medicinal herbs, and traditional O'odham agriculture; there are also in-person classes as well as recorded workshops available to stream.

Info:

Mission Garden
946 West Mission Lane
Tucson, AZ 85745
520-955-5200

TUMAMOC HILL

ON THE WEST SIDE of Tucson, located on Sobaipuri and Tohono O'odham ancestral lands, sits Tumamoc Hill, home to the University of Arizona's Desert Laboratory, countless wild species, and culturally significant Indigenous sites. An 860-acre ecological preserve, Tumamoc was deemed a US National Historic Landmark in 1975, noted on a plaque halfway up. The botanical laboratory, active since 1903, contains the world's oldest and still-used permanent plant quadrats (or plots) and leads multidisciplinary projects investigating the future of life in the desert. Even with this notable activity and landmark status, perhaps the biggest draw for the 1000+ people who visit Tumamoc Hill daily is simply the experience of climbing it—with friends or solo, for exercise or contemplation, amidst flora, fauna, and friendly trail mates.

Fundamentals: Hike; 2.1 miles (3.4 km) northwest of downtown Tucson; moderate to challenging

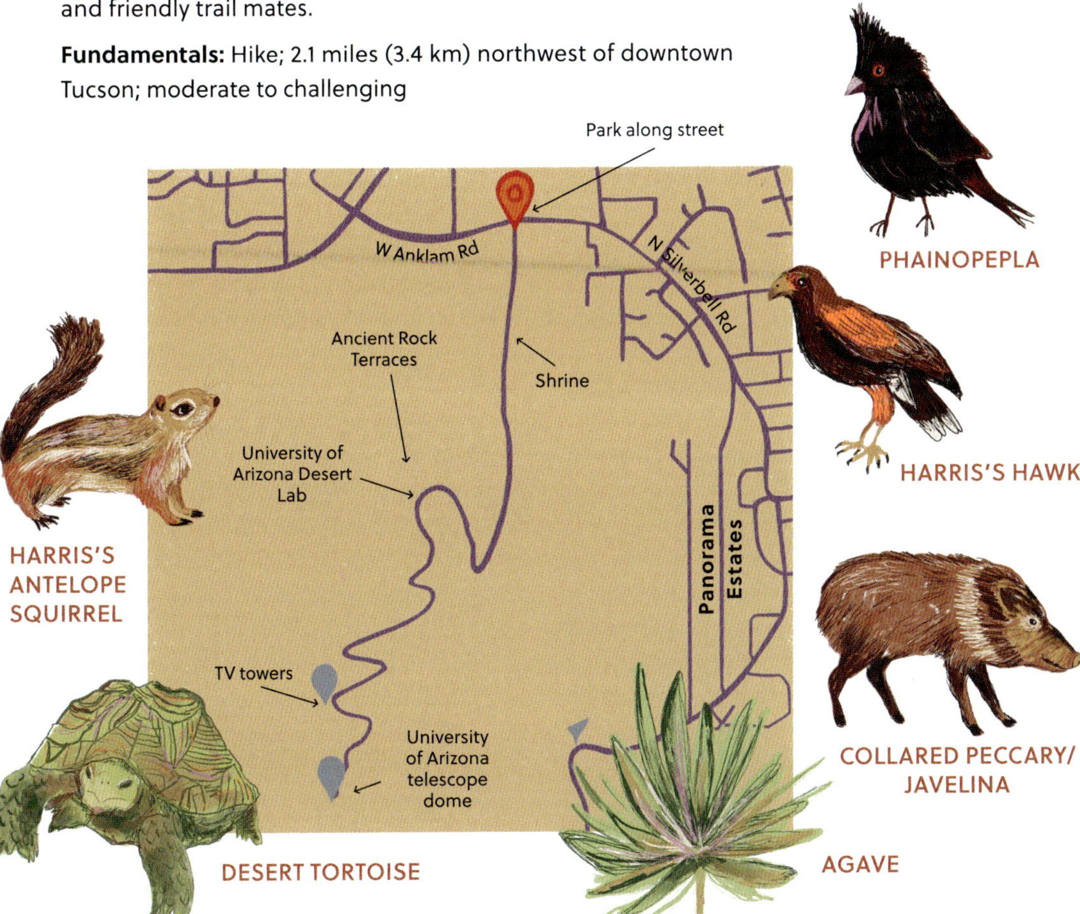

▲ Starting the walk up Tumamoc Hill

◄ The road is very popular with walkers.

SWEAT AND SOCIAL TIME

If you like to rise with the sun, get some exercise, and grab a breakfast burrito before diving into the rest of your day, this is the hike for you. Tumamoc Hill opens at 4 a.m. daily and closes at 10 p.m. Over the years, this healthy hiking/workout option near the heart of Tucson has earned cult-like popularity, with T-shirts, hashtags, and selfies declaring "for the burn, for the view."

Upon arrival, a line of cars—at any time of day—means you've reached the right place. The paved route up the hill begins with a relatively gentle slope with just enough oomph to help you warm up. (It gets steeper later.) If the hilltop is your goal, you're aiming for the metal towers overhead. Double-check the water supply, start your fitness app, and go!

The first half of the hike covers two long segments with benches to rest along the way. At the bend, you'll see Tucson in the distance, a saguaro cactus forest nearby, and likely some animal tracks underfoot. Keep going to the halfway point where there's an agave heritage garden, honoring a plant central to Indigenous cultures for millennia. Just past the garden, you'll find the Desert Lab, greenhouse, and parking lot.

If you choose to press on, go through the next metal gate and mentally prep for "the burn." Six bends lay ahead, and the switchbacks get increasingly steep. (The second is the worst—the climb is easier after that.)

At the summit, celebrate your achievement, take some time to rest, and enjoy the panoramic views—"A" Mountain, the Santa Cruz

◂ There are a few places to sit, rest, and take in the view along the way.

◂ Rainbow from Tumamoc Hill

River, Interstate 10, Mercado San Agustín, downtown Tucson, the University of Arizona, and beyond. Imagine the landscape without the human-made structures and you'll have a sense of the expansive vistas that greeted the original inhabitants over the centuries.

FLYBYS AND ANIMALS IN DISGUISE

Tumamoc hosts a wide range of plant and animal species. Lining the path, interpretive signage (in English and Spanish) encourages you to take notice of the natural world of the hill. Read about phainopeplas (they look like black cardinals!), Harris's antelope squirrels, coyotes, and more. The 13 signs are positioned at suitable resting spots, ensuring that you can simultaneously learn about, and momentarily feel like, a desert tortoise. Download the Tumamoc Tour app for audio edification along the route.

Flanked by brittlebush, palo verdes, white thorn acacia, and creosote, the path is a sensory immersion. The scent of the desert is unmistakable, particularly on misty mornings or during monsoons when the petrichor (that pleasant post-rain smell) is at its most potent.

As you get into the rhythm of your hike, note the sounds around you. Gambel's quail, Gila woodpeckers, creosote bush katydids, and American crows all contribute to the desert's soundscape.

Close inspection of the path and surrounding plants reveals a vast array of invertebrates and reptiles—look for walking sticks, velvet ants, and pollinators—which varies with the season and temperature. Sightings of larger animals, such as javelinas, mule deer, and soaring raptors, are common. In the evening, keep an eye out for black-tailed rattlesnakes, scorpions, camel crickets, and pocket mice.

SAVING THE SAGUAROS

The saguaro—that most iconic of cacti (and the tallest)—is native to the Sonoran Desert while buffelgrass is not. Considered an invasive species in the Sonoran Desert, buffelgrass has overtaken many areas in and around Tucson, outcompeting native plants. The species creates a carpet between saguaro stands (look for dense patches of brown or green knee-high grasses on Tumamoc and nearby "A" Mountain/Sentinel Peak).

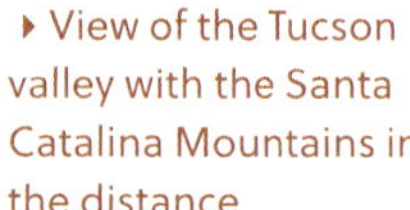

▸ View of the Tucson valley with the Santa Catalina Mountains in the distance

◂ Many of the slopes of Tumamoc Hill and neighboring "A" Mountain are infested with invasive grasses, endangering the saguaros.

A major concern is that, if lightning were to strike one of these patches, buffelgrass would fuel the fire. The after-effects of a July Fourth fire in 2017, caused by fireworks, are still visible on nearby Sentinel Peak. In response to the danger, the Arizona-Sonora Desert Museum, the University of Arizona, and the Desert Laboratory have collaborated to study the impacts of fire on the Sonoran Desert and on saguaros. Visit desertmuseum.org to learn more about buffelgrass and support efforts to eradicate it by removing it from your yard or participating in a community pull.

MORE DETAILS

Directions: Head west on West Congress Street, past the freeway, and make a slight right onto North Silverbell Road; a left onto West Anklam Road; and a left onto Tumamoc Hill Road. Park and walk to the trailhead at the base of the hill.

Hike: 3 miles (4.8 km) round-trip to/from summit; 700-foot (213-m) elevation gain to the summit; moderate (up to the halfway mark) to challenging (from the halfway mark to the summit).

Amenities: Free street parking; paved trail; two portable toilets, a water refill station, and benches halfway up; benches at the summit; dogs are not permitted.

Special Features: Agave heritage garden; Desert Laboratory and greenhouses; lab-sponsored public lecture series.

Pro Tips: At any time of day or evening, it's advisable to allow time to park—the street parking is often full and parking in the lots of nearby businesses is frowned upon. On the other hand, stopping for a post-hike refreshment or meal is a great way to support these establishments. Be aware that this steep route can be particularly difficult on the descent—zigzag on the way down to reduce stress on your hips, knees, and feet.

Info:

Tumamoc Hill
Tumamoc Hill Road
Tucson, AZ 85745

University of Arizona Desert Laboratory on Tumamoc Hill
1675 West Anklam Road
Tucson, AZ 85745
520-621-6945

UNIVERSITY OF ARIZONA CAMPUS ARBORETUM

THE UNIVERSITY OF ARIZONA campus is also an arboretum—a living laboratory of hundreds of native and desert-adapted trees and plants—and strolling the grounds is not only a tour of botanical specimens from around the world, it's also a walk through more than a century of research and experimentation dating back to the university's founding in 1885 when botany, agriculture, and land stewardship were major areas of study (as they continue to be). One of the oldest, largest, and most diverse gardens in Tucson, the arboretum itself was established in 2002 to preserve and enhance the historic tree collections on the 392-acre campus and to encourage sustainable horticulture in the Sonoran Desert.

Fundamentals: Urban hike; 1.8 miles (2.9 km) northeast of downtown Tucson; year-round

FIG

UNIVERSITY OF ARIZONA CAMPUS EDIBLE PLANTS (1-15)

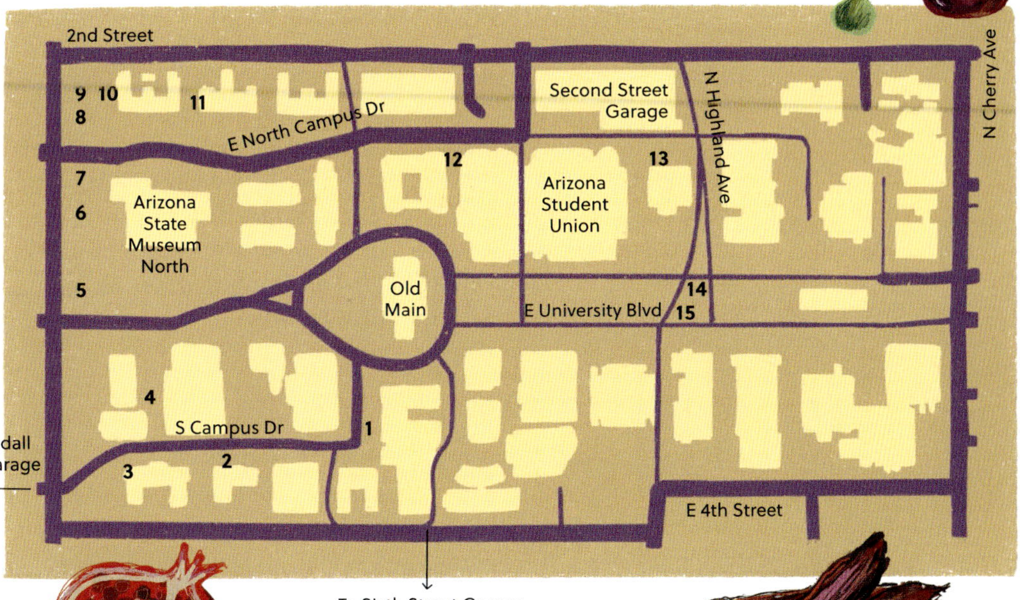

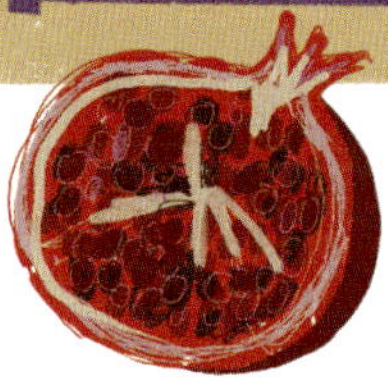

POMEGRANATE

CAROB POD

▸ Aerial view of the University of Arizona campus

OUTDOOR CLASSROOM

Since 1960, the Tucson population has doubled and doubled again, fueling concern about water availability and conservation in a desert city. In response, the University of Arizona campus gardens began to change—drip irrigation gradually replaced flood irrigation; manicured lawns were removed to cultivate native plants; and two decades ago, the arboretum was founded as a research and educational collection designed around conservation and sustainability issues.

The arboretum provides an outdoor classroom for courses in botany, ecology, horticulture, landscape architecture, and anthropology. It also provides data and information to other institutions and the public at large. Check out the arboretum's excellent public tours—offered both virtually and in person—about its history, desert landscaping, native plants, trees of the world, and medicinal plants. Because so many of the plants on campus have been central to the diets and nourishment of the region's animals and people over the centuries, we include a version of the Edible Landscapes tour to pique your curiosity and possibly your appetite.

EDIBLE LANDSCAPES TOUR

This two-hour loop—one of more than a half-dozen offered by the arboretum and which can also be self-guided—is perfect for locavores (people who prefer locally-grown food) and will introduce you to relevant trees and plants as well as their edible products. More information about all these plants can be found on the Arboretum website (arboretum.arizona.edu/tours/edible-landscapes-tour).

1. ARGENTINE MESQUITE (SOUTH AMERICA)

Location: Forbes Building

Highly nutritious, tasty, and sweet, mesquite pods have long been a staple food for local Indigenous people, who used them to make fermented beverages and milled them into flour for atole (porridge) and baking.

2. FIG (MEDITERRANEAN)

Location: Saguaro Hall

Introduced by Jesuit missionaries in the late 1600s and popular ever since, figs, especially the Black Mission variety, are well-adapted to the Tucson environment.

3. TRUE DATE PALM (MIDDLE EAST)

Location: Cochise Hall

Another remnant of the Spanish colonial period, date palms are almost always grown as ornamental plants; although they're well suited to the desert climate, considerable knowledge and labor are required to cultivate them for food production.

4. POMEGRANATE (IRAN TO NORTHERN INDIA)

Location: Women's Plaza

Since Spanish colonial times, Tucson has been home to many pomegranate varieties; today, it's considered a quintessential backyard and public garden tree.

▾ Date palm

▸ Olive and palm trees line some of the paths on the older parts of campus.

5. EUROPEAN OLIVE (MEDITERRANEAN)

Location: Olive Walk

Today a Pima County ordinance prohibits the cultivation of olive trees due to severe pollen allergies, but these specific trees were planted in the 1890s to assess their potential as a commercial crop for the region.

6. WEEPING MULBERRY (EAST ASIA)

Location: Green Belt

Although there are many varieties of mulberries that produce tasty fruit, this species is primarily grown as an ornamental plant.

7. CHINESE JUJUBE (CHINA)

Location: Green Belt

Drought-tolerant and sometimes invasive, the jujube (also called Chinese date) is a popular backyard tree in Mexican and Chinese American homes, producing fruits that taste like apples when fresh and like dates when dried.

8. ITALIAN STONE PINE (MEDITERRANEAN)

Location: Green Belt

High in protein and fiber, pine nuts have a delicate flavor and buttery texture suitable for pesto and gluten-free foods.

9. CAROB (MEDITERRANEAN)

Location: Green Belt

The pods of this stately evergreen leguminous tree can be used as a sweetener or low-calorie chocolate substitute.

Mulberries

Mesquite beans (seed pods) ripening

10. HACKBERRY (US MOUNTAIN SOUTHWEST)

Location: Gila Hall

Native to riparian habitats and a common landscaping choice for its intricate branches and hardiness, this tree is an important food source for wildlife, especially birds, and people also enjoy its miniature red berries.

11. SOUR ORANGE (EAST ASIA)

Location: Gila/Maricopa Hall Alley

Because this robust edible citrus has been a favorite landscape plant for generations, many people mistakenly refer to it as an ornamental, but it's a favorite for marmalade and widely preferred over lemons in Middle Eastern cooking.

12. TEXAS HONEY MESQUITE (TEXAS/NORTHEAST MEXICO)

Location: Student Union Alley

The Texas honey mesquite lives up to its name—its pods are high in sugar and protein—and because it produces fruit even in drought, Indigenous people and wildlife alike have relied on it as a food source.

13. CENTURY PLANT/AGAVE (MEXICO/US DESERT SOUTHWEST)

Location: Administration building

This impressive succulent, known as *el árbol de las maravillas* (the tree of marvels), holds a special place among Tucson's xeriscape plants (those adapted to arid climates) due to its multiple uses—as a food, fiber source, building material, and mezcal distillate.

14. SAGUARO (SONORAN DESERT)

Location: Krutch Garden

An icon of the Sonoran Desert and the epitome of extreme drought and heat adaptation, this majestic columnar cactus is a keystone species (one that defines an ecosystem), blooming at the height of the dry season and producing brightly colored fruit that nourish a wide range of desert creatures, including humans.

15. PRICKLY PEAR (WESTERN HEMISPHERE)

Location: Krutch Garden

The pads (*nopales* in Spanish) and juicy fruit of this abundant cactus are staple foods for desert-dwellers, from insects and birds to reptiles and rodents to mammals, including humans.

MORE DETAILS

Directions: The University of Arizona Campus Arboretum is just northeast of downtown Tucson and can be accessed by car, public bus, bicycle, wheelchair, or on foot. The parking garages closest to this tour are the Sixth Street Garage (1201 E. 6th Street) and Tyndall Garage (880 E. 4th Street).

Amenities: Garage, lot, and street parking; food concessions, shops, and restrooms in the Student Union; free Wi-Fi; campus grounds open 24/7 year-round.

Accessibility: The university ensures disability access to the campus; for more information, contact the Disability Resource Center at 520-621-3268.

Pro Tips: Stop by the Arboretum office in Herring Hall, directly south of Old Main (the university's inaugural building) to learn more about the plants on campus and pick up informational materials.

Info:

University of Arizona Campus Arboretum
Educational Research Center
1140 E. South Campus Drive
Tucson, AZ 85719
520-621-7074

SWEETWATER WETLANDS PARK

LOCATED BETWEEN THE SANTA Cruz River and Interstate 10, Sweetwater Wetlands is an easily reachable and extraordinarily biodiverse hot spot in Tucson for desert exploring and bird-watching. The Tucson Audubon Society has recorded more than 300 bird species. Every time you visit, you'll see something new and incredible.

Fundamentals: Hike; 5.7 miles (9.2 km) northwest of downtown Tucson; spring/fall/winter

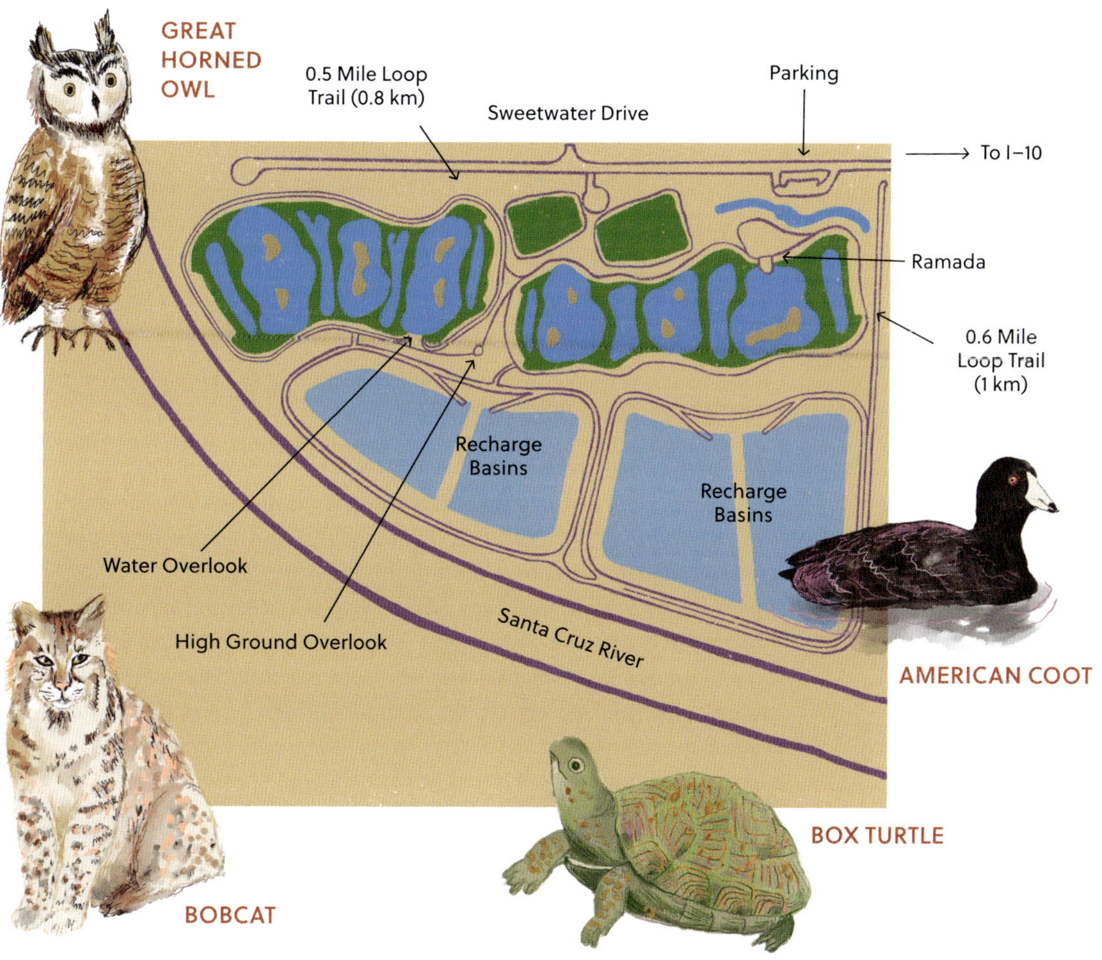

▸ Sweetwater wetlands is an oasis in the desert.

▸ Cottonwood and palo verde trees frame the entrance to Sweetwater Wetlands.

THIRST IMPRESSIONS

The wetlands are, well, wet and function as a natural water treatment facility, receiving wastewater and filtering it through basins for later reuse in city parks, schools, and golf courses. From a naturalist's perspective, they're a dream destination, with ample opportunities for close encounters with resident urban wildlife and migratory species.

Some of the mammals that you're likely to see, depending on season and time of day, include javelinas, raccoons, round-tailed ground squirrels, coyotes, and cotton rats. The bobcats are a particular draw. Visitors photographed one beloved wildcat for more than seven years, each year zooming in for close-ups of her kitty offspring.

The wetlands are rich in herpetofauna (reptiles and amphibians) as well. Resident aquatic species—bullfrogs, red-eared sliders, and, darting in the water, mosquitofish (all non-native)—are ever-present, with a range of other native species passing through:

Clockwise from upperleft:
Bobcat checking the map?

Red-eared sliders are not native to the region. They probably got here when pet turtles were released.

American bullfrogs are not native to the region and have become invasive, devastating native aquatic species.

Clark's spiny lizard

American coot

Western diamondback rattlesnakes, gopher snakes, king snakes, spiny lizards, tree lizards, and Sonoran Desert toads. Less frequently, you may find red-spotted toads, softshell turtles, and box turtles.

Then there are the birds. Grackles and red-shouldered blackbirds create a cacophony that may at times overwhelm the experience. But an attentive birder can learn to discern the various calls and tune in to the tweeting melodies of the song sparrows; staccato cheeps of the verdins; and squawks and peeps of the Gila and ladder-backed woodpeckers, respectively. Splashing bullfrogs join the boisterous fray along with honking American coots and sleepy buzzing cicadas.

PHOTOGRAPHER'S DELIGHT

If you'd like to try your hand at wildlife photography, the wetlands offer subjects in every direction. Macro photographers will delight in the abundance of insects—praying mantises, fig beetles, giant mesquite bugs, and dragonflies mating in "wheel" position. Birders with telephoto lenses can capture images of a distant American bittern or the details of a green heron's iridescent feathers. You'll also find raptors in flight, yellow-headed blackbird murmurations, and the occasional bobcat, poised as if posing.

HOW I FELL IN LOVE WITH BIRD-WATCHING

Not many love stories start with an owl, but my long-term relationship with Sweetwater Wetlands does.

In the birding world, a "spark bird" is that first feathered creature that transforms a hiker or nature lover into a birder, someone consistently on the lookout for new species (and old friends) and regularly recording their sightings. I met mine on my very first trip to the wetlands.

Looking up, I came face-to-face with a great horned owl perched in a cottonwood tree, an encounter that forever changed my naturalist trajectory. Unseen by anyone else and minding its business, this majestic bird of prey rested within sight of a parking lot, right off a major interstate.

I'll always be grateful to that owl—it's the spark bird that's turned me into a wetlands "frequent flyer," returning to that beautiful and inspiring spot whenever I can.

—Catherine Bartlett

◂ Great horned owl

REGULARS AND RARITIES

If you're a local or repeat visitor to Southern Arizona, the best way to experience the wetlands is frequently. Explore the park at different times of day and various days of the week to truly see all the magic on display. You'll get to know the regulars by sight and sound and become familiar with the seasonal changes (phenology) of vegetation and wildlife. There's a duck season, warbler season, migratory season, and reptilian season. Perhaps you'll discover your own spark bird, and your naturalist hobby will take flight.

GOTTA LET IT BURN

A controlled burn occurs at the wetlands annually to remove the dead or overgrown bulrush and cattail and is utilized as a training opportunity for the Tucson Fire Department. Check the City of Tucson's website for dates. Please take note that the biodiversity will be lower for a month or two following a controlled burn as the water and wildlife seep back in.

MORE DETAILS

Directions: From Interstate 10W, get off at Exit 254/Prince Road. Turn left onto West Prince Road; right onto North Business Center Drive; right onto North Commerce Drive; left onto North Benan Venture Drive; and left onto West Sweetwater Drive. The park entrance is on your left.

Hike: 2.5 miles (4 km) of trails, including 1.1-mile (1.8-km) loop; 9-foot (2.7-m) elevation gain; easy.

Amenities: Free street parking and extra parking lot; covered ramada for shade; benches; 1000 feet (305 m) of paved trail; drinking fountain with water bottle refill and restrooms at park entrance; ADA accessible; family-friendly. Please note that dogs, horses, bikes, and fishing are prohibited.

Pro Tips: If you'd like to expand your outing, the wetlands are in striking distance of Saguaro National Park West, Gates Pass, and the Arizona-Sonora Desert Museum.

Info:

Sweetwater Wetlands Park
2511 West Sweetwater Drive
Tucson, AZ 85745
520-791-4331

HIDDEN CANYON AND BOWEN TRAIL LOOP

LIKE MANY TRAILS IN the Tucson Mountain range, the Hidden Canyon and Bowen Trail Loop is scenic and awe-inspiring, abundant with vegetation and wildlife. What sets it apart is its proximity to downtown—a short ride to the trailhead delivers you right to the tranquility, rich biodiversity, and immersive experience of the Sonoran Desert.

Fundamentals: Hike; 5.9 miles (9.5 km) west of downtown Tucson; spring/fall/winter

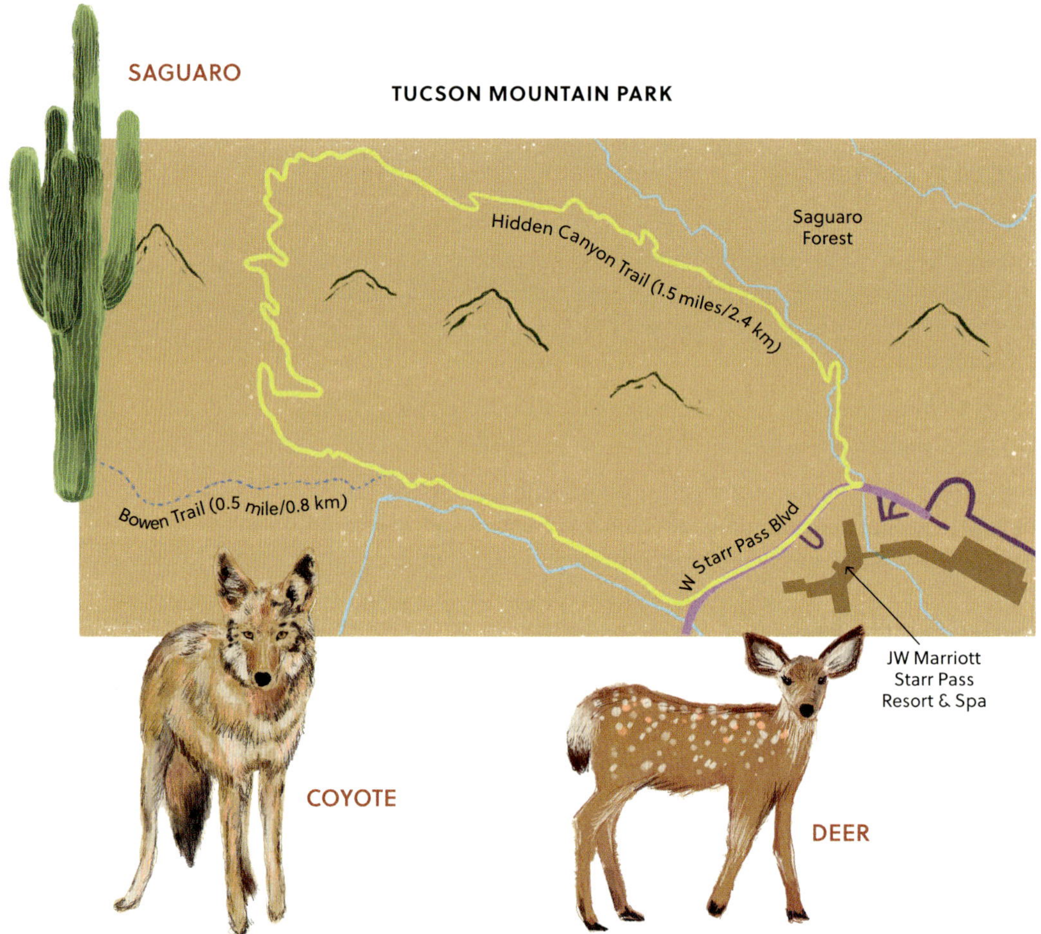

ADVENTURE 6

A HIDDEN TRAIL

Just 20 minutes from downtown, tucked behind the JW Marriott Resort at Starr Pass, the Lorraine Lee Hidden Canyon Trail (named for a local community activist) and Bowen Trail (so called for the family who established a nearby homestead in the 1930s) intersect and circle along the base of the Tucson Mountains. (You can reach the Bowen Stone House ruins via the intersecting Yetman Trail.)

This 2-mile (3.2-km) loop traverses the Arizona Uplands region of the Sonoran Desert, showcasing gorgeous mountain views and providing opportunities for close encounters with local birds, mammals, and reptiles. Resident species are most active in the morning and evening, and you may well glimpse the occasional deer, coyote, or bobcat during those hours. Because this is rattlesnake habitat, stay alert and steer clear—remember they are as eager to avoid us as we are to avoid them, and we are much bigger than they are.

Stroll among the stately saguaros, and admire lush patches of vivid-white purple-flecked mariposa lilies in bloom after the fall and winter rains. Stop at the saddle to take in the expansive views before descending the trail. Be sure to allow time to enjoy the trail's solitude and peacefulness; despite the nearby hotel, foot traffic is minimal—don't be surprised to find yourself alone for most of the hike.

View from Hidden Canyon trail

Magnificent older saguaros

HIDDEN BEAUTY

Each season offers a unique sensory experience that makes a lasting impression. In winter and early spring, temperatures are cool to moderate throughout the day. Winter rains provide moisture to every living organism along the trail and bring to life winter-adapted species of plants and plant-like organisms, such as lichens and living soil crusts dominated by cyanobacteria (blue-green algae) as well as mosses, microfungi, and bacteria. Depending on rainfall, springtime can usher in a wide array of desert wildflowers, making these areas a prime destination for wildflower enthusiasts from around the world.

Summer and fall offer a completely different experience, one that highlights the resilience of the region's plants and animals. Due to the near-zero relative humidity and monthslong lack of rain, every plant along the trail is adapted to these dry conditions, not only surviving but often thriving. Summer monsoon storms, typically starting in early July, are a game changer. The desert bursts into new life, and the clouds, skies, and smells of the desert after a rain are unforgettable.

UNHIDDEN FLORA

The 20,000-acre Tucson Mountain Park, on traditional Tohono O'odham lands, is home to almost 62 miles (100 km) of trails and, like the others, the Hidden Canyon and Bowen Trail Loop meanders through a magnificent saguaro cactus forest rivaling those in nearby Saguaro National Park. These spectacular cacti, considered ancestors and relations by the O'odham, will be your companions along the route along with other fascinating cacti—barrel cacti, prickly pear, and chollas, including the jumping cholla with segments that detach upon the slightest contact. At various times during spring and early summer, all burst forth with vibrant blossoms in shades of bright red, yellow, orange, magenta, and white, followed by fruits ideally timed to the needs of hungry wildlife.

Interspersed with the cacti, a great diversity of leguminous (bean-producing) trees and shrubs support the rest of the desert ecosystem. Some trees resemble bushes rather than typical towering species in other parts of the United States, though acacias, palo verde, and mesquite may grow as tall as 20–50 feet (6–15 m). These leguminous trees function as "nurse plants" to young, vulnerable cacti, especially slow-growing saguaro, and protect the cacti under their shady foliage. Scanning through the canopy levels, you'll discover a universe of other prickly plants, shrubs, and bushes peppering the entire hillside—spindly olive-colored ocotillo, lime-green jojobas with their leathery leaves—creating the most amazingly verdant collage you've ever seen.

REVEALED SCENERY

Jumping cholla

Look for American kestrels perching high on saguaros.

On the drive to the trailhead, over the Tucson Mountain foothills, majestic vistas will welcome you. This Sonoran Desert scenery is the more panoramic version of what awaits you on the trail, where you'll become part of the landscape and can examine it from within.

An overlook near the high point of the trail reveals saguaro-spiked ridges and faraway hills. Rounding back to the trailhead and at higher elevations along the route, you'll also see occasional houses and parts of downtown, a reminder of how extraordinary this hidden gem is, right on the edge of a bustling urban area.

MORE DETAILS

Directions: Access the trails via the service drive of the Starr Pass Resort (3800 W. Starr Pass Boulevard). Follow the winding drive 0.4 mile (0.6 km) to the well-marked Hidden Canyon Trailhead on the right, across the street from the resort's main entrance. After 1.5 miles (2.4 km), the trail joins the Bowen Trail, which completes the loop back to the resort. However, be aware that the trail intersection is unmarked.

Hike: 2 miles (3.2 km) round-trip; 357 feet (109 m) elevation gain; easy to moderate.

Amenities: Free street parking; family-friendly.

Pro Tips: Wear proper footwear, sunscreen, and a hat. Always bring water.

SO CLOSE, WITH A FARAWAY FEEL

10–20 MILES (16–32 KM) FROM DOWNTOWN TUCSON

SABINO CANYON RECREATION AREA

SOUTHERN ARIZONA OFFERS DOZENS of gorgeous locales, and one of the most beautiful and accessible is Sabino Canyon in the Santa Catalinas. Cooler, scenic, and nearby, it encapsulates why so many people love Tucson. Of course, this means it's extremely popular—people flock to this destination. For peace and solitude, choose one of the less popular trails from a network of more than 30 miles (48 km).

Fundamentals: Half-day trip; 15 miles (24 km) northeast of downtown Tucson; year-round

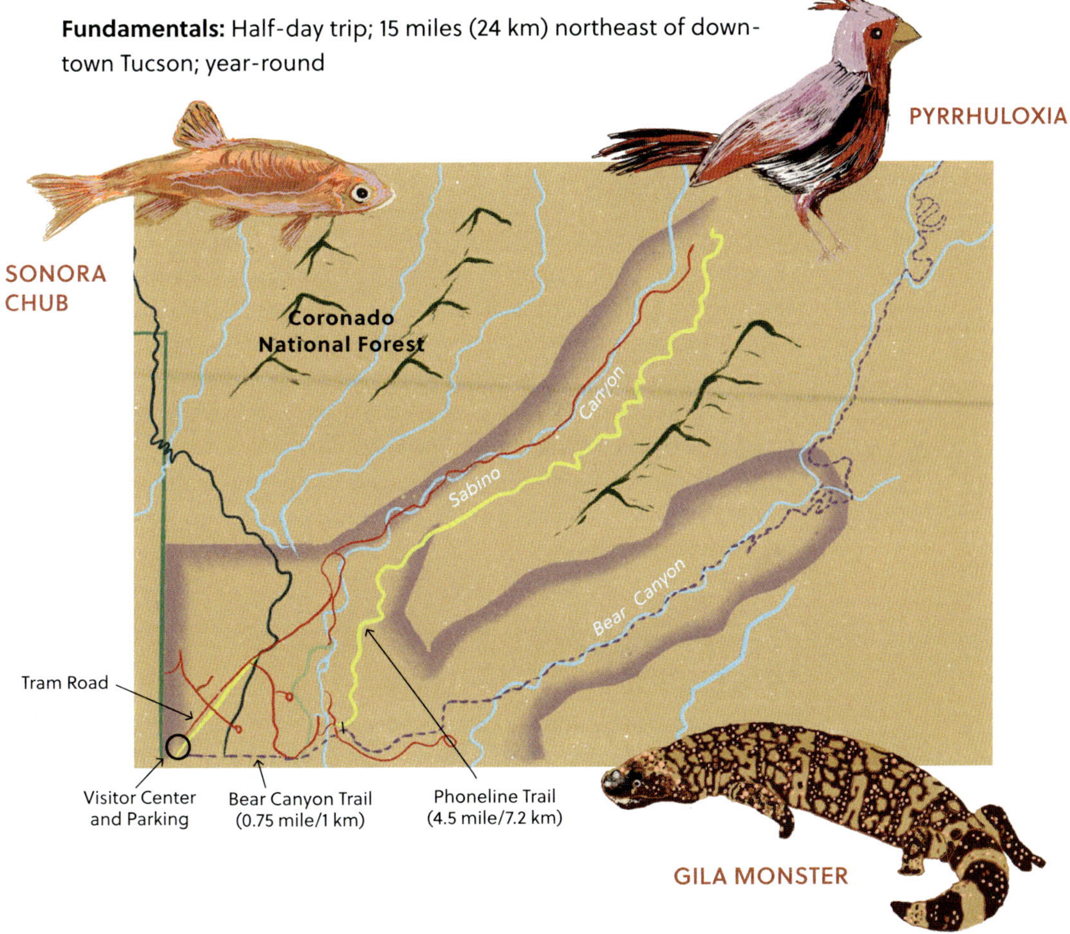

◂ Large flat rocks in the creek offer many places to rest or have a picnic.

▲ Seven Falls Trail is a popular 8-mile (13-km) out-and-back hike with this wonderful reward at the end.

◄ The main path up the canyon is paved. A hop-on, hop-off shuttle bus is available for a fee as well.

IT'S ALL ABOUT THE VIEW—AND THE WATER

Simply put, Sabino Canyon is visually stunning. In the canyon, regardless of where your eyes wander, you'll encounter iconic, awe-inspiring views—truly the stuff of Southwestern landscape art and postcards. The Santa Catalina Mountains rise to the north, east, and west, their hillsides covered in palo verde trees, majestic saguaros, and purplish cholla, barrel, and other cacti. Steep water-carved granite cliffs and beautiful riparian vegetation flank Sabino Creek, portions of which are perennial, a rare, life-sustaining gift to desert plants, animals, and people. During the rainy season, the creek can become a raging river!

A PLETHORA OF PLANTS AND WILDLIFE

Sabino Canyon is a prime location to see many of the plants and animals of the Sonoran Desert. With more than 500 types of plants (including statuesque trees, such as sycamore, cottonwood, hackberry, four types of willows, ash, black walnut, rosewood, alder, cypress, juniper, and several types of oaks; 15 types of cacti; dozens of shrub species; nearly 70 varieties of grass; and a profusion of seasonal wildflowers), the canyon is a botanical paradise. In addition, wildlife is both abundant and diverse. Many mammals—among them mountain lions, bobcats, deer, skunks, raccoons, ringtails, coatis, rabbits, and rodents—call Sabino Canyon home.

Like all riparian areas, it's a birder's paradise, with myriad species frequenting the canyon, including year-round residents and seasonal species, some arriving in winter (the real "snowbirds"), such as hermit thrushes, green-tailed towhees, and Lawrence's goldfinches. Summer visitors include elf owls, northern beardless tyrannulets, Bell's vireos, hooded orioles, Lucy's warblers, and broad-billed hummingbirds. As for year-round residents, they abound—greater roadrunners, western screech owls, northern cardinals, pyrrhuloxias, and Abert's towhees as well as smaller sparrows.

Herpers will be happy here, too; reptiles and amphibians are abundant, both commonly seen species (side-blotched and spiny lizards, gopher snakes, western diamondback rattlesnakes) and rarer ones (Gila monsters, greater earless lizards, Sonoran mud turtles, black-necked garter snakes). You may even encounter some semiaquatic amphibians near the water's edge, such as canyon tree frogs, which look just like the granite boulders they cling to. Sabino Creek is also home to Sonora chub, a native desert fish.

A DEEPER DIVE

Part of Coronado National Forest, Sabino Canyon offers a number of ways to learn more about the canyon's natural and cultural history. Take a self-guided tour of the visitor center's hands-on exhibits, videos, and displays. Join one of the volunteer naturalists for an interpretive talk, walk, hike, or demo. Finally, ride the electric shuttle for a narrated, educational tour in English or Spanish (earbuds provided to eliminate noise for non-shuttle visitors); it takes about 45 minutes with nine stops, allowing you to disembark for on-foot exploration and get back on later.

CHOOSE YOUR TRAIL

Trails range from easy, wide-open, and paved to challenging, steep, and rocky. A popular, moderately challenging, option, considered by many to be the gateway to Sabino Canyon, is the Phoneline Trail. A 9.4-mile (15-km) round trip with an elevation gain of 1400 feet (427 m), it features uphill sections, a fair amount of moderately rocky segments, and some smoother stretches. This trail follows the shuttle road, easy to access from several points should you wish to shorten your hike. It also connects to other trails, if you'd like a longer hike.

▲ Water levels in the creek vary throughout the year; they are highest in spring and during the monsoon season.

Though there's signage to direct you, it can be confusing. To get to the Phoneline Trail, follow the Bear Canyon Trail slightly downhill, to the east from the visitor center. About 0.75 mile (1 km) down, you cross Sabino Creek and see a trail in front of you—this is the beginning of the Phoneline Trail. Here the climbing starts as you begin your ascent, picking your way through the rocky terrain. Once on the trail, you can choose to pick up other trails, such as Blackett's Ridge, Phoneline Link, or Historic Sabino Trails.

MORE DETAILS

Directions: Drive west on Broadway or Speedway, then north on Wilmot Road, which turns into North/East Tanque Verde Road. Turn left onto North Sabino Canyon Road, which takes you to the recreation area.

Hikes: 30 miles (48 km) of trails; 1400 feet (427 m) elevation gain for Phoneline Trail; easy to challenging.

Amenities: Dedicated parking lot; accessible visitor center; restrooms; picnic tables; water; drinks and snacks; gift shop; electric shuttle; accessible, paved paths; nearby campgrounds; service animals permitted but no pets; family-friendly.

Pro Tips: Like most desert hikes, October through May are best. If you visit from July through September, go early in the morning, and pay close attention to the weather. If storms are forecast, avoid the canyon due to the danger of flash floods, which make the creek impassable, and lightning strikes.

A Cautionary Note: Mountain lions are common in Southern Arizona, but rarely seen due to their secretive nature and nocturnal hunting routines. Though you can never count on seeing one, Sabino Canyon is notable for its number of sightings. This majestic animal, weighing 100–200 pounds (45–90 kg), is truly impressive, and if you see one, you will never forget it. Remember, mountain lions are not aggressive, and negative interactions with them are extremely rare. However, due to sharing their habitat with people, some resident mountain lions lose their fear of humans. Though we are not on their menu as prey, they are apex predators and can cause grave bodily injury, so pay attention to where you are walking and, if you encounter one, *never* approach the animal.

Info:

Sabino Canyon Recreation Area
5700 North Sabino Canyon Road
Tucson, AZ 85750
520-749-8700

Day-use fee and weekly pass for Sabino Canyon; annual pass available, which also permits entry to Mount Lemmon and Madera Canyon.

SAGUARO NATIONAL PARK EAST

HIGHLIGHTED IN A HANDFUL of nature documentaries, westerns, and television programs—*America's National Parks*, *Tombstone*, and *Reading Rainbow*, to name a few—the landscape of Saguaro National Park is iconic largely due to those familiar desert denizens, the saguaros. Split into two districts—east and west—Tucson lies in the valley between and is perfectly located for outings in either direction. Whether you're in the mood for a scenic drive, easy hike, intense workout, cycling adventure, or overnight backpacking trip, this eastern portion of the park at the foot of the Rincon Mountains is full of options. You can check out seasonal waterfalls, abandoned dams, ridgeline trails, and other remarkable sights. This adventure focuses on Cactus Forest Scenic Loop Drive, which circles through the park, and a few adjacent trails.

Fundamentals: Hike/drive/bike; 16 miles (25.7 km) east of downtown Tucson; year-round

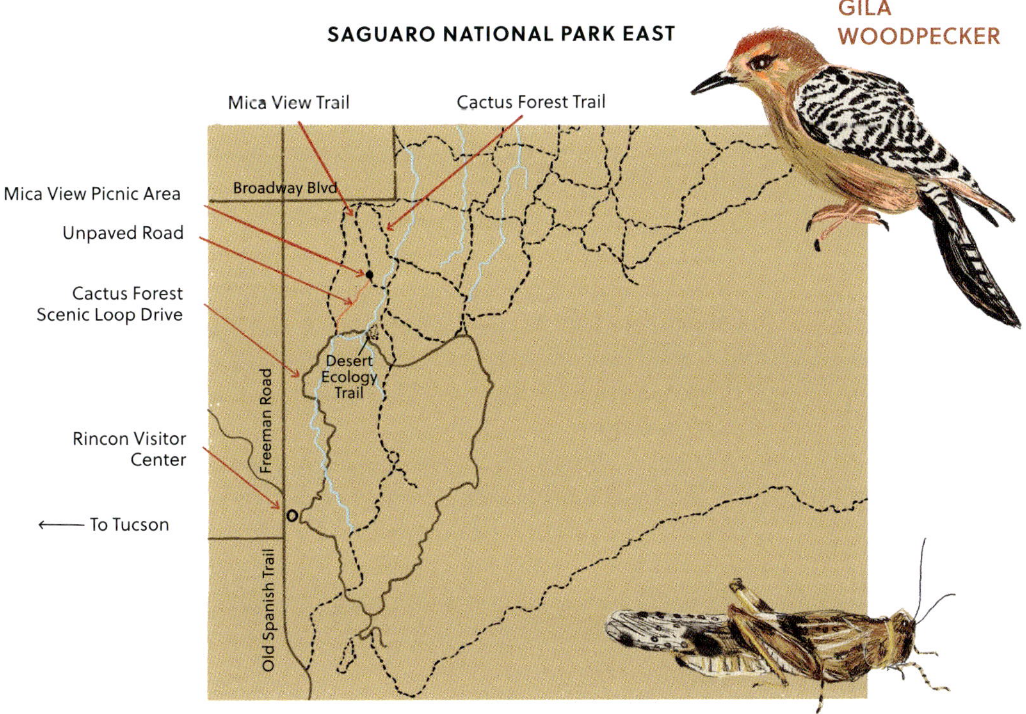

Above, left to right: Saguaro National Park East is set in the Rincon Mountains, with a maximum elevation of 8666 feet (2642 m).

Cactus Forest Scenic Loop Drive

Rufous-winged sparrow at Saguaro National Park East

TRAIL CHAT AND ANIMAL SCAT

Open from dawn to dusk, Cactus Forest Scenic Loop Drive covers 8 miles (13 km) of magnificent views and offers an immersive experience from the comfort of a vehicle (especially suited to Sonoran summers) or the up-close access of a bike. The winding one-way road begins at the visitor center, just past the fee station. Turn left and you're on your way.

Washes crisscross the paved route—watch out for wildlife, hikers, and bikers. Stop at the pullouts to read the interpretive signs, snap a pic, or take a break to marvel with your companions at the extraordinary nature around you. After about 2 miles (3.2 km), keep left and head down the gravel road to Mica View picnic area, equipped with tables, fire grills, and pit toilets (but no water).

After getting your gear in order, start your hike at the Mica View Trailhead. The trail is graded and paved until you reach the Broadway Trailhead. For a shorter, accessible 4-mile (6-km) round trip, you can turn around here and head back to the picnic area. Alternatively, at the Broadway Trailhead, take the unpaved Cactus Forest Trail to explore the park further.

You'll spend much of your hike looking out and up at the mountains and vegetation, but don't forget to look down at the scats and tracks on the ground. In the sandy washes or off to the side of the paved trail, you may find signs of animal life. Bring along a scats and tracks guide and have fun identifying who traveled this trail before you. Don't be surprised to learn that you're following in the footsteps of a gray fox, javelina, or coyote.

A DESERT MEDITATION

If you look and listen attentively, you may well encounter the hammering cousins—gilded flickers and Gila woodpeckers. These conspicuous cavity nesters can be seen pecking away at saguaros or heard noisily calling to each other. Between their chattering, pecking, and flying, you're sure to spot more than a few beautiful birds.

Far from Tucson noise and traffic, each sound is amplified. Listen for the shuffling chirp of creosote bush katydids and the snap-and-pop of the pallid-winged grasshoppers. Cactus wrens and seasonal sparrows round out the desert concert. Human voices, too, may be part of the spontaneous composition, in languages from across the globe, representing the diversity of visitors to the park.

As you walk along, perhaps passing or falling behind other hikers, enjoy the quiet space and let the stillness of the desert envelop you. This trail, nestled against the looming Rincons and bordered by age-old saguaros, can encourage contemplation, particularly if you're hiking solo.

Find a favorite saguaro and ponder its vast lifespan, sometimes as long as 250 years. If it has arms, it's likely much older than most people alive. How many human generations has it lived through? Consider the countless hikers who have passed under its shadow; hawks that have perched on its crown; birds that have hollowed out shelter in its trunk. How many millions of seeds, thousands of fruits, and liters of cactus flower nectar has this single plant produced over the years and centuries? You are now part of that extensive and shared history.

▲ Some saguaros, like the one in the center, have a wavy surface. The cause is unknown.

WHERE HAVE ALL THE SAGUAROS GONE?

Saguaros (*Carnegiea gigantea*), North America's largest cactus, fill the park as they have for millennia. But in 1937, a cold front brought record low temperatures to Tucson, devastating the saguaro population. After another extended cold spell in 1962, researchers discovered that freezing temperatures for more than 20 hours was the cause of the population's decimation. Additionally, heavy cattle grazing, since banned, destroyed nurse trees and young saguaros.

In more recent decades, the park and its researchers have been actively working to preserve and protect saguaros from human interference, invasive species, and climate change with promising results. Today, there's a hopeful trend of baby saguaros growing under nurse trees and beside their 150-year-old forebearers. These young saguaros are the ancestors of tomorrow.

MORE DETAILS

Directions: To get to the park entrance, take Arizona State Route 210E (East Aviation Parkway) to East Golf Links Road. Turn left onto South Houghton Road and turn right onto East Old Spanish Trail. Continue and turn left onto Cactus Forest Drive to enter the park.

Drive/Hike/Bike: Cactus Forest Drive, 8 miles (12.9 km) for cars and bikes; 128 miles (206 km) of hiking trails; elevation gain varies by trail; easy to challenging hikes.

Amenities: Free parking; visitor center with restrooms and water refill station; gift shop; interpretive pollinator garden; two picnic areas with restrooms, tables, and ramadas; helpful volunteers; paved and accessible trail (Mice View Trail); leashed dogs permitted on Desert Ecology Trail and paved section of Mica View Trail only; family-friendly.

Pro Tips: Continue your drive to the Javelina picnic area where a crested saguaro stands tall on the south side of the road. Bring plenty of water.

Info:

Saguaro National Park East
3693 South Old Spanish Trail
Tucson, AZ 85730
520-733-5153

Weekly and annual passes available (can also be used at Saguaro National Park West).

SAGUARO NATIONAL PARK WEST

YOU WON'T COME ACROSS many cities smack in the middle of a national park, but Tucson is just that. Split into two districts by the city, Saguaro National Park is located in both the Rincon Mountains to the east and the Tucson Mountains to the west. Hundreds of miles of trails attract both local and visiting hikers, and one of the most fascinating in Saguaro National Park West is the King Canyon Trail to Wasson Peak. Starting in a canyon and ascending to 360-degree mountaintop views, the trail provides glimpses into the geologic and human history of this area, including a 100-million-year-old lake, the summit of a volcano, ancient petroglyphs, and abandoned mines.

Fundamentals: Hike/drive; petroglyphs, 360-degree views, Arizona-Sonora Desert Museum nearby; 14 miles (22.5 km) west of downtown Tucson; fall/winter/spring

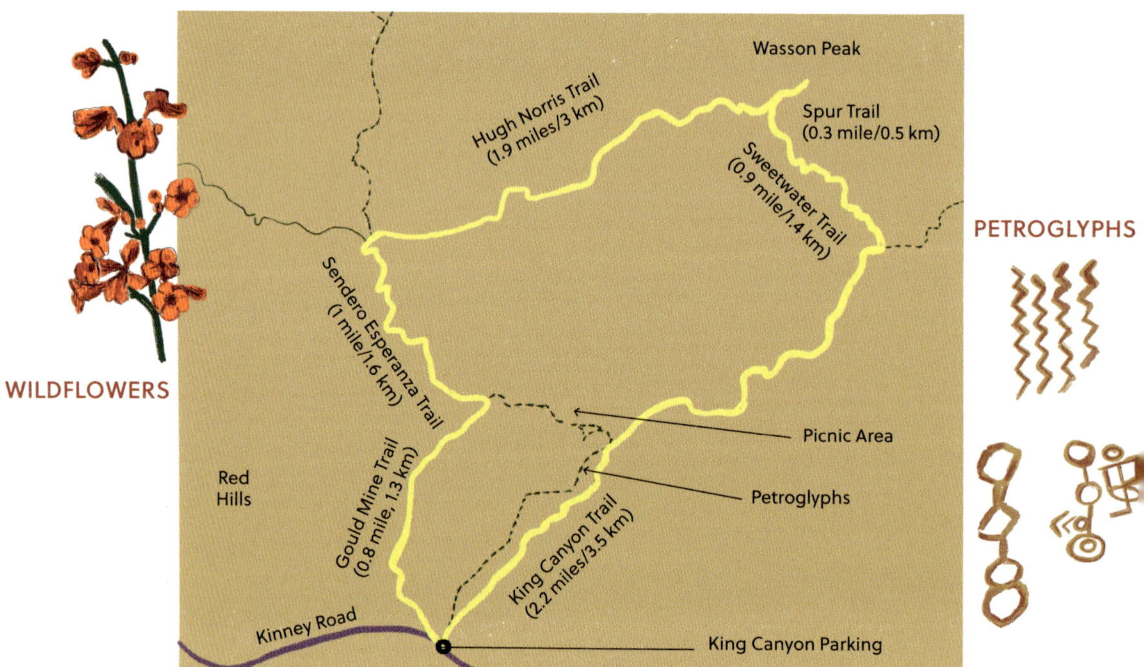

TRAVEL BACK IN TIME: CANYON WASH TO PETROGLYPHS

Just beyond the trailhead, look for the path that goes down into the wash. This portion of the hike runs 0.9 mile (1.4 km). Imagine a much wetter time, about 100 million years ago, when rivers coursed through the region and you might swim in a large freshwater lake. These waters are memorialized in the rocks all around you, layered with sediment. Walking up the wash, you'll encounter a series of large "steps" or ledges. You can scramble over them or climb the easier routes alongside them.

Start looking for petroglyphs on both sides of the canyon at the 0.75-mile (1.2-km) point. Many are quite faded, but the more you look, the more you will find. People decorated these rocks during the Hohokam Period (about 300 to 1450 CE). You'll also pass an old stone-walled restroom building, built in the 1930s by the Civilian Conservation Corps. Next, you can leave the wash for a lunch break in the Mam-A-Gah picnic area, then continue on the King Canyon Trail toward Wasson Peak or, for a shorter outing, return to the trailhead via the old mining road above the wash.

▸ Starting the walk up King Canyon wash

▲ Petroglyphs

‣ This resilient saguaro took root in a boulder in the middle of the canyon.

CLASSIC SONORAN DESERT: KING CANYON TRAIL TO SWEETWATER TRAIL

Stay to the right to continue up the King Canyon Trail for another 1.4 miles (2.3 km). The trail is fairly steep here and takes you through prime saguaro habitat. This area is called the Arizona Upland, the highest and coldest part of the Sonoran Desert. The numerous saguaros and palo verde trees give this region its other name, the saguaro–palo verde forest. Look closely and you'll see a remarkable diversity of plants—more than 630 species in the small mountain range. When you arrive at the junction with Sweetwater Trail, pause to take in the epoch-straddling views—modern Tucson to the east and 200-million-year-old red hills to the west.

▲ View from the trail junction

SWEETWATER TRAIL TO WASSON PEAK

Along this 1.2-mile (1.9-km) portion of the route, you'll ascend some steep switchbacks, passing a couple of closed mine shafts. One of these, the Old Yuma Mine, was active from the 1880s to the 1950s. It was the most successful mine in the Tucson Mountains, producing copper, silver, gold, molybdenum, lead, and zinc. It is also known for impressive wulfenite and vanadinite mineral specimens, some of which are often on display at the Arizona-Sonora Desert Museum across the road.

You'll next come to the intersection with the Hugh Norris Trail. Here, a short spur trail leads to Wasson Peak. At 4687 feet (1429 m), it's the highest point in the Tucson Mountains. At the summit, enjoy the sweeping views as you stand on a volcanic caldera, the remains of a tremendous eruption that occurred 70–75 million years ago. Wasson Peak was one of at least seven explosive volcanoes active in this region at that time.

To return, you can either retrace your path or take a slightly longer route to complete the loop. For the loop option, follow the Hugh Norris Trail to the Sendero Esperanza Trail. Next, the Gould Mine Trail will bring you back to the parking lot.

MORE DETAILS

Directions: To get to the King Canyon Trailhead, drive west on West Speedway Boulevard, which turns into West Gates Pass Road and dead-ends at Kinney Road. Turn right onto North Kinney Road and continue for 2.5 miles (4 km) to the trailhead, located on the right, just beyond the entrance to the Arizona-Sonora Desert Museum.

Drive/Hike: King Canyon Trail to Wasson Peak, 7 miles (11.3 km) round-trip with shorter 2-mile (3.2-km) option and 1800-foot (548.6-m) elevation gain. To explore more of the park, drive north on Kinney Road to the Red Hills Visitor Center. There are 43 miles (69 km) of hiking trails with easy to challenging hikes.

Amenities: Free parking; restrooms and water refill station at the Red Hills Visitor Center a few miles north on North Kinney Road and at the Arizona-Sonora Desert Museum across the road; exhibits and Western National Parks Association bookstore in visitor center; five picnic areas; dogs not permitted.

Pro Tips: After a wet winter, you may see a profusion of wildflowers on King Canyon Trail. There's very little shade after the first mile, so it's best to do this hike in cooler weather or early in the day. Wear sturdy boots and sun protection, and bring lots of water. If it's raining, stay out of the wash!

Info:

Saguaro National Park West
Red Hills Visitor Center
2700 North Kinney Road
Tucson, AZ 85743
520-733-5158

Weekly and annual passes available (can also be used at Saguaro National Park East).

HONEY BEE CANYON PARK

A SHORT DRIVE FROM metro Tucson, in the town of Oro Valley, the trails of Honey Bee Canyon Park wend their way between the Santa Catalina and Tortolita mountain ranges, an area where the people of the Hohokam period once lived and farmed. The park trails take you to ancient petroglyphs (carvings in stone) they left behind as well as the later ruins of a nineteenth-century dam. Because the elevation is almost 1000 feet (305 m) higher than that of the Tucson Basin, it's an ideal place to hike when it's just a little too hot in the valley.

Fundamentals: Hike; petroglyphs, historic dam; 19 miles (30.6 km) north of downtown Tucson; late spring/late summer/fall/winter

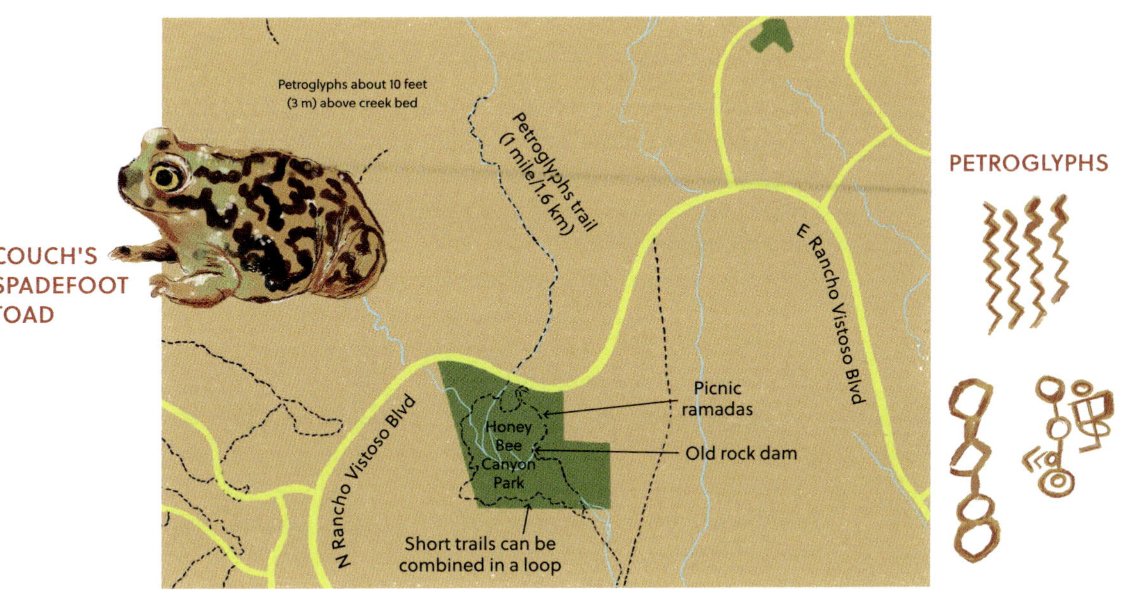

▲ Honey Bee Canyon wash

SO CLOSE YET SO FAR AWAY

Upon arrival, you'll immediately notice the cooler temperature and stunning views of the Santa Catalina Mountains to the east and northeast. Though adjacent to residential areas and nearby roads, Honey Bee Canyon Park is unexpectedly quiet and secluded, with about 2 miles (3.2 km) of trails, which run mostly within the dry riverbed (also called a desert wash or arroyo) of Sausalito Creek, taking hikers from urban interface to desert immersion. Because the silty sand is well-compacted and elevation gain is modest, hiking here is relatively easy and family-friendly.

After parking, you can either drop into the wash just south of the road or head north under the bridge and onto the main trail. The lower portion has several short extensions that cycle back to the northern route and create a loop. Alternatively, deepen your experience and extend your time in the desert by traveling along the higher portion of the trail. And don't miss some of the prettiest and most peaceful portions of the trails, which lie to the south.

WATER IN THE DESERT

Surface water in the Sonoran Desert is rare and usually seasonal. The summer monsoon provides well over half the region's rainfall, sometimes delivered in a few violent and short-lived storms, which can be dangerous due to flash floods and lightning strikes. Though these storms are a sight to see from a safe enclosure, be sure to time your hike to avoid them. Afterward, the rainpools left in their wake offer a temporary home to several species of amphibians that rely on the puddles for reproduction.

Honey Bee Canyon Park hosts several desert-adapted species in the area, including the Couch's spadefoot, which grows from egg to froglet in as few as nine days, about five times faster than their closest competitors, the true toads. If you want to see these spotted desert jewels, head out in the morning in late August or early September, when the monsoon rains end—you're likely to encounter them, along with several species of other desert amphibians, especially recent metamorphs (species changing from one stage of life to the next). The spadefoots are tiny and hard to see—imagine small pieces of gravel that suddenly hop around—so watch where you step.

WALKING BACKWARD (THROUGH TIME)

Haling along the center or eastern trail, you'll come across a rocky dam dating back to the late 1800s, likely built to collect water for livestock. Upon entering this structure, the feel of the canyon will instantly surround you. Heading north, you'll travel under the bridge that supports the main road. This longer in-and-out trail rises ever so slightly in elevation and, about a mile in, leads you to a number of petroglyphs on the wash's west side, believed to have been created during the Hohokam period by people who inhabited this region between 300 and 1450 CE.

◣ Rock wall in the canyon

▾ Gambel's quail family

These inhabitants were some of the earliest farmers and the only people native to North America to design, construct, and relied on irrigation canals to direct water to their crops. They were also excellent artisans, producing the tools required to carve the petroglyphs in Honey Bee Canyon.

SEASONS IN (AND OUT OF) THE SUN

Plants in Honey Bee Canyon Park include saguaros and barrel cacti; palo verde and mesquite trees; and a variety of shrubs, such as brittlebush and ragweed. When winter rains are abundant, you'll discover stunning displays of wildflowers in spring. Short of that, many desert plants have beautiful and colorful flowers that bloom in May and June.

As for animals, a wide variety roam this area, such as javelinas, deer, cottontails, and coyotes, and you'll be able to identify a host of bird species, including hummingbirds, Gambel's quail, Gila woodpeckers, and roadrunners. Honey Bee Canyon is also prime turf for reptiles, including the greater earless lizard, the rarely seen Gila monster, and snakes ranging from large western diamondback rattlesnakes and gopher snakes to thin sand snakes. Snakes are commonly found during the wet summer months, especially at night, while lizards are more prevalent in spring.

MORE DETAILS

Directions: The park is easily accessed from the east via Oracle Road (Highway 77) or from the west via I–10 (Tangerine Road exit).

Hike: 2 miles (3.2 km); 200-foot (61-m) elevation gain; easy.

Amenities: Free parking at park entrance; picnic tables and barbecues by reservation; restrooms and water at trailhead; family-friendly; dogs permitted on leash.

Pro Tips: The trail is not consistently marked, making it difficult to know which trail you're on. Fortunately, the trails are short, and you can easily locate a road or a house nearby to reorient. If hiking during monsoon season, make sure to bring extra shoes for later, in case the sand is wet.

Info:

Honey Bee Canyon Park
13880 E. Rancho Vistoso Boulevard
Oro Valley, AZ 85755
520-229-5050

TORTOLITA PRESERVE TRAILS

PACK SOME SNACKS, FILL the water bottles, grab your dog, and drive! This secluded destination, about 30 minutes north of downtown Tucson in Marana, is a perfect excuse to escape the city for an immersive hiking getaway. For guests of the local Ritz-Carlton, the network of trails in the Tortolita Preserve, accessed via the Wild Burro trailhead, is right outside your door. Let the attendant at the security resort's kiosk know you're a day hiker and follow the drive to the large dirt lot on the right to access the trails.

Fundamentals: Half-day trip; house and well ruins, Hohokam petroglyphs; 20 miles (32 km) northwest of downtown Tucson; fall/winter/spring

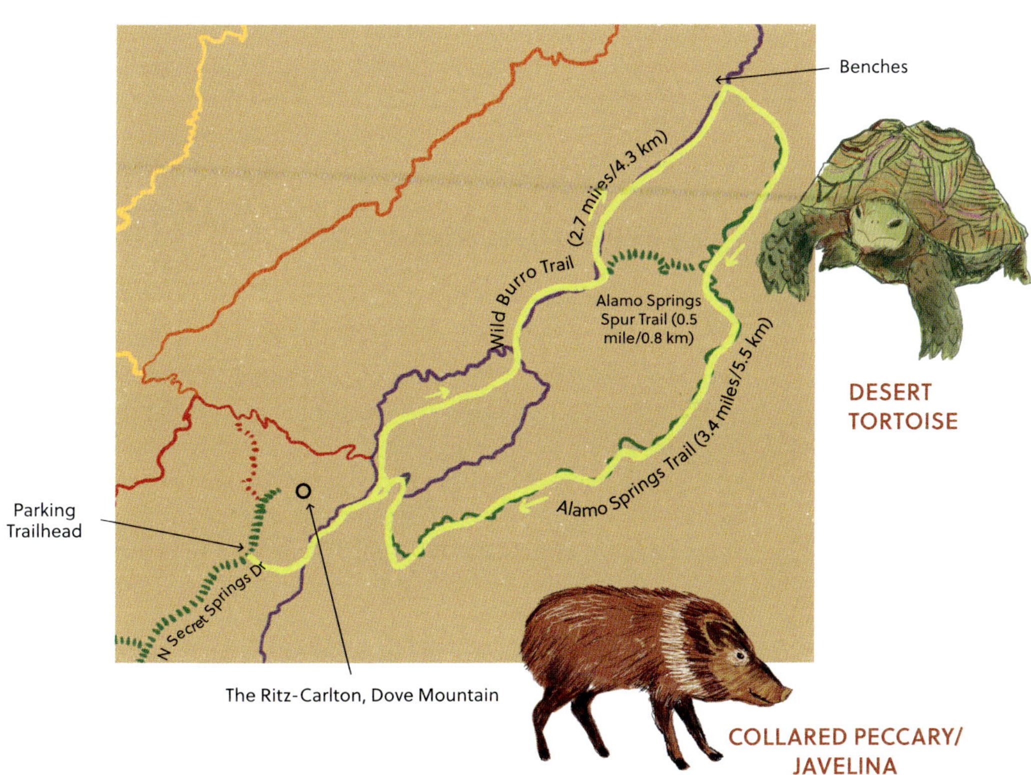

▸ Parts of the trail are steep as you climb out of the wash.

CHOOSE YOUR HIKE

The Tortolita Preserve, a 2400-acre area ensconced in in the Tortolita Mountain range, has approximately 29 miles (46.7 km) of interconnected trails, so you can build your own hike. (*Tortolita* means little mountain dove in Spanish, and this location is often referred to as the Dove Mountain area.) For a moderately challenging, fun, and nature-rich experience, follow the Wild Burro Trail to the Alamo Springs Trail. The hike is about 6.8 miles (10.9 km) round-trip with an elevation gain of nearly 1000 feet (305 m) and can be done in around three hours, depending on pace and breaks. Meet up early with friends and break for lunch after.

SCENIC VISTAS AND SORE LEGS

Just past the trailhead, the route immediately dips into a wash with the resort on the north side and steep mountains to the south. Walking in the sandy wash, appreciate the canyon walls on either side of you for about a mile as you warm up for the longer stretch. After 1.7 mile (2.7 km), you'll reach the remnants of an old ranch cabin (see map) indicating where the structure once stood near a dilapidated cattle tank. This is a great spot to hydrate both yourself and your pup in anticipation of the climb.

Stay to the north side of the trail and begin the steep 0.3-mile (0.5-km) climb in a clockwise direction. If you enjoy strenuous ascents, this is arguably the most satisfying part of the hike (and much easier than the descent). After negotiating the up and downs

◂ Remnants of ranch cabin

of the trail, you'll cross a wash; pay close attention to the trail markers and continue on.

At the midway point, you'll encounter the Alamo Springs Trail. *Alamos* is Spanish for cottonwoods, and these huge trees offer a welcome respite to rest and enjoy the shade and birdsong. There are rocks to explore, a bench to take in the views, and interpretive signs to edify. Wander around and you could encounter signs of earlier human habitation, such as grinding holes or even petroglyphs. From this vantage point on a clear day, peer at Baboquivari Peak in the west, which holds a great importance to the Tohono O'odham people as the center of their universe, home to their creator I'itoi.

NO BURROS, BUT LOTS OF BIRDS

After your break, proceed on the Alamo Springs Trail to loop back through grassy areas dotted with abundant plant life. Naturalists will appreciate the incredible biodiversity of the preserve, where more than 600 plant species can be found. Enjoy the rolling trail and changing views amidst the company of agaves, ocotillos, ironwood trees, palo verdes, jojobas, even the occasional crested saguaro.

In addition, more than 100 bird species have been documented in Wild Burro Canyon, including canyon and rock wrens, flickers, turkey vultures, and 11 different kinds of sparrows. As for land creatures, it's common to spot wild desert tortoises on this part of the trail. Also, look for centipedes, tarantulas, snakes, deer, roadrunners, javelinas, bobcats, and mountain lions.

▸ View to the east of the Santa Catalina Mountains

MORE DETAILS

Directions: Take Interstate 10W and get off at Exit 244. Follow city streets approximately 9.3 miles (15 km) to reach the Wild Burro Trailhead.

Wild Burro/Alamo Springs Hike: 6.8 miles (10.9 km) round-trip; 1000-foot (305-m) elevation gain; moderate to challenging.

Amenities: Large dirt parking lot; well-maintained restrooms with flush toilets, soap, and hand dryers, water station, and trail maps at trailhead; unpaved trails not ADA accessible; mountain biking and leashed dogs permitted (dog bags available at trailhead); horseback riding permitted on selected trails.

Pro Tips: Please note that it's easier on the knees to hike the Alamo Springs and Wild Burro Trails in a clockwise direction; going in a counterclockwise direction is much more difficult, and hiking poles can help with going up and down the steep grades. The trails offer little shade, so be sure to carry water, wear sun protection, and time your visit for cooler times of day.

Info:

Wild Burro Trailhead
14810 N. Secret Springs Drive
Marana, AZ 85658
Town of Marana Parks and Recreation: 520-382-1950

CATALINA STATE PARK AND ROMERO POOLS

CATALINA STATE PARK, DUE north from downtown Tucson, covers 5500 acres of foothill and canyon habitat on the southwest side of the Santa Catalina Mountains. With so many outdoor adventures to choose from, why here? Sweeping desert views; rocky desert canyons; a range of trails; refreshing bodies of water in certain seasons; incredible bird-watching; and plenty of Sonoran Desert plant- and wildlife. The Romero Canyon Trail, detailed here, offers the chance to experience all of these.

Fundamentals: Day trip; eight trails to choose from; pools, ruins, bird-watching; 15 miles (24 km) north of downtown Tucson; year-round

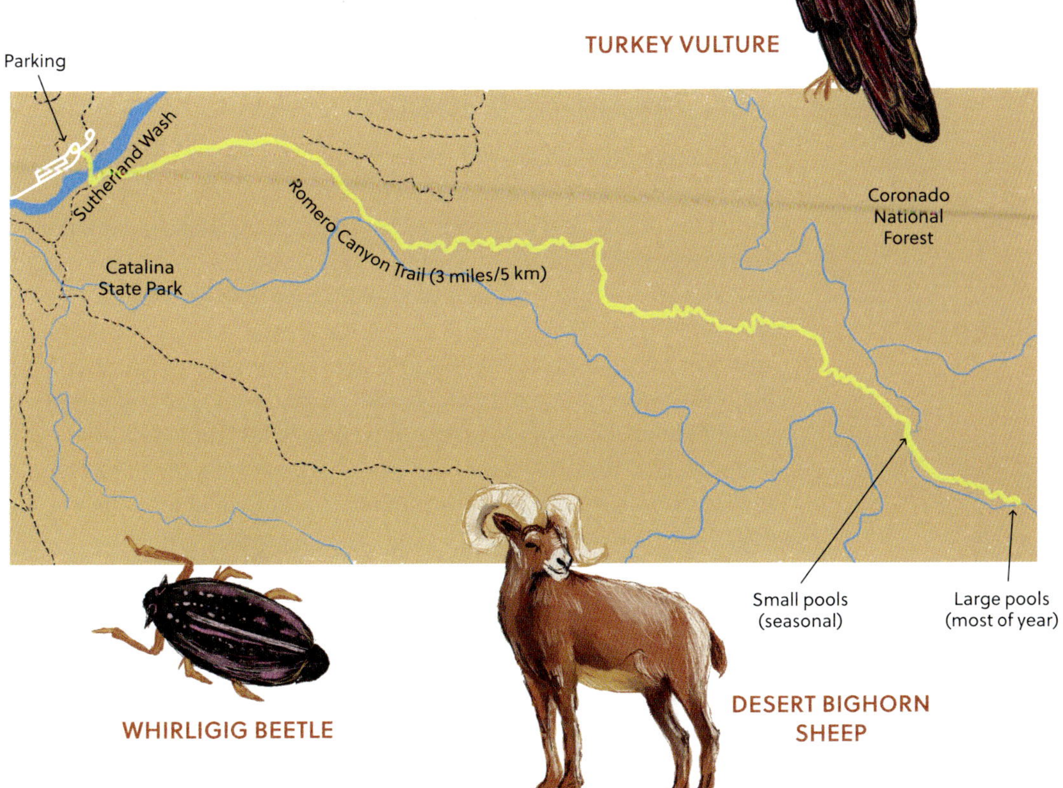

Clockwise, from left: A magnificent old multi-armed saguaro

View of Pusch Ridge in the Santa Catalinas from Catalina State Park

Romero Canyon Trail

SAGUAROS AND SHEEP

This is a true desert hike, with all the usual desert suspects in attendance—mesquite and palo verde trees, ocotillo, desert spoon (a yucca-like shrub from which sotol, an alcoholic beverage is derived), prickly pear, cholla, and sizable saguaros. Wildlife is plentiful and all around, but often well hidden. Funnel-web, net-web, and black widow spiders; scorpions; several species of lizards; and diamondback, black-tailed, and tiger rattlesnakes all live here, but (except for the lizards) don't readily reveal themselves. White-winged doves, Gila woodpeckers, and curve-billed thrashers are common and more apparent. Turkey vultures and red-tailed hawks soar above while packrats, rock squirrels, ringtails, and other mammals work the ground.

Perhaps most exciting is the possibility of seeing desert bighorn sheep, which disappeared from the Catalina Mountains in the late 1990s until their reestablishment in the early 2010s. Though bighorn are native to this location, reintroducing them was controversial—the demise of the original population wasn't fully understood and restoring it required removing some of the resident pumas, natural

◂ Romero Pools are a welcome break and reward before heading back down the trail.

predators of the sheep that would compromise the project. Be sure to stop occasionally and glance up at the surrounding slopes in case one or a few might be grazing. It's truly awe-inspiring to glimpse these magnificent animals in the wild.

THE POOLS

For desert dwellers—and visitors, too—water is an unparalleled treasure, making the pools one of the special, if seasonal, benefits of this trail. While you can't count on water year-round, heavy winter rains (producing snow, followed by snowmelt higher up) or summer storms fill the pools. When water is present, you may see a variety of aquatic invertebrates, including giant water bugs that cling to rocky pool edges (beware their stabbing mouthparts if you're inclined to handle them) and whirligig beetles that swim in frantic circles at the surface. The pools also serve as a wet nursery for spadefoot and true toads—look for tiny dark tadpoles swimming around or recently metamorphosed froglets around the pool's perimeter.

FIRE FOOTPRINTS

Fortunately, you're not likely to come across an actual wildfire, but you will see the footprint that past fires have left behind. Wildfires have heavily impacted the Romero Trail, resulting in occasional closures. An extended closure occurred in 2020 after the devastating Bighorn Fire, which burned for six weeks and consumed nearly 120,000 acres.

As you hike, scan the hillsides for charred trees and shorter new plant growth. Wildfires, especially those fueled by invasive species like buffelgrass, often burn hotter, destroying a tremendous amount of habitat. On occasion, they can spur positive results. Such was the case with some fires that cleared out thick vegetation and created more open space for reintroducing bighorn sheep.

Beyond visually noting the signs of past wildfires, you're likely to *feel* the burn—in your legs and overall. The pools are about 3 miles (5 km) up the trail and, though this hike is considered moderate and initially flat, open, and sandy, portions of the trail are steep and rocky, making it overly arduous or a great workout, depending on your perspective. In addition, the route is largely unshaded—be sure to liberally apply sunscreen beforehand, wear a hat, and take plenty of water, because you are likely to need it.

MORE DETAILS

Directions: From downtown Tucson, head north on North Granada Avenue, which quickly turns into North Main Avenue, then North Oracle Road (Highway 77). Drive 14 miles (22.5 km) and turn right at Catalina State Park.

Day Trip: Eight trails with varying degrees of difficulty. For the Romero Canyon Trail to Romero Pools, 3 miles (5 km) one-way to the pools; 1318-foot (402-m) elevation gain; challenging.

Amenities: Parking; visitor center and park store; restrooms; vending machines; programs and events; campsites with picnic tables, grills, electricity, water, flush restrooms, and showers; RV hookups; horses, bikes, and leashed dogs permitted, with some exceptions, such as the Desert Bighorn Sheep Management Area along the Romero Canyon Trail (check website).

Pro Tips: Though the Romero Canyon Trail rises above the Tucson Basin, leading to slightly cooler temperatures, like most exposed trails in this area, it's best to hike this trail in late fall through early spring. To check for or report any fire danger, call 623-582-0911 or 1-800-309-7081.

Info:

Catalina State Park
11570 North Oracle Road
Tucson, AZ 85737
520-628-5798

Fee station at park entrance to collect vehicle (1–4 adults) or individual entrance fee.

VENTURING OUT

20–70 MILES (32–110 KM) FROM DOWNTOWN TUCSON

RAÚL M. GRIJALVA CANOA RANCH CONSERVATION PARK

CANOA RANCH LIES IN the Santa Cruz River Valley, which occupies a unique place in Southern Arizona's prehistoric and recorded history—as a vibrant ecosystem supporting vegetation and wildlife; a fertile region supporting human habitation and shifting populations; and an international watershed linking two modern-day nations. You can learn all about this fascinating past and present—and take in the magnificent nature and views—at the Raúl M. Grijalva Canoa Ranch Conservation Park.

Fundamentals: Day trip; guided tours, bird-watching, gardens, exhibits, nearby trails; 33 miles (53 km) south of downtown Tucson; year-round

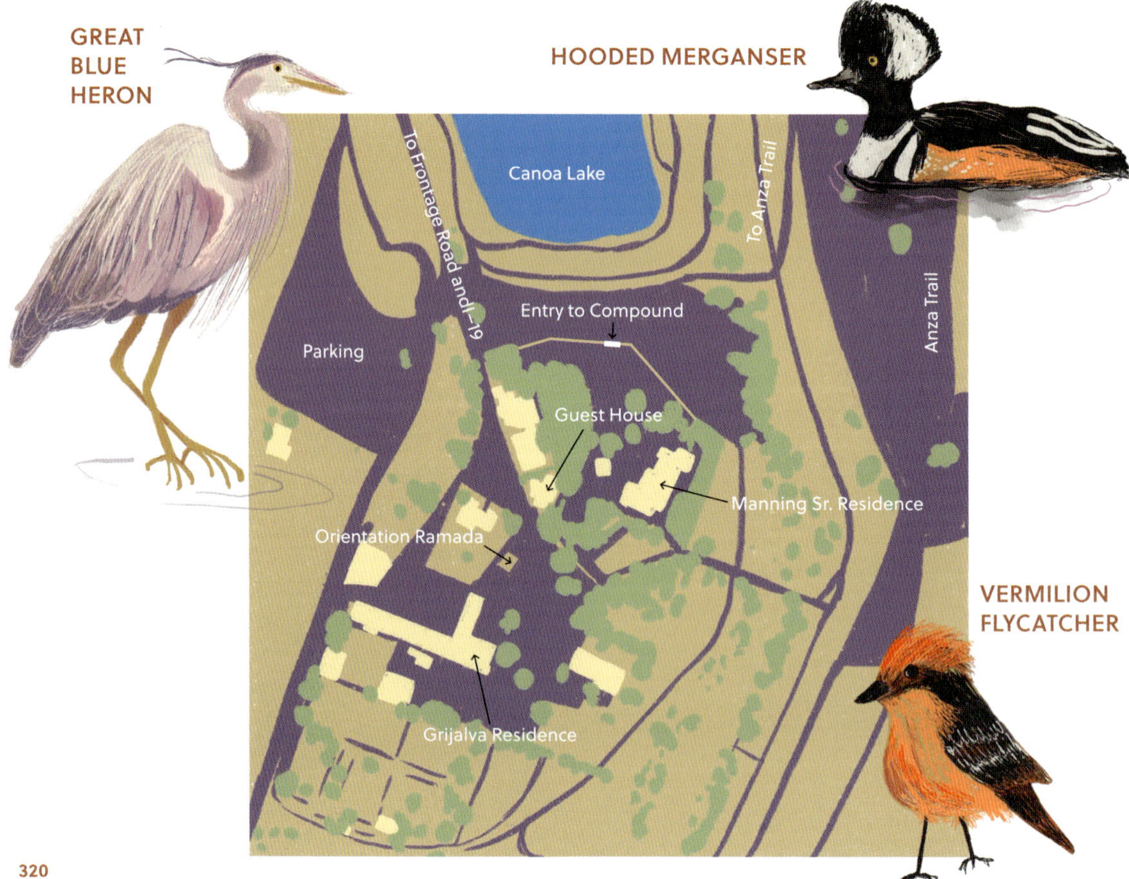

ADVENTURE 13

WHERE HISTORY AND ECOLOGY MEET

Above, left to right:
Canoa Ranch house

Great blue heron

Canoa Lake

Covering 4800 acres, the park's grounds provide plenty of opportunities—and the smooth, level trails—to explore the area's history and nature. Check out the various exhibits and chat with volunteers about the land's earlier eras and people as well as more recent ranch life. Consider signing up for a tour of the renovated ranch buildings and corrals or the reestablished gardens and orchard.

With the natural environment attracting more than 160 avian species, Canoa Ranch also offers birding tours. Of course, birders can venture forth independently, checklist in hand, to note their discoveries, such as vermillion flycatchers, yellow warblers, green herons, and gray hawks. Stroll the 1-mile (1.6-km) perimeter of the restored lake to encounter some of Southern Arizona's amazing waterfowl, shorebirds, raptors, and other species and rest under a lakeside ramada to enjoy the cottonwoods, willows, and other landscaping that enhance the habitat for both people and wildlife.

IF THE RIVER COULD TALK

Indigenous peoples inhabited the Santa Cruz River Valley from as early as the Paleolithic period, about 10,000 years ago. During this time, people lived in small, dispersed, nomadic family groups, subsisting primarily by hunting the large animals that roamed the area, such as mammoth and bison. Over millennia, this river valley supported an evolving succession of intricate human land arrangements, giving rise to population growth, socioeconomic systems (from hunter-gatherer to early farming), and the earliest known domestication of food crops (corn, squash, beans) in North America.

Agriculture and a more sedentary lifestyle brought new challenges, such as war and raids by non-sedentary groups. Archaeological evidence also points to intermittent and drastic population declines; in some cases, populations vanished altogether, likely due to changing environmental conditions caused by prolonged drought. Over time, the Tohono O'odham (Desert People) and the Sobaipuri O'odham (River People) adapted to the new conditions and inhabited the valley when the first Europeans arrived in the late 1600s.

EUROPEAN PRESENCE IN THE VALLEY

By the mid-1700s, European expeditions up the Santa Cruz River Valley became routine. Jesuit missionaries (Eusebio Francisco Kino and others) established the mission system, which spread northward along every river valley in the Sonoran Desert. The Santa Cruz (Spanish for "holy cross") was no exception as missions grew in both size and number at the river's permanent water holes where Indigenous villages had flourished. As the Catholic Church expanded its influence and Spain lay claim to foreign lands, the missions served as religious and colonial outposts, simultaneously amassing converts and new subjects.

Often organized as haciendas (large farms or plantations), the missions attracted even more Europeans. To defend territory and protect the largely unwelcome colonists, Spain oversaw the construction of presidios (forts), like the Tubac Presidio established in 1751. The Spanish population continued to increase and, by the next century, new homesteads called ranchos appeared up and down the river valley. Rancho La Canoa (Canoe Ranch) was one of these, sharing the Spanish name for the region, originally derived from the canoe-like water troughs carved from cottonwood trees and used to transfer water or feed cattle.

FROM RANCH TO LANDMARK

One hundred years before Arizona became a state (1912), Rancho La Canoa was already a working cattle ranch. In 1821, Tomás and Ignacio Ortiz paid $250 to Spain for the original 17,000-acre San Ignacio de la Canoa land grant. Over the course of several generations, as possession transferred to a series of Anglo families, local politicians, and entrepreneurs, Rancho La Canoa remained a

▲ Anza Days cultural celebration at Canoa Ranch

working ranch until the 1970s. In 1997, recognizing the site's historical, cultural, and environmental importance, Pima County purchased the ranch and began restoration in 2004.

At the height of its 1950s productivity and prominence, the ranch complex included workshops, stables, corrals, several service buildings, a forge, a school, and homes for 40 vaqueros (cowboys) and their families. This legacy is commemorated in interpretive exhibits (of furnishings, tools, and equipment) and signage, educating visitors about ranching life and culture. Many of the facilities have been restored to their original condition or rebuilt utilizing traditional methods; the renovated corrals, for example, were constructed using a colonial-era retaque technique (from the Spanish, *retacar*, meaning "to fill"), tightly stacking native mesquite wood between vertical posts to create strong and secure holding areas for cattle.

The site is named for the late US Representative Raúl Grijalva, an avid supporter of the project who lived at Canoa Ranch until the age of five. (His father came to Arizona in the 1940s to work as a vaquero on the ranch.) He credits his childhood experience with instilling in him a great reverence for open space and, in his later work, an ongoing passion for public lands and conservation. In honor of his advocacy, the park was renamed for him in 2007, the same year it entered the National Register of Historic Places.

MORE DETAILS

Directions: Take Interstate 10E to Interstate 19S. Get off at Exit 56, follow East Canoa Ranch Drive to traverse the highway, and turn left onto the frontage road. You'll reach Canoa Ranch in 1.8 miles (2.9 km).

Day Trip: Walking tours; historic buildings; bird-watching; pollinator and other gardens; orchard; plant nursery; Canoa Lake; access to the Anza Trail.

Amenities: Parking; visitor center with exhibits and restrooms; ramadas; picnic tables; family-friendly.

Accessibility: The lake walkway is wheelchair accessible.

Pro Tips: A modest fee is charged for walking tours; call ahead for the schedule and information about required online registration.

Info:

Historic Canoa Ranch
5375 South Interstate 19 Frontage Road
Green Valley, Arizona 85614
520-724-6680

CATALINA HIGHWAY AND MOUNT LEMMON

VISIBLE FROM ALMOST ANYWHERE in the Tucson Basin, the Santa Catalina Mountains are often associated with their tallest and best-known peak, Mount Lemmon. The winding 25-mile (40-km) journey to the top on the Catalina Highway (also called the Mount Lemmon Highway) offers shifting panoramic vistas and, in terms of climate zones and native vegetation, is equivalent to driving from Mexico to Canada. In fact, the mountaintops are called Sky Islands (see the section "Sky Islands" on page 19) for their high-altitude isolation from and sharp contrast with the desert valley below.

Fundamentals: Day trip; scenic drive; hiking trails at every elevation; southernmost ski area in the United States; 45 miles (72.4 km) north-east of downtown Tucson to the top of Mount Lemmon; year-round

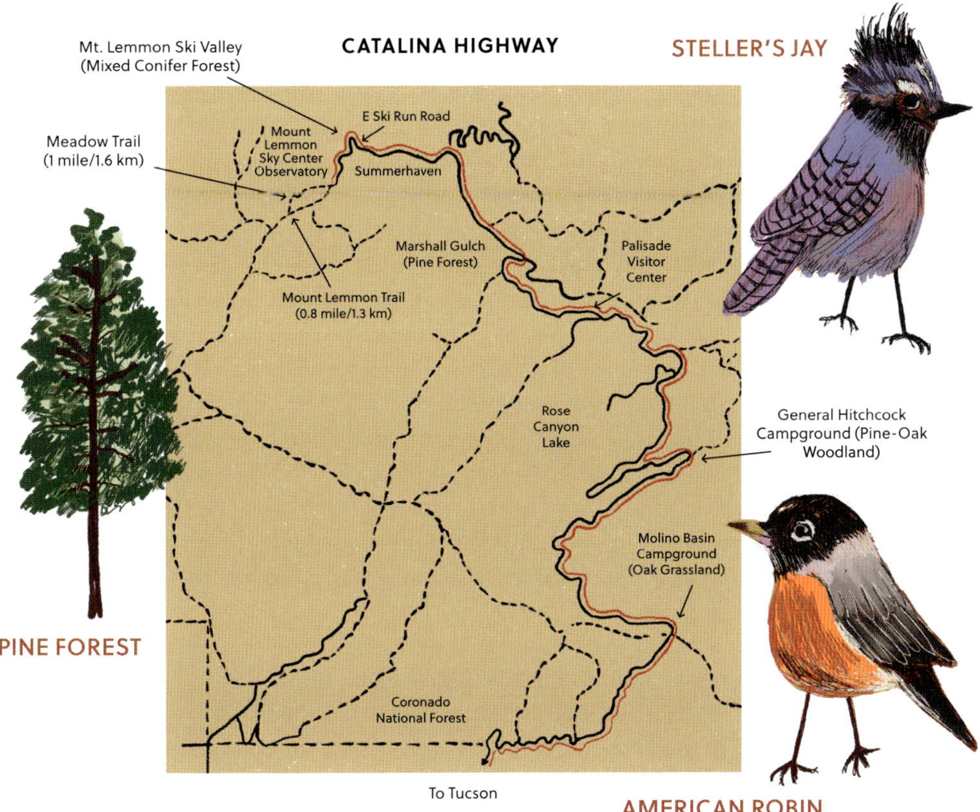

A JOURNEY TO A DIFFERENT CLIMATE

The shops in Summerhaven, at the top of Mt. Lemmon, benefit from many an ill-prepared day-tripper leaving 90°F (32°C) heat in the valley and then needing a jacket. The temperature change from valley floor to mountaintop is about 30 degrees, or a 5°F (2.8°C) drop for every 1000-foot (305-m) rise in elevation. The cooler air at higher altitudes increases precipitation, which leads to differences in plant and animal life along the route.

LIFE ZONES

Driving up to Mount Lemmon's peak, you'll pass through six distinctive life zones, areas uniquely characterized by specific plants, animals, temperatures, and moisture levels:

Desertscrub: At the base of the mountain, Sonoran desertscrub, often described as a "saguaro–palo verde forest," differs from desertscrub elsewhere in the world in the dominance of legume trees (like palo verdes and mesquites) and tall columnar cacti. You'll also see a wide variety of other cacti and desert shrubs.

Oak-Grassland: Saguaros disappear as you reach oak-grassland (4800 feet/1450 m), as they can't survive the winter freezes. Here, the open landscape supports a greater variety of plants than other biomes on the mountain. Look for the Emory oak's sweet acorns (*bellotas* in Spanish), an edible treat for people and a major food source for jays, woodpeckers, and other birds.

Pine-Oak Woodland: Next, you'll enter pine-oak woodland (5900 feet/1800 m) where evergreen trees, including juniper, Arizona cypress, and a variety of pines and oaks, overtake shrubs and grasses. The tree canopy of woodlands lets in sunlight, but the canopy of forests blocks out most of the sky.

Chaparral: The mountain includes a relatively small chaparral zone (6600 feet/2011 m) characterized by dense evergreen shrubs with leathery, shiny, resinous leaves. These resins help prevent water loss in the hot, dry summers but are also highly flammable. This biome is adapted to fire, and many plants require fire to germinate their seeds.

Pine Forest: Higher up (7300 feet/2225 m), you'll see pine species common to both the Rocky Mountains, north of the Santa Catalinas (such as ponderosa pine), and the Sierra Madre Occidental plateau to the south (such as Arizona pine). The combination of these

Above, left to right: Catalina Highway

Mount Lemmon is home to the southernmost ski area in the United States.

Hiking by some dark granite crisscrossed with veins of lighter quartz and feldspar

"influencer" species underlies the biological diversity of the Santa Catalina woodlands and forests.

Mixed Conifer Forest: At the very top (9100 feet/2770 m), you'll enjoy cool mixed conifer forest, with pine and fir trees as well as high-elevation maples and oaks. Quaking aspens occur in patches and provide a brilliant splash of yellow in fall. With a warming climate, it's likely that this mountaintop will become inhospitable to a mixed conifer community; several studies show that plant communities are already migrating upward as temperatures rise.

ON THE ROCKS

About 35 million years ago, the Santa Catalinas were formed as part of the extension along fault lines that led to the formation of the Basin and Range Province to the west and north (see the section "Making and Moving Mountains" on page 28). The road cuts along the highway display evidence of the great heating forces that pulled the western continent apart. Older, darker granite (1.4 billion years old) swirls with younger, paler granite (45 million years old) like chocolate and vanilla in a marbled cake. In some places, thin bands of large multicolored rocks reveal the mountain's geological past; look closely and you'll see flattened and stretched individual crystals. For another glimpse at the mountain's natural history, check out the hoodoos (rock towers formed by millions of years of erosion) at Windy Point pullout, halfway up to the top.

▸ Mount Lemmon Trail

MOUNT LEMMON AND MEADOW TRAILS

Treat yourself to this mellow 2.1-mile (3.4-km) loop through mixed conifer forest, featuring scattered meadows, great views and, in summer, throngs of lady beetles (ladybugs) congregating on trees. Near the end of the highway, take a right and follow signs to Ski Valley. Continue on Observatory Road for about 1 mile (1.6 km) to the trailhead parking area next to a power substation. If this lot is full, you can backtrack a short way to the larger lot.

Hiking the trail, you'll quickly come to a convergence of paths. Go straight to where the Mount Lemmon and Meadow Trails meet, and turn right on the Meadow Trail.

Walk along the fence of the Mount Lemmon Observatory, a University of Arizona facility housing the Catalina Sky Survey, a project that identifies asteroids that could potentially collide with the earth.

Past the observatory, enjoy picnic-perfect meadows interspersed with cool forest. If you plan to picnic, bring a blanket—the grasses here can be prickly.

You'll soon reach another junction with the Mt. Lemmon Trail. You can either return the way you came or follow the Mount Lemmon Trail (more exposed with sweeping valley views) to finish the loop.

WHAT'S IN A NAME?

- **Mount Lemmon:** Named for Sara Plummer Lemmon, a botanist, botanical illustrator, and Civil War nurse who was the first white woman known to summit Mount Lemmon on foot and horseback in 1881.

- **General Hitchcock Highway and Campground:** Yet another name for the Catalina/Mount Lemmon Highway. Frank Harris Hitchcock was US Postmaster General from 1909 to 1913 and established the country's first airmail service. He supported the construction of the Catalina Highway as well as the formation of the Saguaro National Monument and died in Tucson in 1935.

- **Babad Do'ag Rest Stop and Trail:** Honor the Tohono O'odham name for the Santa Catalinas—Frog Mountain, for the shape of the mountain range's silhouette.

- **Gordon Hirabayashi Campground:** Named for a University of Washington student—and other conscientious resisters—who challenged the constitutionality of Japanese American internment camps during World War II and refused to report to one when ordered. His case went all the way to the Supreme Court, which did not rule on constitutionality but instead sentenced him to prison for his disobedience. He chose to serve time in a prison road camp and hitchhiked from Spokane to the Catalina Federal Honor Camp. After the war, Hirabayashi earned a PhD in sociology. His conviction was overturned in 1987.

MORE DETAILS

Directions: Follow East Catalina Highway to head up the mountain.

Scenic Drive/Hike: Catalina Highway drive is 29 miles (46.7 km); 9157-foot (2791-m) elevation gain; winding road. Mount Lemmon/Meadow Trail loop is 2.1 miles (3.4 km); 360-foot (109.7-m) elevation gain; easy.

Amenities: Restaurants, stores, and gift/souvenir shops in Summerhaven; overnight accommodations; campgrounds; leashed dogs permitted on some trails; family-friendly.

Pro Tips: The chairlift at Ski Valley runs most of the year, offering a fun excursion to the top of the ski runs. Before embarking on your trip, it's advisable to check current road and weather conditions, especially during winter months when the road may be closed to motor vehicles (hotline number below).

Info:

Pima County Sheriff's 24-hour year-round Road Condition Hotline: 520-547-7510
Santa Catalina Ranger District Office: 520-749-8700
Ski Valley for skiing fees and conditions: 520-576-1321

CIÉNEGA CREEK NATURAL PRESERVE

IN 1986, THE CIÉNEGA Creek Natural Preserve was established to protect the creek, riparian vegetation, and surrounding areas and has been a destination for hikers, bird-watchers, and wildlife enthusiasts ever since. The main trail traversing the preserve is part of the historic Arizona National Scenic Trail. Easy to reach and yet off-the-beaten-path, it's an ideal place to spend a morning or afternoon in quiet contemplation, surrounded by nature.

Fundamentals: Half-day trip; 24 miles (38.6 km) southeast of downtown Tucson; year-round

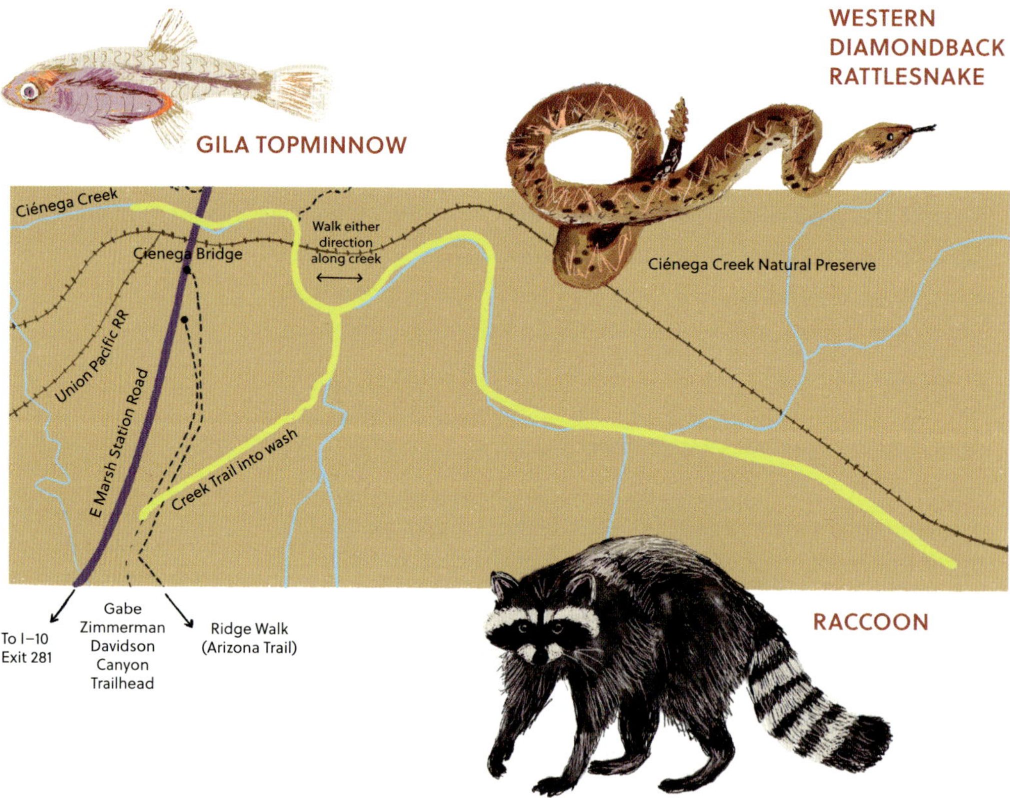

A DESERT HAVEN

The drive to the Ciénega Creek Natural Preserve is a half-hour tour of the topography and nature of the area; the Santa Catalina Mountains loom large to the north and, as you travel down the interstate, desertscrub gives way to desert grassland dotted with statuesque soaptree yuccas. Variations in vegetation is one of the more remarkable features of the preserve. It covers more than 4000 acres, stretching for about 12 miles (19 km) along Ciénega Creek from Colossal Cave to the headquarters of Empirita Ranch, an active cattle ranch. Located in a zone that transitions from Sonoran to Chihuahuan Desert, the preserve contains no fewer than nine distinct plant communities. Once in the parking lot, impressive views of the Rincon Mountains will greet you as well as striking views of the canyon and the riparian zone fed by the creek below.

You have your choice of hiking trails. The first is the Arizona Trail, a narrow ridge trail that cuts through expanses of desert grasses and impressive stands of ocotillo and creosote overlooking Davidson Canyon. It's an easy walk through the desert with some interpretive graphics about the viewshed along the route, but lacks shade, at least for humans. Tall grasses provide shade—and great hiding spots—for western diamondback and Mojave rattlesnakes. Remember, rattlesnakes aren't a reason to avoid the hike, just a reminder to pay attention to your surroundings and stay on the path.

The other option is the creek trail, which descends from the parking area but, once there, provides an easy hike and has much to offer. There are stretches where the creek runs continually; however, its flow is shallow, narrow, and intermittent, allowing for unimpeded walking. If you choose this trail, head north from the creek bed to experience the sights and sounds along the way, such as the cascading song of a canyon wren and stands of cottonwood, willow, and mesquite trees offering significant shade.

Ciénega Creek

Creek flow is intermittent, and water levels vary throughout the year.

LOCAL HISTORY AND NATIONAL IMPORTANCE

The Arizona Trail is part of the Arizona National Scenic Trail, an 800-mile (1287-km) nonmotorized path stretching north-south across Arizona from Mexico to Utah and crossing a range of ecosystems and geographical areas (deserts, mountains, canyons, forests) as well as historically significant sites and modern-day communities. Consider that this hike will give you bragging rights—you can say you've hiked (at least part of) the Arizona Trail.

It is also a place for solemn reflection. At the top, take note that the trailhead is named after Gabe Zimmerman, who was killed during the assassination attempt on US Representative Gabrielle Giffords on January 8, 2011. Nineteen people were shot, six of whom died. Gabe had a deep love for this area and enjoyed hiking and biking through the mountains and canyons you see from this vantage point.

SOMETHING FISHY GOING ON

Despite being a relatively dry state, mostly in the southern half, there are more than two dozen species of naturally occurring fish in Arizona, some of which swim in Ciénega Creek. If you peer into the water, especially in deeper pools, you're likely to find tiny Gila topminnow and other rare minnows, many endangered. Depending on season, temperature, and rainfall, you may see different size classes of the same species and even spot a number of tadpoles (larval amphibians).

During the summer rains, several species breed in and around the creek, and year-round you may identify lowland leopard frogs (or hear them plunk into the water as they seek escape from you). You'll also see an abundance of aquatic invertebrates, particularly in backwater pools. All the above are obligate (freshwater dependent) aquatic/semiaquatic species, at great risk as climate change, development, and invasive species overtake riparian habitats and eclipse the native species that have relied on these water sources for thousands, if not millions, of years.

A DESERT OASIS

Throughout the preserve, wildlife abounds, even if not immediately visible. Grasshoppers, dragonflies, tarantula hawks (a type of spider wasp), antlions, various lizard species, several types of snakes (such as semiaquatic garter snakes), and a wide variety of mammals (including raccoons, coatis, and skunks) are common in or near the creek.

◂ Ciénega Creek is also a great train-spotting location, as the Union Pacific Railroad crosses over the creek.

Like other riparian habitats, the preserve is a great place for bird-watching and is home to smaller songbirds, ravens, vultures, and other birds of prey. The creek and surrounding valley provide abundant habitat and important wildlife corridors for larger mammals, such as mule deer, javelinas, coyotes, bobcats, and mountain lions. In all, more than 280 species of native wildlife, including 150 species of birds, either live in or visit the preserve.

MORE DETAILS

Directions: Take Interstate 10E to the State Route 83N exit, sharp right onto Frontage Road/E. Marsh Station Road. Follow this 3 miles to the Gabe Zimmerman trailhead parking lot.

Amenities: Two parking areas; portable toilets; no water fountains; not ADA accessible; leashed dogs are permitted and you must remove their waste.

Special Features: Nearby attractions include Colossal Cave, one of the largest dry caves in North America, showing evidence of human use as far back as 900 CE.

Pro Tips: Hikers, mountain bikers, and equestrians are welcome. For the protection of the preserve, the number of daily visitors is limited and a permit is required (available through the Pima County Natural Resources, Parks and Recreation Department), so plan ahead. Because water from four mountain ranges drains into the Ciénega Creek watershed, it easily floods after even a modest rainfall. Use caution during the rainy season (July through early September) or reschedule your visit. Be sure to bring everything you might need, including water, snacks, sunscreen, layered clothing, and a hat, along with a mobile phone.

Info:

Ciénega Creek Natural Preserve
15865-15887 E. Marsh Station Road
Vail, Arizona
Permits: 520-725-5000

BUENOS AIRES NATIONAL WILDLIFE REFUGE

THE BABOQUIVARI MOUNTAINS, sacred to the Tohono O'odham people, mark the western edge of Southern Arizona's Sky Islands. At the base of their eastern slope, Brown Canyon nestles within the Buenos Aires National Wildlife Refuge (BANWR) in Altar Valley. With views of surrounding oak woodland above as well as sycamore, willow, and cottonwood lining the canyon, this area is home to many species that populate both sides of the international border. The drive itself is a scenic treat, passing through one of the largest undeveloped grasslands left in this region and offering sweeping valley views that include Baboquivari Peak, jutting 1000 feet (305 m) above the surrounding wilderness, and the shiny domes of Kitt Peak National Observatory.

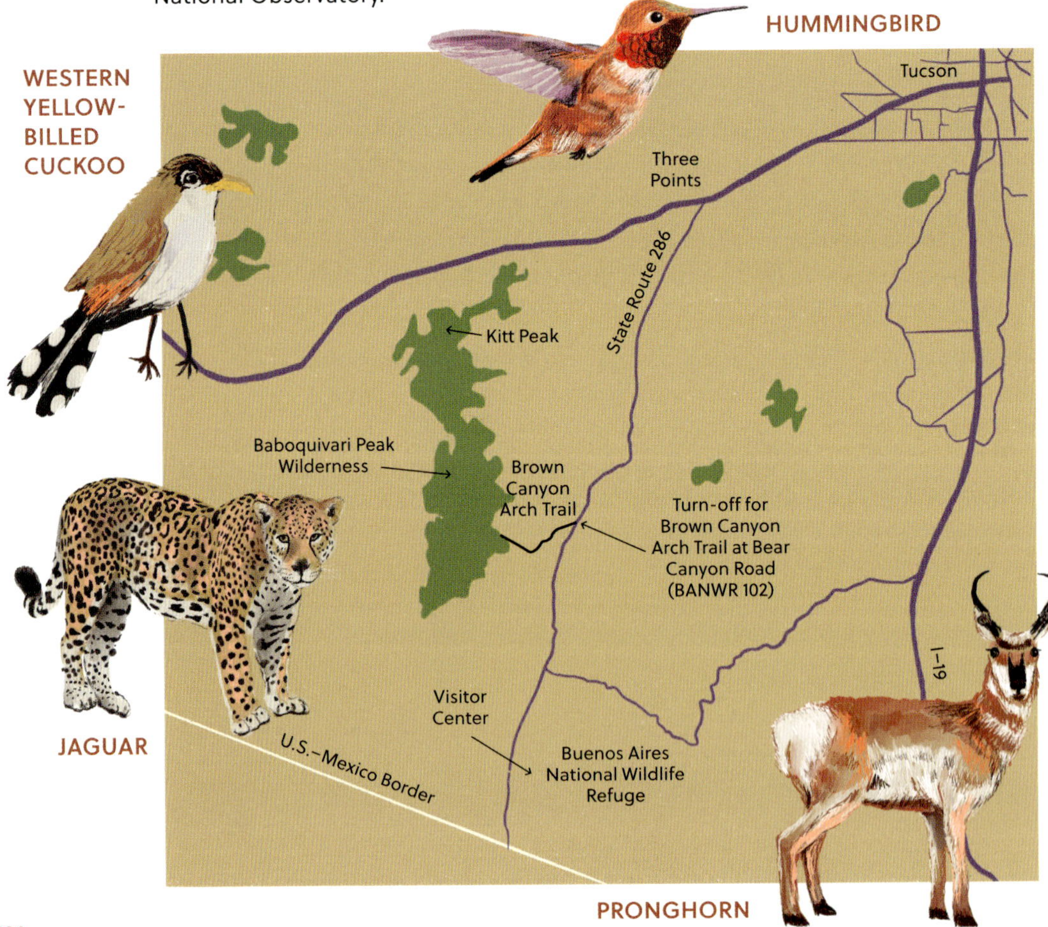

Fundamentals: Day trip; scenic drive and hike; 64 miles (102 km) southwest of downtown Tucson; sites include Brown Canyon, Baboquivari Peak, Arch Rock; BANWR guide required (call ahead to schedule); high-clearance vehicle required; fall/winter/spring

A TASTE OF NORTHERN MEXICO

BANWR's 117,464 acres are habitat for more than 300 kinds of birds and 130 other wildlife species. Depending on the season or specific day of your visit, you may see summer poppies, sunflowers, five species of oak, rainbow cacti, horse lubbers (massive grasshoppers!), pronghorns, pumas, ringtails, and coatis. Gila monsters, desert tortoises, lesser long-nosed bats, rufous hummingbirds, and Wilson's warblers scuttle, plod, and perch here, too. Several rare species live in or pass through the refuge: masked bobwhite quail, Chiricahua leopard frog, Northern Mexican garter snake, western yellow-billed cuckoo, southwestern willow flycatcher, Pima pineapple cactus, Kearney's blue-star, and even jaguar. Neotropical birds, such as the

◂ Boardwalk over Arivaca Cienega (wetlands) in the refuge

◂ Vast grasslands of the refuge with Baboquivari Peak in the distance

▲ Chiricahua leopard frog with transmitter

▼ Masked bobwhite quail

gray hawk, black-bellied whistling duck, green kingfisher, tropical kingbird, thick-billed kingbird, northern beardless tyrannulet, and sora are also regular residents.

A QUAIL TALE

Spotting any of these native species would be a high point of your hike to share with friends, but perhaps the most interesting story—one that touches on diversity and scarcity simultaneously—is about the quail of this area.

A unique feature of this valley is that four species of quail—Montezuma, Gambel's, scaled, and masked bobwhite—live here. The last is a critically endangered species, native to Southern Arizona and northern Mexico, and BANWR staff have invested decades of hard work to save it from extinction. More than 100 years ago, ornithologists noted the masked bobwhite's diminishing population; in the subsequent decades, it nearly disappeared from the landscape. BANWR sustains the last known wild population.

Though the early days of the recovery were very challenging, from 2018 to 2022 BANWR released 1800 chicks, many of which survived. Staff hope to reestablish this beautiful bird well beyond the boundaries of the refuge. To help make this happen, the small, dedicated refuge team is working with the Altar Valley Conservation Alliance (a consortium of conservation-minded ranchers) to develop a Safe Harbor Agreement that would encourage ranchers to allow the quail to be established on their ranches. Refuge staff are working with ranchers in Mexico to restore habitat and reestablish the quail there, too.

▲ Access to much of the refuge is on well-graded dirt roads.

A BIT OF THE OLD (AND NEW) WEST

Rock art documents thousands of years of human habitation in these Tohono O'odham ancestral lands (today part of the refuge is co-managed by the Tohono O'odham Nation). In the late 1600s, Padre Kino passed through, making note of Baboquivari Peak, a landmark used by people throughout recorded history. Though treeless grassland for millennia, Altar Valley's ecosystem shifted in the 1800s with the introduction of ranching and impact of prolonged drought; sightings of many native species became a rarity.

By the end of that century, the drought had decimated livestock and those that survived consumed much of the remaining vegetation. With little vegetation to hold soil intact, the returning rains created deep washes and gullies in the area for the first time, and these waterways have impacted the valley ever since, continually carving deeper channels into the landscape. These events made the valley vulnerable to the invasion of non-native mesquite trees, further disrupting the grassland ecosystem.

Despite its challenges, ranching has continued in Altar Valley, and today ranchers and Indigenous peoples may hold the key to preserving what's left of the original grassland habitat by keeping it free of large-scale development and working together to understand how to balance human needs and landscape use with long-term natural resource sustainability.

TAKING A HIKE

Choose from 1200 miles (1931 km) of hiking trails to explore. Brown Canyon Arch Trail, just under 4 miles (6.4 km) round-trip, is a wonderful introduction to the refuge and begins in flat open terrain at slightly above 4000 feet (1219 m) in elevation. As you proceed into the canyon, the winding path narrows and steepens, offering amazing views of Baboquivari Mountain. Investigate a connecting trail, such as Jaguar Canyon Trail, or continue on to Arch Rock, a natural rock bridge 47 feet (14.3 m) high.

MORE DETAILS

Directions: West on Ajo Road (State Route 86), then south on State Route 286 to milepost 7.5. BANWR stretches along both sides of the road. To arrive at the refuge headquarters, head east from Route 286 and follow the signs. Brown Canyon Arch Trail access is between mileposts 20 and 21.

Hike: 4 miles (6.4 km), round-trip; 650-foot (198-m) elevation gain; moderate.

Amenities: Restrooms or portable toilets and water available in the visitor center and the Brown Canyon Education Center and Lodge, where the Friends of BANWR host educational programs. Call ahead to check refuge and facilities hours, canyon access, and educational programs as well as make reservations for hikes, which require a staff guide.

Pro Tips: The best seasons for hiking in this area are fall through spring. When temperatures are warmer, hike in the morning; if severe weather events are forecast, reschedule your trip. Depending on the season and time of day, some trails are shaded by trees and canyon walls. While the refuge is open 24 hours, the visitor center has limited hours that vary by season. Keep in mind that you are very close to the international border and are likely to see border patrol vehicles and personnel.

Info:

Buenos Aires National Wildlife Refuge
7.5 miles (12 km) North of Sasabe on State Route 286,
Sasabe, AZ 85633
520-823-4251

KARTCHNER CAVERNS STATE PARK

KARTCHNER CAVERNS IS A remarkable, 200,000-year-old living cave system. While most public caves are "dead"—their minerals are no longer growing due to air and light exposure—this natural marvel has been preserved with meticulous care; bats and other cave critters (troglofauna) can thrive, and cave formations (speleothem, such as stalactites and stalagmites) are ever-growing. You won't detect any crystal growth during your short visit, however—they grow a mere inch (2.5 cm) every 750 years.

Fundamentals: Day trip; natural cave formations, tours, special events; 54 miles (87 km) southeast of downtown Tucson; year-round

CAVE MAP

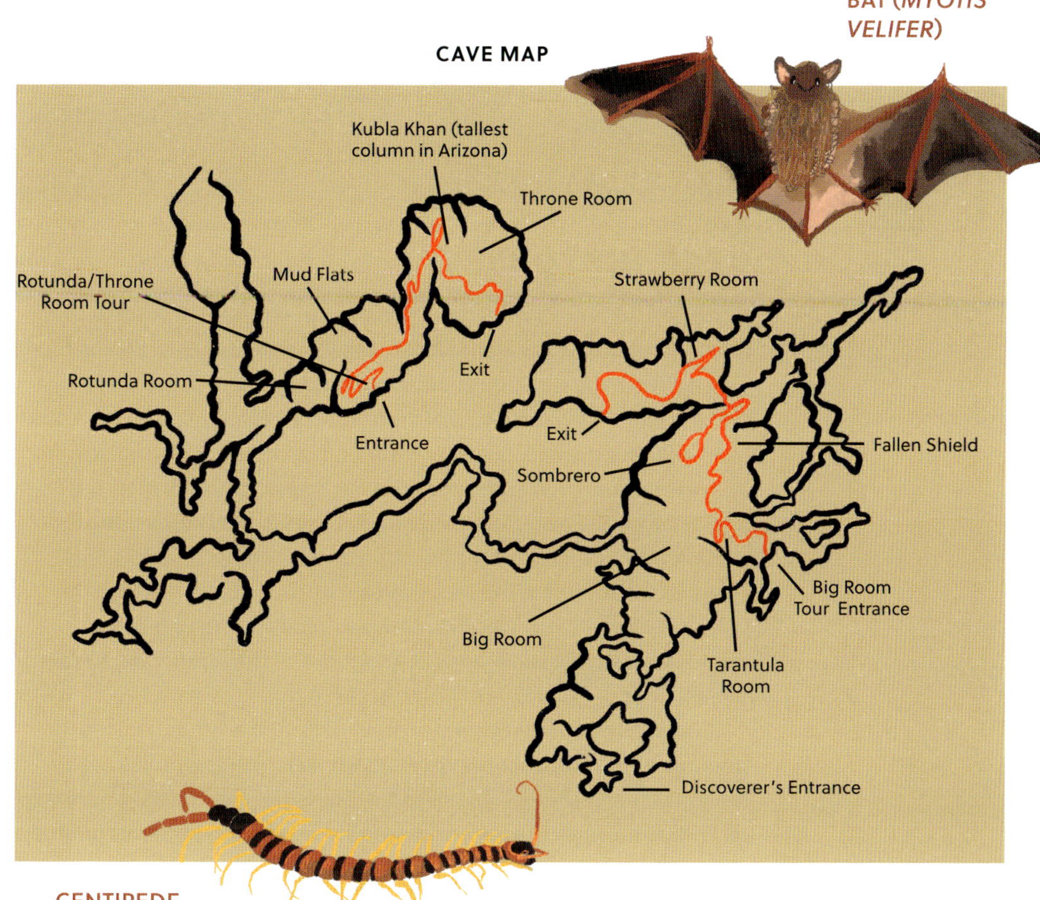

▸ Whetstone Mountains

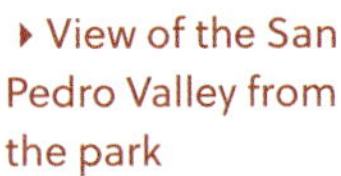

▸ View of the San Pedro Valley from the park

DEEP HISTORY

Burrowed under the Whetstone Mountains, with their entrance overlooking the broad San Pedro River Valley to the east, the caverns provide a clue to the geological drama behind this landscape. Like most caves, Kartchner was formed in limestone, a sedimentary rock created from the fused shells of sea creatures. These rocks formed about 330 million years ago when the area was covered by a shallow sea.

Fast-forward hundreds of millions of years, several cycles of mountain-building, oceans flooding and receding, and this limestone block settled in the mountains, hundreds of miles from the nearest ocean. Slightly acidic rainwater filtered through cracks in the rock, slowly dissolving more and more of the limestone. Cracks became passageways, and holes became huge caverns.

Eventually, most of the water drained from the caves, leaving underground rooms for nature to adorn with the incredible cave formations (speleothems) we see today. These are created as groundwater moves through the cave and evaporates, leaving minerals behind.

THE BEST KEPT SECRETS

When Randy Tufts and Gary Tenen stumbled upon an elaborate cave system in 1974, they kept their find under wraps, fearful that this subterranean wonder would be overrun with curious or unscrupulous cavers, trampling through and chopping up stalagmites and stalactites to sell. They'd seen this happen to other caves and decided the best way to preserve the caverns was to garner formal protection of them. The question was how.

In 1978, they informed the property owners, James and Lois Kartchner, about the caves and, in 1984, approached the Arizona State Parks Department about establishing a park. Still "obsessively secretive," according to Tufts, the pair persuaded an agreeable (and blindfolded) Parks official to accompany them to the cave under cover of night. That visit sparked sufficient interest to move the project along, through the agency, governor's office, and state legislature, all the while maintaining the utmost secrecy.

Funding came through in 1988, and planning began in earnest. Over the next 10 years, the Parks Department designed and built a system that would allow the public to experience these magnificent caves while minimizing the impact of construction and ongoing visitation. Small group tours are conducted with care (no one is permitted to touch any surfaces, minimizing the introduction of new microbes); walkways and railings keep visitors from straying; and although the entrances were greatly modified to allow access (tours are fully accessible), multiple doors maintain crucial humidity. In addition to humidity, carbon dioxide and other gas levels are actively monitored and managed. Lighting is carefully designed to be as cool as possible, activated only when people are present, and several ultraviolet light scans per year identify fabric lint, dust, hair, and other human residue for removal.

CAVE DWELLERS

Come spring and through early fall, the Big Room hosts more than 1000 female cave myotis bats (*Myotis velifer*) that use the room to birth and rear their pups. Moms move in around the end of April, each giving birth to a single pup in late June/early July. Over the next three to four months, the moms leave the roost nightly to eat, collectively consuming about 1000 pounds (454 kg) of insects over the summer. To protect the colony, human visitors are prohibited in the Big Room during this time.

‣ Numerous types of cave formations (speleothems), such as these shields, soda straws, and stalactites, are on display.

‣ The Big Room

‣ Tasteful lighting highlights the varied features of nature's artwork.

Guano (bat poop) is the base of the food web for most other cave critters. Fungi and bacteria feast first, then are eaten by a host of animals—nematodes, mites, isopods, amphipods, spiders, centipedes, millipedes, crickets, beetle larvae, and more. These invertebrates and the microbes they consume are extensively researched and monitored as part of the National Science Foundation's worldwide network of Microbial Observatories; these studies help us better understand the diversity of microbes as well as their essential functions and interactions with all other life forms on the planet.

Kartchner has also served as the final resting place for other animals over the millennia. Archaeologists have unearthed the fossilized remains of an 86,000-year-old Shasta ground sloth, a 34,000-year-old horse, an 11,000-year-old bear, and many other smaller animals.

TOURING THE CAVES

The number of daily visitors to Kartchner Caverns is limited, so reserve your tickets well in advance, especially during the busy winter and spring seasons. Two regular cave tours are offered—for the Rotunda and Throne Rooms (year-round) and the Big Room (from mid-October to mid-April only; not available for children under seven). Tours cover about a half mile (0.8 km) and take 1.5–1.75 hours. Specialty tours are also available.

The underground temperature is about 70°F (21°C) year-round, with nearly 99 percent humidity, so dress in layers. Note the wet sheen on many surfaces (a sign that dripping water is slowly building on existing speleothems and creating new ones) and the bands of color created by the groundwater's changing chemistry.

COLOSSAL CAVE: AN ALTERNATIVE CAVING EXPERIENCE

For families with young children, or if you have less time, Colossal Cave on the southeast outskirts of Tucson is a good option. It's a dry cave with now-dormant formations. Visitors can take a 50-minute guided tour (0.5 mile/0.8 km) or a number of specialty tours. Please note that the cave tour is not wheelchair accessible. The surrounding park has picnicking and camping areas as well as trails for hiking, biking, and horseback riding.

MORE DETAILS

Directions: Take Interstate 10E to Interstate 19, getting off at Exit 302 for State Route 90E, then travel along State Route 90S about 9 miles (14.5 km) to the park.

Day Trip: Campsites, camping cabins, and RV sites available; 8.4 mi (13.5 km) of hiking trails with 360–2345 ft. (109.7–714.8 km) elevation gain, easy to challenging.

Amenities: Parking; Discovery Center with museum, video presentations, hands-on, child-friendly exhibits, restrooms, gift shop, and Bat Cave Café; shaded picnic tables; hummingbird garden; ADA accessible; pets allowed in the park, but not the caves.

Pro Tips: Booking tickets in advance, online or by phone (877-MY-PARKS, #2), is highly recommended. Check the website for current visitor information, fees, tour schedule/reservations, and pre-visit instructions and precautions.

Info:

Kartchner Caverns
2980 State Route 90
Benson, AZ 85602
520-586-4100

MADERA CANYON

THE STRIKING SANTA RITA MOUNTAINS border the Tucson Basin to the south, with their highest peak, Mount Wrightson (or "Old Baldy"), towering among them at 9452 feet (2881 m) and about 100 miles (161 km) of trails to explore. A frequent destination for locals, the mountains provide a cool escape from the valley heat and are often accessed via Madera Canyon on Mount Wrightson's northern slope, popular for its amenities and easy paved-road approach. Pack a picnic and make a day of it.

Fundamentals: Day trip; scenic drive, picnic area, bird-watching, hiking trails; pass required; 40 miles (64.4 km) south of downtown Tucson; year-round

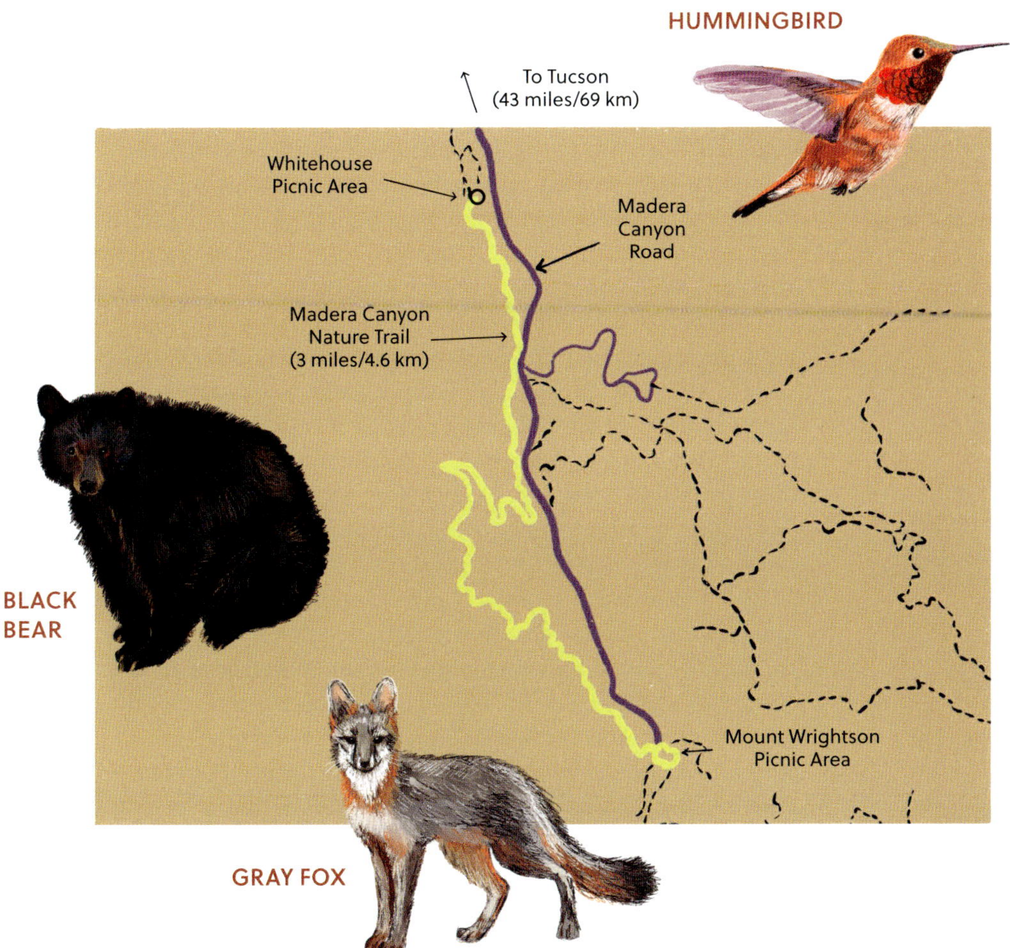

▲ Road to Madera Canyon in the Santa Rita Mountains

VISTAS, VISTAS EVERYWHERE

The drive from Tucson to Madera Canyon packs plenty of visual impact. To the southeast, the Santa Rita Mountains stretch toward the international border while Mission San Xavier Del Bac, built in the late 1700s, sits to the west on the Tohono O'odham Nation. Along the way, you'll see mine tailings (impressive flat-topped mounds of discarded earth from mining) to the west. They represent an essential chapter of Arizona's cultural story and one of the ongoing environmental issues in the region.

Once you're off the freeway and heading into the mountains, signs will direct you to the Santa Rita Experimental Range and Wildlife Area, the longest continuously active rangeland research facility and one of the five oldest biological field stations in the United States. To reach the canyon, follow the road as it slices through several plant biomes, including Sonoran desertscrub, semi-desert grassland, oak/juniper woodland, and more. The canyon floor is dominated by streamside riparian woodland and populated with beautiful cottonwood and sycamore trees, fed by Madera Creek's intermittent stretches of surface flow.

Note the pullouts and camping areas en route, some at lower elevations and others much higher up. All are gateways into the natural world of the Santa Ritas and, depending on the season and temperature, one of these might be your choice on a given day. Here, we are zeroing in on the Madera Canyon Nature Trail, a beautiful all-purpose trail and a good year-round option as long as you visit when temperatures are tolerable.

MILE-HIGH HIKE

The nature trail starts at 4600 feet (1400 m) and stays relatively close to the creek, a refreshing course for a summer hike but one that will remind you of what breathing at higher elevations feels like. The trail passes through Mexican blue and Arizona oaks, manzanitas, and alligator junipers, along with a mixture of cottonwood, sycamore, ash, and walnut trees, which provide intermittent shade, in and along the stream. Ferns, Madrean yuccas, bear grass, agaves, and some cacti abound here as well.

◤ Madera Creek

▲ View from higher elevations in the canyon

The canyon places you in prime habitat for bobcats, pumas, ringtails, javelinas, squirrels, raccoons, and skunks. At this elevation, white-tailed deer, black bears, and gray foxes are common, too, as are coatimundis (or coatis, for short) and their racoon relatives. Even if you do not spot them, these animals are present—they see and hear (and smell) you—so stay aware of your surroundings. If you are camping, follow protocols for bear country. Finally, keep in mind that biting chiggers live in the grasses—stay away from those areas to avoid unwelcome souvenirs (itchy rashes) of your visit.

THE BIRDS AND THE BEETLES

Home to around 250 species, including 15 types of hummingbirds—both year-round residents and seasonal migrants—Madera Canyon is one of the top birding areas in the United States, drawing people from around the world. By day, you may encounter elegant trogons, sulfur-bellied flycatchers, zone-tailed hawks, and more. By night, you may see (or more likely, hear) Western and whiskered screech owls, elusive elf owls, and even occasional flammulated or spotted owls. If you're an avid birder looking for specific birds, you'll want to check birding websites beforehand for any species you might soon be able to add to your birding life list.

▲ Elegant trogons are year-round residents in Mexico but migrate to mountain canyons in Southern Arizona and New Mexico for spring and summer. Their range appears to be expanding northward as the climate warms.

Alternatively, take advantage of the canyon's "no-hike" birding option. Park at the Santa Rita Lodge Gift Shop and pick up a drink, snack, birding guide, hat, or other memento, then settle on a bench and let the birds come to you. Our feathered friends have reason to stop and linger—the wide range of seed feeders, hummingbird feeders, and suet and peanut butter blocks that attract them. The feeders also attract hungry coatis, and there's a special feeding station for them to keep them from climbing the trees and emptying the bird feeders.

Lovers of other flying creatures will want to keep an eye out for jewel scarab beetles during the rainy season. With their shiny green and gold elytra (hard outer wing coverings that resemble liquid metal), they are every bit as beautiful as the birds.

Anyone herpetology-inclined will appreciate that Madera Canyon is also a haven for some rare reptiles, including mountain spiny lizards, Sonoran mountain kingsnakes, and green rat snakes. In rocky outcrops, you may catch sight of any one of three rare and protected rattlesnakes—rock, Arizona ridge-nosed, and twin-spotted. Several of these species barely enter Arizona in Sky Island habitat, with the bulk of their ranges east, west, and south of the state. For a challenge, look along the creek for canyon tree frogs, well-camouflaged with speckled skin that blends with the granite boulders they rest on.

MORE DETAILS

Directions: Take Interstate 10E to Exit 260 for Interstate 19S. Get off at Exit 63 for Continental Road, turn right onto Madera Canyon Road, and drive 12.2 miles (19.6 km) to the canyon. Park at the Whitehouse Picnic Area for Madera Canyon Nature Trail.

Day Trip: Day pass required; Madera Canyon Nature Trail is 5.8 miles (9.3 km) round-trip with 921-foot (280.7-m) elevation gain, moderate. There are multiple places to access and/or turn around on this out-and-back trail to shorten or lengthen the hike.

Amenities: Parking; picnic areas with grills; a campground and private lodge; restrooms; refreshments available; leashed dogs permitted; family-friendly.

Pro Tips: Spring and fall afternoons or summer mornings are the best times to hike the canyon. If it's chilly or raining in Tucson, there's a good chance you'll see some Southern Arizona snow. For more hiking options, you can easily access the Santa Rita Mountains trail system from the canyon. Consider a visit to Tubac, a delightful town known for its arts and crafts, just to the south. Besides Madera Canyon, there are other points of entry into the Santa Ritas—many dirt roads offer access to quieter, less frequented trails—but most require high clearance and/or four-wheel drive.

Info:

Madera Canyon
Green Valley, AZ 85614
Nogales Ranger District: 520-281-2296

TOHONO O'ODHAM MUSEUM AND OBSERVATORY

THIS JOURNEY TO A SOVEREIGN Indigenous nation and an astronomy research center provides new perspectives on the land and the skies around it as well as ourselves and our cultures through time.

Fundamentals: Scenic drive; cultural museum; telescope complex and optional night viewing program; southwest of downtown Tucson, 70 miles (113 km) to the Cultural Center and 54 miles (87 km) to Kitt Peak; year-round

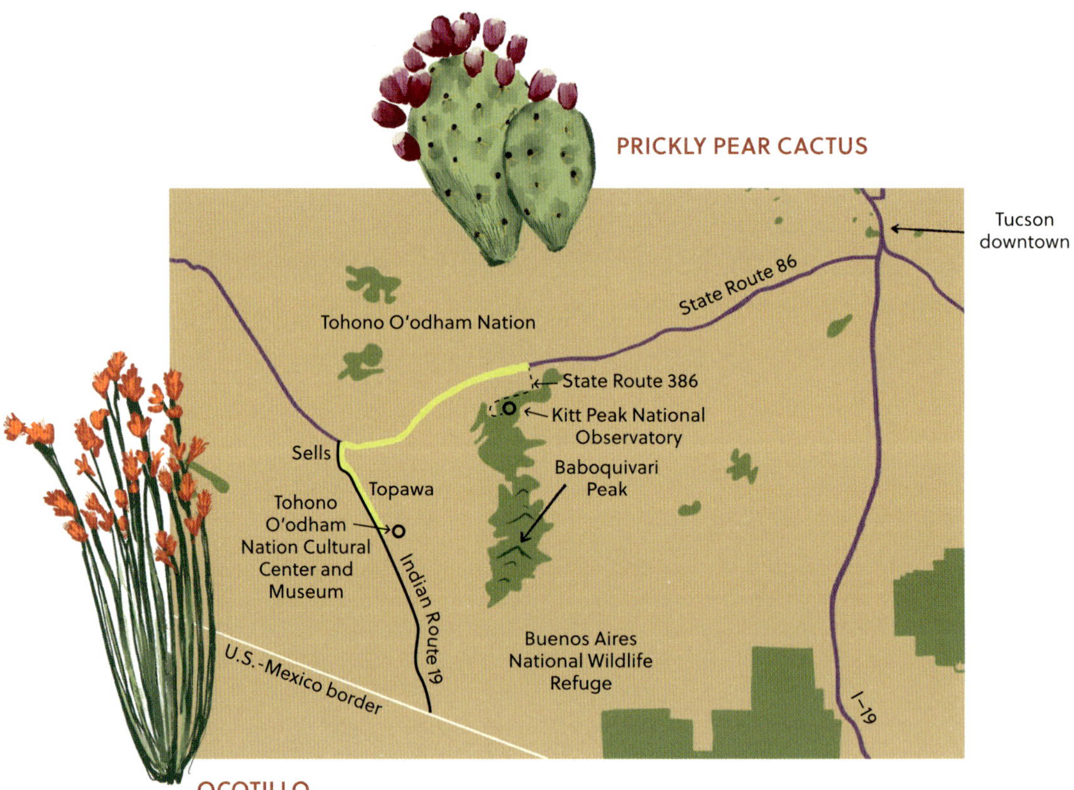

◂ Tohono O'odham Nation Museum and Cultural Center (Himdag Ki:) entrance

TOHONO O'ODHAM NATION CULTURAL CENTER AND MUSEUM - HIMDAG KI:

Tohono O'odham means "desert people," and O'odham ancestral lands stretched (using present-day place names) across the Sonoran Desert, from north of Phoenix, south into Sonora, west to the Gulf of California, and east to the San Pedro River. In 1854, when the United States acquired what is now Southern Arizona from Mexico, the international border was established, dividing O'odham lands and people. Today, the Tohono O'odham Nation, one of the largest Indigenous sovereign states in the United States, governs an area approximately the size of Connecticut and has about 30,000 members, many of whom live outside of tribal lands. There are four federally recognized O'odham tribes in Arizona, each one governed separately as a sovereign nation: the Tohono O'odham Nation west of Tucson, and three communities farther north—Gila River Indian Community, Ak-Chin Indian Community, and the Salt River (Pima Maricopa) Indian Community. In addition, there are nine communities in Mexico, and the Hia-Ced O'odham in southwestern Arizona.

Start your day by driving west on Arizona State Route 86 to Sells, the capital of Tohono O'odham Nation. In spring and following summer rains, the road is often lined with brilliant orange poppies and other wildflowers. About 9 miles (14.5 km) south of Sells on Indian Route 19 (San Miguel Road), in the tiny town of Topowa, you'll find Himdag Ki: (Way of Life House). The architecturally striking museum houses fascinating exhibits about Tohono O'odham culture and

Above, left to right: Garden (*oidag*) at the Cultural Center and Museum

Traditional ramada (*watto*) at the Cultural Center and Museum

Baboquivari is framed in this window in the Elder's Room. The design on the window (often referred to as "Man in the Maze") represents a person's journey through life in Tohono O'odham culture.

Baboquivari Peak

history in a setting that honors the land and its inhabitants. Drawing on its extensive collection of artifacts and archives, the exhibits and programs tell authentic stories of the Tohono O'odham. Himdag Ki: primarily serves as an educational and cultural resource for the O'odham and other visitors.

Plan to spend one to two hours exploring the museum. The Himdag Ki: complex also includes nature paths and a cultural center. To the east, you'll see a prominent granite monolith, known as Baboquivari Peak. Its name comes from *Waw Giwulk*, O'odham for "constricted rock." In O'odham cosmology, the peak is the center of Mother Earth and the home of I'itoi, the creator. A prominent feature of the western horizon from many places in and around Tucson, it also appears in the center of the Nation's Great Seal.

If you've worked up an appetite, head back to Sells where there are a couple of options, including a supermarket.

KITT PEAK NATIONAL OBSERVATORY (KPNO)

After visiting Himdag Ki:, return to State Route 86 heading toward Tucson. About 20 miles (32 km) east of Sells, turn south on State Route 386, which will take you to the highest point of the Quinlan Mountains, Kitt Peak. In 1958, Kitt Peak was chosen from more than 150 sites to be the first national astronomical observatory in the United States due to its dark skies and reliably clear weather. Since then, KPNO has assembled one of the largest collections of telescopes in the world. Operated by the National Science Foundation, it's still the US national center for ground-based, nighttime optical

astronomy and, in 1964, opened its visitor center, dedicating three of its telescopes solely to nightly public programs.

As you drive up the mountain, the daytime views of the Sonoran Desert are as impressive as the stars and planets at night (although there may be astronomers who would debate this). The paved road heads south toward the mountain through prickly pear and cholla cacti, which grade into ocotillos and yuccas along the climb.

The winding road presents new vistas around each bend. To the east, you'll see the steep and rugged Coyote Mountains Wilderness. From a north-facing pullout at 3 miles (4.8 km), look for a white strip in the Silverbell Mountains; this is the Silverbell copper mine located about 20 miles (32 km) away. At 8.5 miles (13.5 km), you'll get a clear view to the west of the alternating basins and ranges for which this geological province (Basin and Range) is named. Then, curving south, the distinctive profile of Baboquivari Peak will come into view, followed 1 mile (1.5 km) later by the white telescope domes. Toward the top of the mountain, you'll find a picnic area and finally the parking lot for the visitor center at a heady elevation of 6875 feet (2096 m).

In addition to the telescopes, you'll immediately notice the temperature difference from the valley below; it's typically 15–20°F (8–11°C) cooler on the mountain and often windy. Enjoy KPNO's exhibits and a daytime or self-guided tour. If your schedule allows, attend a nighttime viewing program—they are outstanding, both awe-inducing and informative, offering visitors the chance to speak with expert astronomy educators and peer through or view images from research-grade telescopes. If you aren't already a stargazer, you'll become one.

▸ Moonrise behind the Mayall telescope

▸ The McMath-Pierce Solar Telescope was decommissioned in 2017 and is being repurposed as an outreach center.

▸ The nighttime viewing programs are educational, fun, and awe-inspiring.

▲ Telescope complex at Kitt Peak

MORE DETAILS

Directions: See sections above for specific directions. Please note that the turnoff from Indian Route 19 (San Miguel Road) onto Baboquivari Mountain Road (location of Himdag Ki:) is easy to miss; it's 2.2 miles (3.6 km) past the high school, just before a cluster of district office buildings on the left.

Day Trip: Scenic drive; museum and cultural center; observatory.

Amenities: Visitor services are limited in Tohono O'odham Nation. While gas and food are available in Sells, you won't find much in the way of restaurants and stores, and there are no hotels or motels. Himdag Ki: and Kitt Peak Visitor Center have restrooms and are wheelchair accessible and family-friendly.

Pro Tips: When visiting Tohono O'odham Nation, remember that you're traveling through a sovereign nation with some different laws and cultural norms—be aware that it's unlawful to drive off marked roads, to take any natural materials or human artifacts, or to photograph or video people without their permission. Call ahead to Himdag Ki: before you visit, as their hours may vary from what is posted on the website. Check the Kitt Peak website for new exhibits and programs as well as possible restrictions due to weather or fire damage. If you're attending a night program on Kitt Peak, bring extra layers of clothing—it gets chilly at that high altitude.

Info:

Himdag Ki: (Way of Life House)
Tohono O'odham Nation Cultural Center and Museum
Baboquivari
Mountain Road
Sells, AZ 85639
520-383-0200

Kitt Peak National Observatory
Tucson, AZ 85635
520-318-8726

OVERNIGHT TRIPS

BEYOND 100 MILES
(160 KM) FROM
DOWNTOWN TUCSON

CHIRICAHUA NATIONAL MONUMENT

ESTABLISHED IN 1924, the Chiricahua National Monument encompasses 12,025 acres of native plants, wildlife, and remarkable rock formations—balancing rocks (large boulders precariously perched on a stack of smaller ones) and hoodoos (chimney-like towers of volcanic rock) and more, created over millions of years of geological upheaval and erosion. Located in the farthest corner of southeastern Arizona, this outdoor adventure is worth the two-and-a-half-hour drive for the sheer geological spectacle and immersion in the natural world under a starry sky.

Fundamentals: Overnight trip; 8-mile (13-km) paved scenic drive, rock formations, 17 miles (27.4 km) of trails; 117 miles (188 km) southeast of downtown Tucson; year-round

MEXICAN JAY

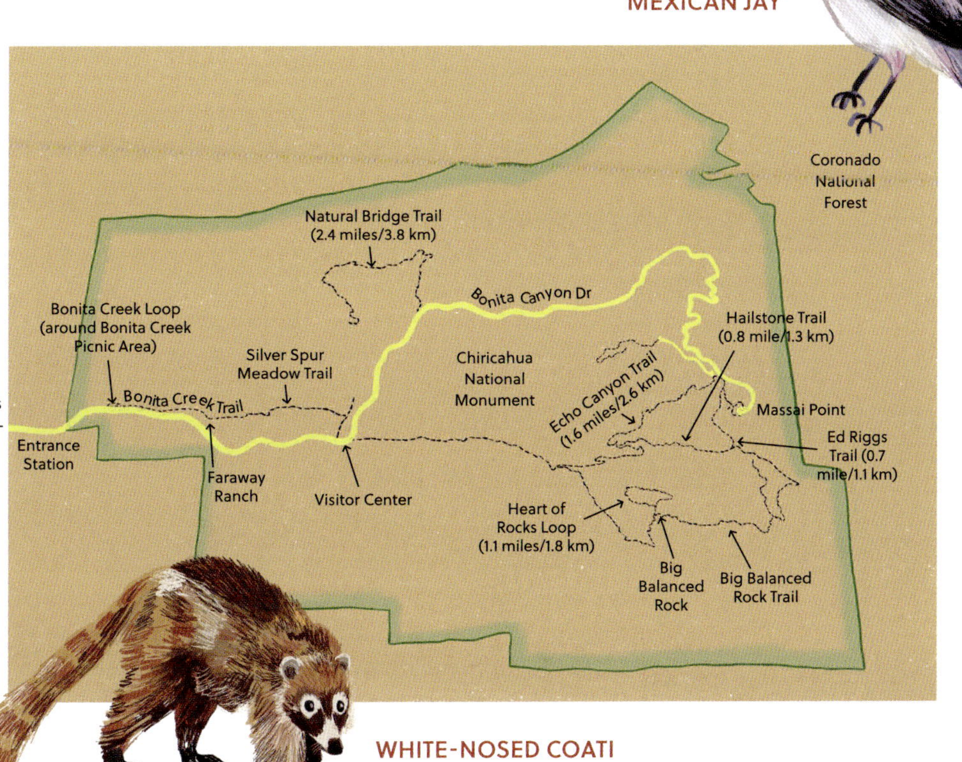

WHITE-NOSED COATI

▲ Big Balanced Rock

◀ Massive hoodoos formed from volcanic deposits throughout the monument.

LAND, WATER, AND SKY

Covering an expanse 35-by-21 miles (56-by-34 km) and peaking at nearly 10,000 feet (3048 m), the Chiricahua Mountains are among the largest of Arizona's Sky Islands. Along the monument's extensive trails, you can explore caves, faults, the remnants of long-ago lava flows, and, just south, the Turkey Creek Caldera, a massive volcanic crater, 12 miles (19.3 km) in diameter.

These mountains helped shape five major watersheds in the region. Water from seeps, creeks, springs, and water-filled pockets called *tinajas* (Spanish for "jars") provides moist habitats for a wide variety of plants and fauna.

With no large cities nearby, you'll experience the wonder of dark, star-stippled desert sky. Millions of stars are visible, making this area an ideal location for some of the world's largest telescopes. The Massai Point and Echo Canyon trailheads are great vantage points for stargazing.

THE NATURAL WORLD OF THE CHIRICAHUAS

The Chiricahuas sit at the crossroads of four major ecosystems—the Rocky Mountains, the Sierra Madre, and the Sonoran and Chihuahuan Deserts. In addition, five biomes (comprised of the living species in a particular location) flourish in and around these mountains: grassland, deciduous and coniferous forest, chaparral, and desertscrub, creating a mosaic of astounding biodiversity hot spots.

▲ Grasslands and desertscrub surround the mountains.

The grasslands are home to almost 1000 species of vascular plants (advanced species with internal circulatory systems) and more than 50 grass species. In the interior chaparral, the dominant plant is pointleaf manzanita. Moving to deciduous forest, oak woodlands take over, with seven oak species as well as madrone and juniper. At higher elevations, conifer forest creates a towering treescape, punctuated by showy Arizona cypress and sycamores. Ferns, mushrooms, and mosses live in shady areas throughout these plant communities, and spring wildflowers burst forth after heavy rains. As you drop in elevation south and east of the mountains, you'll find the arid-adapted plants characteristic of Chihuahuan desertscrub, such as creosote bush.

Though there's much to see on a grand scale, don't forget the smaller organisms. Look for lichens spattered on tree bark and rocks in rich or pale shades of green, amber, brown, and rust. Made up of fungi and algae, these "paintbrushes" of the Sonoran Desert lend an impressionistic flair to everything they touch.

THE UNTAMED WILD

Nearly 200 species of birds have been recorded within the borders of the monument, including 17 raptor species and a dozen species of hummingbirds. This area is also habitat for various rare birds, like the migrating sandhill crane, which summers in northern Canada and Alaska, and Mexican chickadee, a permanent resident you're unlikely to spot anywhere else in Arizona.

▲ Hundreds of hoodoos with a monsoon rainstorm in the distance

You may also encounter any of more than 75 mammal species. Keep your eyes peeled and your binoculars ready. A short list includes coyotes, gray foxes, raccoons, ringtails, mule and white-tailed deer, javelinas, mountain lions, badgers, coatimundis, and long-tailed weasels, not to mention three skunk species and more than 20 types of bats.

If you're into cold-blooded critters, you'll find three dozen reptile species and five amphibian species skittering, slithering, leaping, or paddling here. Reptiles include three protected rattlesnake species and a dozen types of lizards, such as the Great Plains skink, southern alligator lizard, and horned lizards that vary by elevation and habitat. As for invertebrates, they range from the unusual and showy (pleasing fungus beetles, leaf chafers, and jewel beetles) to the seemingly shy and rare, such as fireflies and glowworms. Arizona's only salamander, the tiger salamander, also calls these mountains home.

PEOPLE IN THE CHIRICAHUA MOUNTAINS

The vast human history of this area dates back thousands of years, from the Lithic peoples hunting mammoths, bison, and horses around early Lake Cochise to the hunting/gathering Mogollon, followed by the Chiricahua Apache, Mexicans, Spanish colonizers, and early American settlers of European ancestry. The later groups brought military outposts, ranching, and mining in the mid-to-late 1800s.

Part of the visible human history here is the impact of wildfire, evident in charred tree stumps and cleared brush. Before European settlement, fires were beneficially frequent and the foundation of a

◂ Scenic views in every direction

naturally occurring cycle of clearing, reproduction, and growth. Since then, recurring drought combined with heavy human influence—fire suppression, deforestation, soil erosion, introductions of non-native species, and climate change—have created a more intense and destructive fire regime. Today, fires are larger, hotter, and harder to contain, placing any plants and animals (including humans) in their paths at great risk.

TAKE A HIKE

The Chiricahua National Monument offers dozens of trails and loops to explore, but the surrounding mountains contain hundreds of miles of trails if you wish to go farther afield. They range in length, features, and difficulty, so consider your time, fitness, and spirit of adventure when choosing a route. Short, easy options include Bonita Creek Loop, Bonita Creek Trail, and Silver Spur Meadow Trail; all three of these allow pets.

The Natural Bridge Trail (4.8 miles/7.7 km round-trip) is moderately challenging and, as one of the least used trails, an excellent choice if you're seeking solitude. A more popular trail, Echo Canyon Loop (3.3 miles/5.3 km) winds through breathtaking rock formations; the trail is fairly level but, with a southern exposure, it can be quite hot. For a less taxing approach, take the Ed Riggs Trail heading counterclockwise.

For a longer, more intense hike (7.3–9.5 miles/11.7–15.2 km), consider the Heart of Rocks Loop (no pets allowed here) and spend the day. The loop connects to a range of trails, allowing you to customize your hike based on stamina, interests, and mood.

MORE DETAILS

Directions: Take Interstate 10E to Exit 336; in Willcox, turn right onto State Route 186 and travel 32 miles (51.5 km) to State Route 181. Turn left; the monument entrance is 4 miles (6.4 km) down the road. Gas is not available at the monument; consider filling up in Willcox or Sunizona.

Amenities: Parking; visitor center (constructed by Civilian Conservation Corps stonemasons in the 1930s) with restrooms, exhibits (on geology, natural history, archaeology, and culture), and bookstore; 25 campsites with flush-toilet restrooms, running water, picnic tables, and trash pickup (reservations required—go to recreation.gov); pets permitted on some trails; accessible visitor center, campsite, and picnic areas (call regarding any special needs).

Pro Tips: The best time of day to hike depends on both season and location—at lower elevations, southern-exposure hikes can be hot in summer while high-elevation, northern exposure routes can get cold, especially at night. It's always a good idea to check the weather forecast. For non-camping accommodations, resident-owned short-term rentals and hotels are available, such as the Portal Café, Country Store and Lodge, where you can also stop for a meal or to stock up on hiking/camping necessities. Nearby sites include the American Museum of Natural History Southwestern Research Station in Portal, Arizona and the Chiricahua Desert Museum, just across the state line in Rodeo, New Mexico.

Info:
Chiricahua National Monument Visitor Center
12856 E. Rhyolite Creek Road
Willcox, AZ
520-824-3560

PUERTO PEÑASCO

IF SPENDING A WEEKEND (or a summer!) in Tucson's dry heat conjures escapist dreams of breezy beaches and boundless ocean, relief is a four-hour drive away. Across the international border and tucked along the Gulf of California coast, Puerto Peñasco (Spanish for "rocky cliff port"; Rocky Point in English and *Ge'e Ṣuidagĭ* in O'odham) is a fishing and resort city with sand dunes, beautiful beaches, tide pools, and a renowned research/resource center. Along the way, you can stop at Organ Pipe Cactus National Monument, just before you cross the border. There's also a biosphere reserve halfway between the international border and Puerto Peñasco where you can stop to check out the stark lava fields and dramatic volcanic landscapes—this is where the Apollo astronauts trained for the historic 1969 moon landing.

Fundamentals: Overnight trip; beaches, tide pools, research center, two biosphere reserves; passport required; 211 miles (340 km) southwest of downtown Tucson; year-round

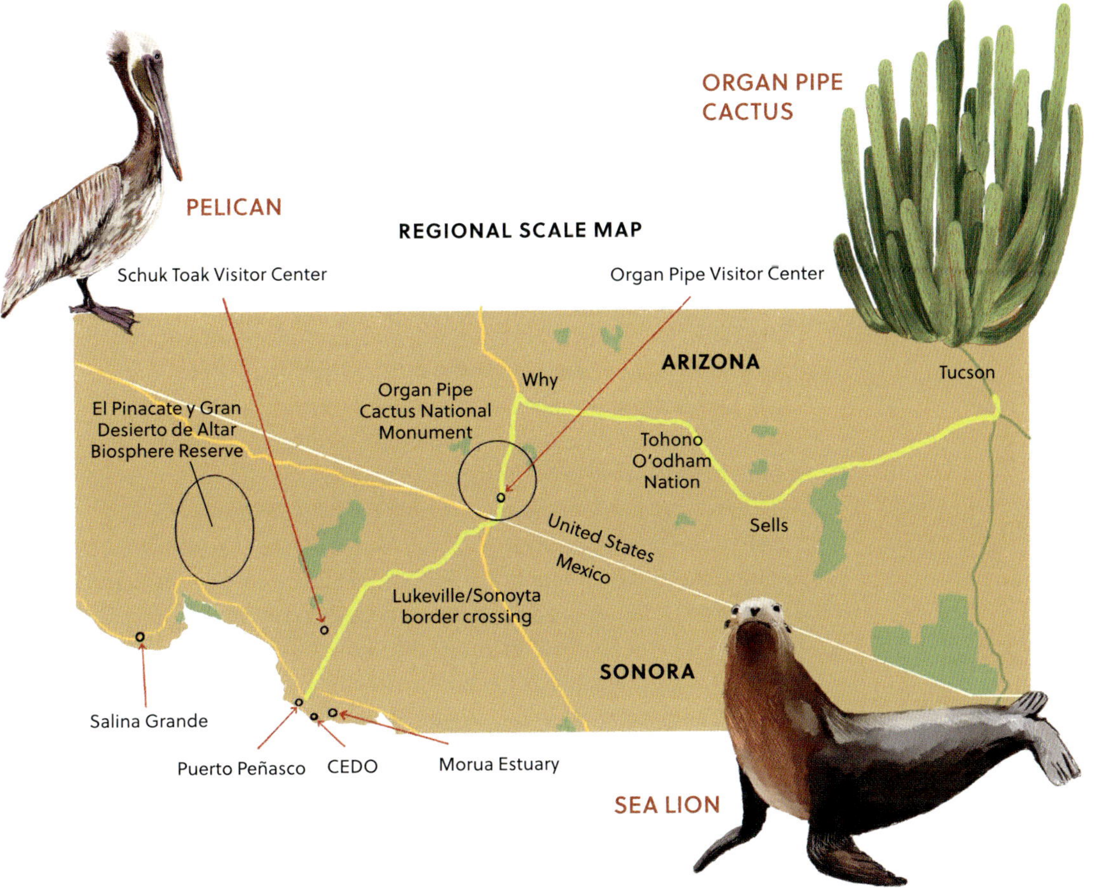

Above, left to right: Organ pipe cactus in its namesake monument

Organ pipe cactus

Downtown Puerto Peñasco with the shrimp fisherman statue

Tide pools

THE CITY SCENE

Puerto Peñasco is the closest coastal city to Tucson and Phoenix. Once a small fishing village, it has grown in recent decades to be a prime tourist destination and port of call for cruises. Visitors come for the warm waters, nearby nature, fresh seafood, and relaxing vibe. Though located in the Altar Desert, the hottest and driest part of the larger Sonoran, Puerto Peñasco's seaside location keeps the weather mostly pleasant, though often humid.

Driving to Puerto Peñasco requires a passport and Mexican car insurance. A Mexican Migration Form (FMM) may be required and can be purchased at border crossings. You'll find plenty of accommodations, including hotels, condos, and homes as well as campsites and RV parks. There are many picturesque beaches to choose from; a waterfront esplanade (*el malecón*) to stroll; and a lively restaurant scene to investigate (where US dollars are accepted and menus are available in English and Spanish).

As you enjoy the local seafood, be mindful to order and buy sustainably sourced options. (Consult Monterey Bay Aquarium's Seafood Watch consumer guide for advice.) Once called "the world's aquarium" by famed oceanographer Jacques Cousteau for its magnificently diverse marine life, today the Gulf of California is suffering the diversity-diminishing effects of overfishing, commercial development, and global warming. We all have a part to play in helping restore it.

WILDLIFE OF THE SEA AND AIR

Some of the world's most extreme tidal fluctuations occur along the rocky coast of Puerto Peñasco—up to 26 feet (8 m) between high and low tides—and tide-pooling is a popular activity. Look closely and marvel at the dazzling marine life in the pools—hermit crabs, sea stars, anemones, urchins, barnacles, seaweed—but don't touch, for both your safety and that of the organisms. Also, remember to practice good environmental ethics—leave what you find in place for others to enjoy and to preserve the interdependent community of marine life and other species.

For avian lovers, birding the beaches and estuaries of Puerto Peñasco is an opportunity to see both migratory and resident species. Non-birders, too, will appreciate tracking the movements of pelicans, gulls, and boobies and watching them fish. Spend some time at Morúa Estuary, east of Las Conchas—thousands of birds live here and, as you look seaward, you may be treated to the sight of dolphin pods cruising in the coastal waters. If you'd like to get closer to the action, consider going on a whale-watching or sunset cruise; they depart from the commercial port where the fishing boats dock.

CONSERVATION AND RESEARCH

Centro Intercultural de Estudios de Desiertos y Océanos (in English, Intercultural Center for the Study of Deserts and Oceans), or simply CEDO, is a nonprofit resource center and field station that seeks workable and ecologically/culturally sensitive solutions to

▸ Fin whale skeleton on CEDO campus

▸ Entrance to CEDO campus

environmental challenges. A collaboration between organizations in Mexico and the United States, CEDO's goal is to promote resiliency, conservation, biodiversity, climate response, and community well-being in the Northern Gulf of California and surrounding regions through research, education, and community development.

CEDO offers public tours, talks, and other programming and maintains a field station with a visitor center, gift shop, botanical garden, and exhibits that include articulated skeletons of a fin whale and vaquita marina. Check out hours and events while you're in the area—a visit to CEDO is an engaging and fun way to learn more about the Sonoran Desert's ecosystems.

◂ El Pinacate y Gran Desierto de Altar Biosphere Reserve

A STARTLING MOONSCAPE

Another remarkable destination within striking distance of Puerto Peñasco is El Pinacate y Gran Desierto de Altar Biosphere Reserve (Pinacate Reserve and Great Desert of Altar). Covering a vast area of over 600 square miles (1600 sq km), the reserve boasts 10 enormous maars (volcanic craters formed by explosions of heated groundwater); hundreds of cinder cones (composed of loose volcanic fragments); and seemingly endless sand dunes. This largely undisturbed ecosystem is habitat to hundreds of plant species as well as myriad mammals, reptiles, and birds. After springtime rains, exuberant clusters of wildflowers dot the landscape with bursts of yellow, orange, and purple against stretches of sand and black and red petrified lava flows.

While at the reserve, be sure to visit the excellent Schuk Toak Visitor Center and Museum. (*Schuk Toak* means "black mountain" in O'odham.) Completely self-sufficient (producing all its energy and water), the museum houses numerous exhibits and interactive displays as well as a gift shop; screens videos about the land, history, and culture of the region; and hosts guided hikes of the surrounding sand dunes. Outside, you'll also find a patio, botanical garden, and three interpretive trails. Call or check online for seasonal hours and entrance fees.

TOHONO O'ODHAM SALT PILGRIMAGE

Sixty-two miles (100 km) northwest of Puerto Peñasco, the Salina Salt Flats (La Salina Grande) are part of Tohono O'odham ancestral lands and the site of their annual Salt Pilgrimage, a rite of passage for young O'odham men. Participants (salt runners) traverse the 300-mile (483-km) route to the ocean and back on foot, accompanied by elders who sing and impart wisdom and fortitude along the way.

Salt is sacred to the O'odham, consumed as a vital nutrient, used in ceremony and, in earlier times, traded for other necessities. Nevertheless, with population dispersal, assimilation, and commercial encroachment, the salt pilgrimage fell off over time. In recent years, tribal leaders have resuscitated the pilgrimage, reinvigorating this annual tradition, preserving cultural knowledge, and affirming their connection to this land.

MORE DETAILS

Directions: Take Interstate 10E to Exit 260 toward Nogales for Interstate 19S, then Exit 99 for Ajo Way/Arizona State Route 86W. Stay on this highway for 107 miles (172.2 km) and turn left onto North Ajo Sonoita Highway/Arizona State Route 85S to enter Mexico. Follow signs for Puerto Peñasco through Sonoita and continue for 60 miles (95.6 km) on Mexico 8 to your destination.

Pro Tips: You will travel through two other sovereign nations on this trip. Research and follow traffic rules and other laws on the Tohono O'odham Nation and in Mexico. US auto insurance is only valid within the United States; most major insurance companies (and some that specialize) offer insurance for driving in Mexico. Mexican law requires liability insurance, and you may wish to get other coverage as well. In addition, before traveling to another country from the United States, it's always advisable to consult—and heed—any travel advisories.

Info:
CEDO México
Edificio Agustín Cortés Sur/Norte
Fraccionamiento Las Conchas
83550 Puerto Peñasco, Sonora
52 638 382 0113

Schuk Toak Visitor Center and Museum
El Pinacate y Gran Desierto de Altar Biosphere Reserve
Carretera Federal 8
Kilometro 72
83550 Puerto Peñasco, Sonora
52 638 383 1433

Organ Pipe Cactus National Monument
10 Organ Pipe Drive
Ajo, AZ 85321
On Arizona State Route 85, 25 miles (40 km) south of Why, AZ and
5 miles (8 km) north of the US-Mexico border
520-387-6849

PHOTO AND ILLUSTRATION CREDITS

Species illustrations by Leigh Kaisen
Map illustrations by Sara Isasi

Arizona-Sonora Desert Museum, 210 (top left), 240 (bottom right)
Arizona State Parks and Trails, 316 (bottom right), 317, 342 (top, bottom)
Catherine Bartlett, 87 (top left), 140 (top middle, bottom left), 152, 154 (left), 155 (bottom right), 157 (left), 160 (top), 179 (top left), 183 (middle right, bottom), 185, 186 (right), 188 (top), 194, 198 (middle, right), 200 (left, middle), 201 (right), 203 (right), 205, 206 (left, top right), 209 (top, middle right, bottom), 210 (middle right), 213 (bottom left), 216 top left), 220 (bottom), 221 (left), 223 (top right), 225, 232 (top), 233 (right), 235, 236, 237 (left), 238, 239 (left), 240 (top left), 242, 243 (middle, right), 264 (right), 270 (left), 271 (bottom), 283 (top left), 289 (right), 298 (left), 299 (right), 300, 303, 309 (right), 321 (middle, right), 347 (right), 359, 361
CEDO Intercultural/Eliud Flores, 366
Daniel Austin, 24 (top)
Gerald Loew, Pima County Communications Office, 46
Glenn Seplak, 151 (bottom left), 153 (left), 154 (right)
Howard Byrne, 189 (top)
Jay Pierstorff, 9 (top), 10–11, 13 (top), 24 (bottom), 48–49, 56, 61 (left), 62 (middle), 63 (bottom), 77, 85 (middle), 87 (top right), 89 (bottom left), 93 (top), 96 (right), 129 (right), 173 (left), 176, 181 (right), 202, 210 (middle left, bottom left), 212, 216 (top right, bottom left), 226 (middle), 228, 230 (right), 231, 237 (middle, right), 239 (top right), 245 (right), 247 (top left, bottom)
Julia Row, 104 (right)
Karen Ramage McCrorey, 210 (bottom right)
Liz Kemp, 243 (left)
Merrian Felix, 351–353 (left)
National Parks Gallery, 29
National Park Service, 29, 44, 58, 60 (left–Alice Wondrak Biel), 69 (bottom), 78 (top–Neal Herbert), 104 (left), 129 (left), 304 (Todd M. Edgar), 356, 358, 360, 364
Randy Metcalf, Pima County Communications Office, 259, 261, 264 (left), 265, 266, 271 (top), 272, 273, 290, 292 (right), 298 (right), 316 (left, top right), 321 (left), 323, 327, 331 (right), 333
Rhonda Spencer, 13 (bottom), 62 (top), 95 (top), 119, 139 (bottom right), 142 (left), 146 (left), 199 (top), 204, 213 (top), 218 (right), 230 (left), 232 (bottom right), 240 (top right), 241, 250 (right), 252 (top, bottom)
Sky Jacobs, 20 (top right)
Steve Hillebrand/USFWS, 336 (right)
Ted Meyers, 89 (middle left), 126, 128 (bottom), 131 (left), 132 (left), 134, 135 (middle), 190 (top), 218 (left)
USGS Southwest Biological Science Center, 335 (bottom)
USGS Southwest Biological Science Center/Brent H. Sigafus, 336 (left)
Wendy Moore, 36

Desert Museum Digital Library

Alex Kerstitch, 169 (left), 181 (top left), 182, 191 (middle left),
Buzz Hoffmann, 143 (left), 146 (right), 183 (middle left), 188 (bottom right), 192 (top, middle),
Carole DeAngeli, 135 (top), 148 (bottom left)
Daniel Austin, 21, 66 (left), 127 (top), 128 (top), 131 (right), 132 (right), 135 (bottom), 139 (bottom left), 226 (top, bottom left), 252 (middle)
Jay Pierstorff, 217 (left)
Jim Honcoop, 89 (top right), 149 (top right), 160 (middle, bottom)
Kike Calvo, 174, 175, 184 (bottom)
Kim Franklin, 143 (top right)
Laura Stafford, 206 (bottom middle)
Manny Rubio, 179 (bottom), 192 (bottom),
Olga Harbor, 140 (top right)
Paul and Joyce Berquist, 23, 234
Rhonda Spencer, 12 (middle, bottom), 61 (bottom right), 89 (bottom right), 96 (left), 106 (bottom), 136, 140 (top left), 143 (bottom right), 146 (left), 147, 148 (top, bottom right), 149 (top left, bottom), 150 (top, bottom left), 155 (top middle), 156 (bottom middle), 157 (bottom right), 158 (right), 166, 168 (LEFT), 169 (right), 170–172, 173 (right), 179 (top right), 181 (bottom left), 184 (top), 188 (bottom left), 197, 198 (left), 199 (bottom), 200 (right), 201 (left), 206 (bottom right), 210 (top right), 213 (third row, bottom right), 216 (top middle), 233 (left), 239 (bottom right), 244, 245 (left), 283 (bottom middle)
Thomas Van Devender, 41 (bottom)
William Hornbaker, 83 (top), 89 (top left), 156 (left), 191 (middle right), 217 (right), 246, 247 (top right),

Flickr

Public Domain

Alan Schmierer, 95 (bottom)
Bill Radke/USFWS, 165 (middle)
Cecelia Alexander, 189 (bottom left)
Kyle Magnuson, 16, 367
UA/USFWS, 240 (bottom left)
U.S. Dept of Energy/ENERGY.GOV, 105 (bottom)
USFWS Mountain-Prairie/Clint Wirick, 232 (bottom left)

CC BY 2.0

Andy Reago & Chrissy McClarren, 223 (bottom)
Bettina Arrigoni, 155 (bottom left)
Brian Gratwicke, 162, 164 (left, middle), 165 (right)
Bureau of Land Management, Bob Wick, 42 (left)
gailhampshire, 97 (right), 144 (top left)
Joanna Gilkeson/USFWS, 123 (top)
John Fowle, 118 (top right)
Katja Schulz, 118 (middle right, bottom left), 168 (right)
Ken Bosma, 91 (bottom)
Kyle Magnuson, 16
Laura Wolf, 85 (right), 221 (right)
Line Sabroe, 151 (top left)
Sébastien FAILLON, 140 (bottom middle)
William Warby, 155 (top right)

CC BY 2.0 Deed
Andy Reago & Chrissy McClarren, 63 (top)
Katja Schulz, 59 (left), 84 (right), 97 (left), 99
Matthew Dillon, 41 (top)
CC BY-NC 2.0
USFWS - Pacific Region, 118 (middle left)
CC BY-SA 2.0
Björn S., 155 (top left)
Dominic Sherony, 107
Gilles San Martin, 151 (right)
PDM 1.0 Deed
Joshua Tree National Park, NPS/Brad Sutton, 33
Public domain, CC0 1.0
Alejandro Santillana (produced as part of the "Insects Unlocked" project, University of Texas at Austin), 139 (top right)

iStock

Jay Pierstorff, 77

Noirlab.edu

Creative Commons Attribution 4.0 International License
KPNO/NOIRLab/NSF/AURA/D. Salman, 355 (middle)
KPNO/NOIRLab/NSF/AURA/R. Sparks, 354 (bottom)
KPNO/NOIRLab/AURA/NSF/P. Marenfeld, 355
M. Hunt/KPNO/NOIRLab/NSF/AURA, 354 (top)

Shutterstock

86Eric_Anthony_Mischke 86, 125 (top)
Adwo, 122
AlexFeder, 213 (second right)
Alybaba, 79 (left)
Ana Mercedes Corona Garza, 12 (top)
Andrew Zavirny, 54
Archaeopteryx Tours, 62 (bottom)
Ariel Celeste Photography, 284
Basin And Range, 328
Beach Creatives, 34, 40
Benny Marty, 42–43
Bierchen, 267
Bill Florence, 116, 120
Bjoern Wylezich, 70 (left)
Breck P. Kent, 70 (right)
Brian Magnier, 139 (middle left)
Charles T. Peden, 106 (top), 159, 183 (top right), 283 (top right, bottom left)
Chris Curtis, 365 (right)
Chris Hill, 84 (left)
Christopher M Hall, 208 (middle left)
Creative Endeavors, 39 (bottom), 80
Danita Delimont, 250 (left), 287 (right)
David G Hayes, 183 (top left)
Dennis Swena, 347 (left)
Dmytro Sheremeta, 124
Erwin Widmer, 365 (left)
Fine Moon Rising, 309 (left)
Florence-Joseph McGinn, 213 (second left)
Flying Mouse, 292 (left)
G Parekh, 348
Gerry Bishop, 153 (right)
Gregg Pasterick, 142 (right)
Griffin Gillespie, 61 (top right)
guentermanaus, 277
GypsyPictureShow, 139 (middle right)
Hans Wismeijer, 337
Ian Peter Morton, 130 (top)
Irina K, 130 (bottom right), 251
James Omlid Photography, 314
Jean C Hebert, 87 (bottom)
Jeremy Christnsen, 289 (left)
John L. Absher, 223 (top left)
Katie Dobies, 127 (bottom)
Kelly vanDellen, 59 (right)
lalcreative, 312
Leonardo Gonzalez, 45
LHBLLC, 9 (bottom), 91 (top), 118 (bottom right), 123 (bottom)
Londowl, 260
Lori Bonati, 283 (bottom right)
Martha Marks, 226 (bottom right)
Mary Sisco, 279 (right)
Matt Jeppson, 190 (center)
Maurizio De Mattei, 144 (right)
Nathan A Shepard, 190 (bottom left)
Ondrej Prosicky, 215
Photos BrianScantlebury, 248
pics721, 308
punkbirdr, 220 (middle)
Rudmer Zwerver, 219 (left)
Sean R. Stubben, 220 (top)
Stanley Ford, 294–295
Stubblefield Photography, 89 (middle right)
Tempus Aura Eugenie R, 130 (bottom left)
Tim Roberts Photography, 53, 109
Tucker Heptinstall, 189 (bottom right)
Underawesternsky, 278
vagabond54, 206 (top middle), 216 (bottom right), 256, 282, 319, 335 (top)
Wangkun Jia, 276
William Cushman, 125 (bottom)
Wirestock Creators, 93 (bottom)
Zane Lewis, 287 (left), 313, 346

Wikimedia

Public Domain
Alan Schmierer, 186 (left)
BLMArizona, 26
Jkan997, 25
John Diebolt, 19
ksblack99, 100–101
Steve Hillebrand/U. S. Fish and Wildfife Services, 353 (right)
Stickpen, 118 (bottom middle)
CC0 1.0 Public domain
Alan Schmierer, 95 (bottom)
Junkyardsparkle, 156 (right)
CC by 2.0
Ken Bosma, 121
Rison Thumboor, 140 (bottom right)
CC by 2.5
Chuck Evans(mcevan), 157 (top right)
Kmusser, 51
CC by-SA 2.0
Brady Smith, Coconino National Forest, 37
Sergio Niebla (from Cd. Victoria, Tamaulipas, México), 123 (top)
CC by-SA 3.0
J Brew, 60 (right)
Johannes Menzel, 305
Kathleen Smith, 20 (top left)
Mcraycroft, 38–39
CC by-SA 3.0 Deed
$1LENCE D00600D, 331 (left)
jkan997, 25
Kati Fleming, 82 (bottom left)
Marine 69-71, 67 (bottom)
Marine discovery, 165 (left)
Stan Shebs, 105 (middle)
WClarke, 110
CC BY 4.0
Kenanhye, 203 (left)
Nmoorhatch, 164 (right)
CC BY-SA 4.0
Gary Tenen, 342 (middle)
Greg Linscott, 150 (bottom right)
Jengod, 144 (bottom left)
Joe Brewer, 158 (left)
Joering, 66 (right), 67 (top)
Josep Gesti, 69 (top)
Miwasatoshi, 118 (top left)
Shaunnamm, 340
Susan Barnum, 78 (bottom)
Wade Greenberg-Brand/Paleontological Research Institution, 21 (bottom)
WendyAvilesR, 43 (right)
xpda, 139 (top left)
CC BY-SA 4.0 Deed
Rhododendrites, 83 (bottom right)
Saplants, 102, 105 (top)
Steve and Kimberly Rader, 64, 76

ACKNOWLEDGMENTS

IN PUTTING TOGETHER THIS BOOK, the authors benefited greatly from the work of our predecessors at the Arizona-Sonora Desert Museum, especially as compiled in *A Natural History of the Sonoran Desert*, written and edited by Desert Museum staff and other scholars (University of California Press, 2000 and 2015). This comprehensive volume is an excellent source for more in-depth information about the region, based on decades of research. We'd like to especially acknowledge these Sonoran Desert experts, on whose shoulders we stand: Linda M. Brewer, Richard Brusca, Mark A. Dimmitt, Margaret H. Fusari, Roseann Beggy Hanson, Jonathan Hanson, Janice Johnson, Ken Kaufman, Karen Krebbs, Howard Lawler, Pinau Merlin, Wendy Moore, Gary Paul Nabhan, Steven J. Phillips, Robert Scarborough, Thomas E. Sheridan, Peter Siminski, and Thomas R. Van Devender.

The authors are grateful to the many people who helped foster a connection to nature throughout their lives and to their closest friends and family who supported them while they were buried in writing this book. In particular, we'd like to thank our Adventure Buddies, Bill and Susan Bartlett, Philip Bottonari, Mordecai Colodner, Dena Cowan, Nicholas Ilka, Rachel Ivanyi, Marcia Lambert, John Leipsic, Hugh McCrystal, Marie McGhee, Stephane Poulin, Susan and Gidget Quinn, the Ramos-Hickman Family, Annie Stowers, Emily Truong, Joan Warfield, and Betty Anne Wheeler.

INDEX